# EXPLORING FAMILY RELATIONSHIPS WITH OTHER SOCIAL CONTEXTS

Edited by

**ROSS D. PARKE**
*University of California, Riverside*

**SHEPPARD G. KELLAM**
*The Johns Hopkins School of Hygiene and Public Health*

 LAWRENCE ERLBAUM ASSOCIATES, PUBLISHERS
1994    Hillsdale, New Jersey                    Hove, UK

Lawrence Erlbaum Associates, Inc., Publishers
365 Broadway
Hillsdale, New Jersey 07642

Cover design by Mairav Salomon-Dekel

**Library of Congres Cataloging-in-Publication Data**

Exploring family relationships with other social contexts / edited by
Ross D. Parke & Sheppard G. Kellam.
p.    cm. — (Advances in family research)
Based on the Fourth Summer Institute of the Family Research
Consortium.
Includes bibliographical references and index.
ISBN 0-8058-1073-0
1. Family—United States.  2. Child development—United States.
3. Child rearing—United States.  I. Parke, Ross D.  II. Kellam,
Sheppard G.  IV. Series.
HQ536.E94   1993
306.87—dc20                                         92-40287
                                                         CIP

Printed in the United States of America
10  9  8  7  6  5  4  3  2  1

# Contents

# EXPLORING
# FAMILY RELATIONSHIPS
# WITH OTHER
# SOCIAL CONTEXTS

# Introduction and Overview

Ross D. Parke
*University of California, Riverside*

Sheppard G. Kellam
*The Johns Hopkins School of Hygiene and Public Health*

In the 1990s it is no longer "news" that families do not operate independently from other social organizations and institutions. Instead, it is generally recognized that families are embedded in a complex set of relationships with other institutions and contexts outside the family. In spite of this recognition, a great deal remains to be discovered about the ways in which families are influenced by these outside agencies or how families, in turn, influence the functioning of children and adults in their extra-familial settings, such as school, work, daycare, or peer group contexts. Moreover, we know little about the nature of the processes that account for this mutual influence between families and other societal institutions and settings. The goal of this volume is to present examples from a series of ongoing research programs that are beginning to provide some tentative answers to these questions.

In this introduction a variety of trends—both demographic and scientific—that have converged since the 1980s to support this view of families' embeddedness in a wider set of societal institutions is briefly reviewed. Finally, the organization of the volume and the highlights of the remaining chapters are outlined.

## SHIFTS IN SOCIAL ROLES AND SOCIAL ORGANIZATIONS

In the 1970s and 1980s, a variety of demographic and social changes have occurred that have altered the family's relationship to other institutions in our society.

Three changes are particularly noteworthy. They are the rise in maternal

1

employment, the increased use of day care for infants and young children, and the rise in the divorce rate. Each of these shifts have consequences for the family's relationships with other social institutions outside the family.

First, there has been a dramatic increase in the percentage of women who are employed outside the home. In 1950, only 24% of married mothers with children under 18 worked outside the home, compared with 41% in 1970. By 1990, 63% worked outside the home (Hayghe, 1990). Among mothers with children under age 6 the increase has been even more dramatic. Among married women with children under age 6, the labor force participation rate was 54% in 1990, compared with 30% and 12% in 1970 and 1950, respectively (Barrett, 1987). These changes have raised a variety of questions about the relationships between family and work. Although the focus was initially on the impact of maternal employment on children's development, the framing of this issue has broadened to include a wide range of questions concerning the reciprocal impact of experiences in family and work contexts on functioning in these settings. Moreover, as research has moved from issues of employment per se to consideration of the impact of quality of work on both women as well as men and how work shapes their family lives (Repetti, 1989).

A corresponding increase has taken place in the rise of out-of-home care for children. Approximately two thirds of children under 5 whose mothers work receive care for some portion of the week from individuals other than their parents, grandparents, and/or siblings (Hayes, Palmer, & Zaslow, 1990). As a result, many young children are exposed to nonfamilial caregivers and unfamiliar peers at earlier ages than in prior decades. This increase in day care has led to heightened interest in the effects of this type of care on young children's social and cognitive development, as well as the relationships between family and day-care settings (Howes & Olenick, 1986). In turn, this sharing of young children's socialization between families and day-care institutions has led to an increased focus on the role of peers in young children's development as well as new questions concerning the ways that families facilitate or impede children's successful adaptation to agemates outside the family (Parke & Ladd, 1992).

A third trend is the rise in the divorce rate in the United States from the early 1960s to the mid-1970s. Since that time, the divorce rate has leveled off, but at a high level, with approximately 50% of all first marriages ending in divorce (Cherlin, 1988). In turn, this has meant an increase in the family's link with a variety of outside institutions. Family involvement with the legal system has increased not only for divorce proceedings per se but also for issues of child custody disputes and the enforcement of child support arrangements (Cherlin, 1988). An increasing number of women are maintaining their own households after separation and divorce, and many of these women and their children endure a reduced standard of living, which, in turn, results in increased reliance on welfare and other government supports for economic survival (Garfinkel & McLanahan, 1986; Hewlett, 1986).

In summary, demographic shifts since the late 1970s have resulted in altered relationships between families and other societal institutions such as the workplace, day-care settings and the legal and welfare systems.

## TRENDS IN THEORY AND RESEARCH

A second set of trends are theory- and research-based. At the theoretical level, there has been an increasing recognition that families are embedded in a variety of social institutions. Perhaps, the most influential theoretical statement is found in Bronfenbrenner's (1979) volume, *The Ecology of Human Development,* in which he argued for recognition that families are linked to other institutions in a variety of ways. His now familiar scheme involving microsystems, mesosystems, ecosystems, and macrosystems (Bronfenbrenner, 1979, 1989) set the research agenda for a more vigorous examination of the ways in which families are linked with other institutions in our society. Whereas Bronfenbrenner offered a perspective from developmental psychology, other disciplinary perspectives were converging to embrace a similar view of family's place in the wider social environment. From the viewpoint of clinical psychology, community psychologists (Cowen, 1985) argued that families and children can only be understood by conceptualizing their relationship to the wider community in which they operate. Systems theory perspectives (Sameroff, 1983) also championed the importance of considering the interdependence among contexts including families. Finally, a new discipline that combines community, family, and developmental epidemiology has emerged in recent years (Kellam, 1990) that again seeks to place the family in its proper environmental mileau. This approach is illustrated by Kellam (chapter 6, this volume). Briefly, this approach deploys techniques of sampling, measurement and analysis that permit the mapping of variation in family form and functioning within well-defined communities.

In summary, a variety of perspectives are converging to provide a foundation on which to build theory and research that addresses the interface between families and other institutions.

Finally, as the chapters in this volume demonstrate, work in this area has moved beyond the descriptive phase and is beginning to focus on the *processes* that will help explain how families are linked with other contexts. In a sense, this volume exemplifies the second stage of research in this area. In the first round, the task involved description of the family's ties to other institutions, whereas in this second round, the explanatory processes that can account for these links are the focus.

## AN OVERVIEW OF THE VOLUME

In this volume, a selection of recent research on this topic is presented.

In chapter 1, Crouter examines the relationship between families and work. Specifically, three issues are explored. First, she describes the processes through which work or family status influences behavior in the other setting. Her chapter sounds a recurring theme, namely the bi-directional nature of the influences between families and other settings. Second, Crouter explores the influences of one linking process, namely the mood generated in one setting on interactions or behavior in the other settings. Third, she examines the ways in which adult development is enhanced—or impeded—in one setting that generalize to behavior in the other setting.

In chapter 2, Chase-Lansdale continues the exploration of work–family relationships by focusing on the issue of maternal employment and child care during the early years of life. Her chapter lays out a framework that links these two domains of research and shows how the limitations (e.g., small and unrepresentative samples and retrospective designs) have limited our understanding of work–family linkage. She argues that it is important to consider the child's experience in both the family and the child-care setting in order to understand the impact of maternal employment. This theme of a dual focus on the family setting and the extra-familial context (such as work) is similar to the message of the previous chapter. Finally, Chase-Lansdale argues for the utility of intervention research for evaluating our assumptions about family–work relationships, but cautions that an exclusive focus on children or mothers alone is insufficient. Interventions that target families—children and parents—are more likely to be helpful than programs that target only single members of the family.

In the next two chapters we begin an exploration of advances in our understanding of the role of marital relationships on children's functioning in contexts outside the family. First, Katz and Gittman (chapter 3) provide a compelling argument that we need to better understand the processes that link characteristics of marital relationships to children's socioemotional development. They outline specific characteristics of the marriage relationship, such as differing affective styles used in resolving marital conflict that, in turn, are linked to parent–child interaction and child outcomes, especially the child's peer relationships. They are able to demonstrate links between marital interaction style and children's emotional functioning both inside the family and with peers. The role of affective regulatory processes emerges as an important link between the marital relationship and children's social behavior with peers.

Cowan, Cowan, and their colleagues (chapter 4) continue exploration of this theme of the links between marriage and social adaptation outside the family by focusing on school settings. Using data from their longitudinal project beginning with the transition to parenthood, these investigators are able to show that a combination of marital quality, life stress, and parenting style can predict both academic achievement and social competence with peers 5 years later in kindergarten. Their work underscores the central role of the parents' marriage in children's development not only for dysfunctional families but for nonclinical families as well. The fact that the production of later adaptation begins with how well couples negotiate the transition to parenthood argues convincingly for the value of focusing on transitions in development for illuminating family processes (Cowan, 1991; Cowan & Hetherington, 1991).

Parke and his colleagues (chapter 5) offer further insights into the mechanisms by which the family facilitates or hinders children's adaptation to their peers. These investigators offer a three-part model of how family and peer systems are linked. Parent–child interaction is the first route by which the family alters children's peer relationships. They argue that emotional regulatory skills as well as cognitive representational models of social relationships are two sets of processes that are acquired in the course of parent–child interaction that in turn may account for variations in children's success with peers outside the family. Second, parents serve as educators by directly teaching children social skills that may be helpful in their peer encounters. Third, parents serve as managers of children's opportunities for contact with other children and in this role may alter children's adaptation to peers. Together these three sets of family processes combine to influence children's relationships with other contexts, especially peer settings.

Kellam (chapter 6) continues the theme of how families, school, and peer contexts interact in determining how well a child adapts to the social and intellectual demands of classroom life. Using a developmental epidemiological strategy, Kellam illustrates the value of this approach for locating the sample under study in its community context. Data from large projects in Woodlawn and Baltimore are employed to illuminate the importance of recognizing the variation in structural composition of families within the same community and how this variation can be helpful in understanding later adaptation in extra-familial settings. Finally, Kellam provides a rich portrait of the classroom as a social field and argues for the value of a close examination of teacher- and peer-based processes as modifiers and consequences of family-based childrearing practices. The interplay among peer, teacher, and family process is illustrated by the use of the differential impact of intervention programs on children from different families and classrooms.

McCarthy, Newcomb, and Bentler (chapter 7) move us along the developmental trajectory by an examination of the impact of personal and family influences on the development of competence in young adults. Their findings suggest that family influences may be developmentally bound and have a greater impact on adolescents than on young adults. The impact of families on the competence of young adults may be mediated by their earlier impact on the personal beliefs, values, and lifestyle of individuals during their adolescent years. The importance of direct and indirect effects as well as the developmental stage of the individual are clearly illustrated by this work.

In chapter 8, Sameroff provides an overview of developmental models that can guide research in this area of family–context relationships. Moving beyond his earlier classic formulations of transactional models, Sameroff offers a dynamic developmental theory that seeks to explain how the individual, the family, and context operate together to produce adaptive or maladaptive functioning. His theory alerts us to the important but often neglected role of culture as a regulatory context for shaping individual and family beliefs and behaviors. Finally, he describes new ways of viewing family regulatory processes including paradigms, myths, stories, and rituals that serve as vehicles for orienting family members relationships with contexts and institutions outside the family.

In the closing epilogue, Parke (chapter 9) outlines a variety of issues that can inform a future research agenda in this area. These issues include an expanded range of contexts, more emphasis on process, the development of a better taxonomy of contexts, and greater sensitivity to cultural and historical forces.

These chapters emerged from the fourth summer workshop of the Family Research Consortium that was characterized by lively exchanges not only between speakers and the audience, but among participants in small group discussions as well. Hopefully, these chapters will communicate some of the dynamism and excitement that was evident at the conference. In the final analysis the goal of the volume is to stimulate further theoretical and empirical advances in our understanding of how families relate to other contexts.

## REFERENCES

Barrett, N. S. (1987). Women and the economy. In S. E. Rix (Ed.), *The American woman 1987–88: A report in depth*. New York: Norton.

Bronfenbrenner, U. (1979). *The ecology of human development*. Cambridge, MA: Harvard University Press.

Bronfenbrenner, U. (1989). Ecology systems theory. In G. J. Whitehurst (Ed.), *Annals of child development* (Vol. 6, pp. 185–246). Greenwich, CT: JAI Press.

Cherlin, A. J. (1988). The changing American family and public policy. In A. J. Cherlin (Ed.), *The changing American family and public policy* (pp. 1–29). Washington, DC: The Urban Institute Press.

Cowan, P. A. (1991). Individual and family life transitions: A proposal for a new definition. In P. A. Cowan & E. M. Hetherington (Eds.), *Family transitions* (pp. 3–30). Hillsdale, NJ: Lawrence Erlbaum Associates.

Cowan, P. A., & Hetherington, E. M. (Eds.). (1991). *Family transitions*. Hillsdale, NJ: Lawrence Erlbaum Associates.

Cowen, E. (1985). Primary prevention in mental health: Past, present & future. In R. Felner, L. Jason, N. Mortsuger, & S. Farber (Eds.), *Preventive psychology*. New York: Pergamon.

Garfinkel, I., & McLanahan, S. S. (1986). *Single mothers and their children: A new American dilemma*. Washington, DC: Urban Institute Press.

Hayes, C., Palmer, J., & Zaslow, M. (1990). *Who cares for America's children?* Washington, DC: National Academy Press.

Hayghe, H. V. (1990). Family members in the work force. In *Monthly labor review*. Washington, DC: U.S. Government printing office.

Hewlett, S. A. (1986). *A lesser life: The myth of women's liberation in America*. New York: William Morrow.

Howes, C., & Olenick, M. (1986). Family & child care influences on toddler compliance. *Child Development, 57,* 202–216.

Kellam, S. G. (1990). Developmental epidemiologic framework for family research on depression & aggression. In G. R. Patterson (Ed.), *Depression and aggression in family interaction* (pp. 11–48). Hillsdale, NJ: Lawrence Erlbaum Associates.

Parke, R. D., & Ladd, G. W. (Eds.). (1992). Family–peer relationships: Modes of linkage. Hillsdale, NJ: Erlbaum.

Repetti, R. L. (1989). Effects of daily workload on subsequent behavior during marital interaction: The roles of social withdrawal and spouse support. *Journal of Personality and Social Psychology, 57,* 651–659.

Sameroff, A. (1983). Developmental systems: Contexts and evolution. In P. H. Mussen (Ed.), *Handbook of child psychology* (Vol. 1, pp. 237–294). New York: Wiley.

# 1 Processes Linking Families and Work: Implications for Behavior and Development in Both Settings

Ann C. Crouter
*The Pennsylvania State University*

About 200 years ago, industrialization began to revolutionize the nature of work and its place in society, gradually bringing about the geographic separation of work and family for most sectors of society (Hareven, 1982). The nature of work changed as new technologies lead to the segmentation of work activities into smaller, more routinized functions. The workplace changed as well, with many work settings becoming increasingly large, complex, and hierarchical.

Families adapted to the changes wrought by new means of economic subsistence. In the United States, as in virtually all industrialized countries, fertility rates dropped as families came to the realization that children represented a very different economic and emotional investment than they had in an agriculturally based economy (Zelizer, 1985). Roles and opportunities for women also shifted markedly. In particular, rates of labor force participation for women have increased steadily since the 1950s, both in the United States and in other industrialized countries. Smaller families, increased job and educational opportunities, and changing gender role norms about the "place" of women in society all contributed to this trend (Davis, 1984). Women's participation in the paid labor force has also become increasingly continuous over the years, as fewer women have elected to stay home to care for young children. Indeed, the subgroup of women to experience the greatest increase in participation in the labor force in recent years has been mothers of children under 1 year of age (Hayghe, 1986).

As more women have entered the workplace, scholars have become increasingly interested in the interconnections between the workplace and families (Kanter, 1977). Researchers have approached this issue from several angles, three of which are discussed in this chapter. First, there has been increased interest in families in which both mother and father work outside the home (Hoffman, 1989). These studies have focused primarily on the psychosocial functioning of children experiencing maternal employment. A number of recent studies have gone beyond simply identifying similarities and differences between children as a function of their social address (i.e., dual-earner vs. single-earner family; Bronfenbrenner & Crouter, 1982) and begun detailing the processes within these contrasting family contexts that appear to impede or enhance children's psychological well-being and development. A strength of this set of studies is that the studies illuminate the dynamics of family life. They pay little attention, however, to the nature of the work that parents do.

A second domain of research has focused on the emotional state of the worker/family member as he or she moves back and forth across the settings of work and home. The emphasis here is on short-term psychological processes operating within the individual who traverses the settings. In these studies, there is generally less attention to the properties of the settings themselves—to the roles, relationships, and activities therein—and to long-term processes of individual development.

The third set of studies revolve around work and family as settings for adult development. Both work and family are contexts that offer the kinds of activities that are likely to promote new skills and ways of looking at the world. To the extent that an individual's work, for example, encourages the development of a set of new skills or perspectives, these new abilities or viewpoints are likely to be generalized to life at home as well. These issues lie at the heart of the ecological perspective on development (Bronfenbrenner, 1979, 1989), and represent a promising research frontier for those interested in the interrelationship between work and family life.

In all three areas of research, few studies have paid equal attention to both settings. All too often, one setting is the primary focus, whereas the other is treated as a status variable or as a general source of stress. As Kline and Cowan (1989) explained, "studies from the employment or family perspectives, like maps drawn from the viewpoints of inhabitants from particular regions, show one domain occupying the foreground, while the other is represented only in sketchy outline" (p. 62). In part, this distortion in perspective is due to the complexity of the issues. It is difficult to conceptualize and design research that does justice to both settings. The uneven conceptualization and examination of work and family is also a product of the way in which the scientific disciplines have carved up the social world. Developmental researchers are trained to conduct research in laboratories, schools, and families, but rarely factories and offices. Organizational behavior experts, however, seldom follow their subjects past the boundaries of the workplace. Moreover, interdisciplinary collaboration in this domain of study is rare.

Paying equal attention to both settings provides some valuable insights that can sometimes be too easily glossed over when, for example, family is in the foreground, with work simply seen as a background characteristic (e.g., dual-earner family). It is important to recognize, for example, that work and family are reciprocally interrelated. Although it is generally recognized that work has a powerful influence on family life, the workplace is not immune from effects emanating from workers' family lives (Kanter, 1977). In addition, work and family are not simply settings in which individuals are located. There is a planfulness behind individuals' choices of work and family roles that cannot be overlooked. Many people thoughtfully select a course of study to prepare themselves for a certain kind of job or career. Others turn down job opportunities for family reasons. Increasingly, women in fast-track occupations are postponing parenthood, and when they do have children, they tend to have smaller families than was the case for their mothers' generation. The point here is that individuals actively sort themselves into work and family settings on the basis of their interests, preferences, resources, skills, values, interpretations of prevailing social norms, and best guess about how to maximize future opportunities (Gerson, 1985). This issue of selection adds another layer of complexity to this area inquiry. It forces us to realize, for example, that dual-earner families may differ from their single-earner counterparts on a host of dimensions (e.g., gender role attitudes, educational background) in addition to the wife's employment status. For the field to progress, we must, in Elder's (1981) words, "discover the complexity."

This chapter examines recent developments in the three areas just described: (a) processes through which work or family status influences behavior in the other setting, (b) influences of mood generated in one setting on interactions or behavior in the other setting, and (c) ways in which adult development is enhanced—or impeded—in one setting that generalize to behavior in the other setting. These issues are explored first from the perspective of work's impact on the family and subsequently from the vantage point of studies on the influence of families and family life on the workplace. This structure is simply an organizational device, glossing over the fact that, in reality, the interrelationships between these primary settings of adult life are complex and reciprocal.

## INFLUENCES OF WORK ON FAMILIES AND CHILDREN

### Single- and Dual-Earner Families as Settings for Development

Since the 1930s, developmental researchers have been interested in how the paid employment of mothers influences the psychological well-being and development of their children. As Bronfenbrenner and Crouter (1982) explained, early studies in this area had a social problems focus; maternal employment was assumed to have negative effects on children. Research designs were quite simplistic, employing a "social address model" in which children in traditional, father breadwinner families were compared with children in dual-earner families on a host of outcomes such as school achievement and social adjustment. By the 1960s, studies had become somewhat more sophisticated, building social class and the child's gender into their designs and, occasionally, whether the mother worked full or part time (Bronfenbrenner & Crouter, 1982). Even by the 1980s, however, when well over 50% of all mothers with children under 18 were in the paid labor force (Hayghe, 1986), little research had focused on the critical task of identifying the familial *processes* through which parents' work situations influence their children.

Attention to processes within families is essential for understanding the conditions under which parental work influences children. For example, several studies conducted in the 1960s and 1970s (e.g., Banducci, 1967; Gold & Andres, 1978) reported that boys from middle-class families in which mothers worked outside the home performed less well in school than their peers whose mothers were homemakers. A process-oriented approach focuses on how a differential outcome like this one arises in the first place. Process questions require that one attend to the activities, roles, and relationships that occur within contrasting family contexts (Bronfenbrenner, 1979).

*The Penn State Family Relationships Project.*    Elaborating processes within dual- and single-earner families with school-age children has been the central agenda of the Penn State Family Relationships Project, a longitudinal study that I co-direct with Susan McHale. Since 1987, we have been following approximately 150 families, charting the interconnections between parents' work situations, patterns of daily family life (e.g., children's involvement in various activities; parents' monitoring of children's daily experiences), and the psychological adjustment and development of children moving through the late school-age years. Identified through several school districts in central Pennsylvania, the sample was selected based on several criteria. We sought two-parent, intact families in which our "target child," a fourth or fifth grader, was the oldest child with at least one younger sibling. All fathers were employed full time, but we allowed mothers' work hours to vary. At the first phase of the project, in the winter of 1987, about one third of the mothers worked outside the home full time, one third worked part time, and one third were homemakers. The sample is predominately middle class. Families live in the small cities, towns, and rural areas that are characteristic of central Pennsylvania.

Two recent studies from the project reveal the extent to which a focus on family process illuminates the conditions under which parental work status influences school-age children. The first investigation examined the connections between children's involvement in daily household tasks and their sense of competence, feelings of stress, and closeness to parents (McHale, Bartko, Crouter, & Perry-Jenkins, 1990); the second study focused on parental monitoring and its links to children's school competence and conduct (Crouter, MacDermid, McHale, & Perry-Jenkins, 1990).

At each phase of the project, two different types of data were collected from participating families. In home interviews, mother, father, and target child were interviewed separately about work (e.g., parents' work schedules, feelings of role strain, work preferences), family relationships (e.g., feelings of closeness to other family members, views on the parents' marital relationship), and individual well-being (e.g., sense of competence, anxiety, depression). Through the eyes of the three family members, a triangulated portrait of work and family was developed. In the following several weeks, families were telephoned on 7 different evenings (5 week nights and 2 weekend nights) and asked in detail about a variety of activities that may have occurred on that specific day. Three of these calls were with mother and child, three were with father and child, and the final call was with all three family members. The telephone interviews with the child were designed to elaborate more specifically on children's roles in household chores, their involvement in activities with parents (e.g., leisure activities, homework, clubs and organizations), patterns of activity alone and with peers, the tenor of parent–child interactions, and the extent to which parents were knowledgeable about the child's experiences that particular day (i.e., monitoring). The telephone interview with the parent covered many of the same issues, allowing us to assess interrater agreement on shared activities. We also asked each parent about his or her involvement in household chores that day, as well as a variety of questions about that day's work schedule, child-care arrangements, marital interactions, and other matters. These data provided a window into the dynamics of daily life for children and parents in single- and dual-earner family contexts.

*Involvement in Household Chores as a Mediating Process.*    Children's involvement in housework represents a family process with potentially quite different meanings in dual- and single-earner families. Although previous research has documented that children in dual-earner families perform more housework than their peers whose mothers are full-time homemakers (Hedges & Barnett, 1972; Propper, 1972), little is known about the links between involvement in housework and children's psychosocial functioning. Our ongoing research specifically examines this issue. In addition, we have asked whether the family process in question (i.e., involvement in housework) has different consequences in single-earner than in dual-earner family contexts, an example of what Bronfenbrenner and Crouter (1983) referred to as the "person–process–context model."

We reasoned that children's contributions to the division of labor may be particularly valued in families in which both parents work outside the home. Elder (1974) argued that sons who experienced their adolescent years during the Great Depression actually flourished under conditions of economic deprivation because their involvement in paid work and household chores were valued by their parents as meaningful contributions to the family economy. Although contemporary dual-earner families are not experiencing the dire circumstances many Depression Era families faced, the involvement of children in family work may be particularly needed and valued in these "time-poor" environments. Families are also important settings for gender socialization (Huston, 1983). Thus, children probably take their cues about the appropriateness of being assigned household tasks from their parents, especially the parent of the same gender. We expected to see positive associations between involvement in housework and children's sense of competence and closeness to parents in dual-earner households, particularly when the child's level of involvement was congruent with the gender role attitudes and pattern of involvement in housework of the same-gender parent.

The results mirrored our expectations for boys, but not for girls (McHale et al., 1990). Boys from dual-earner families who were highly involved in household tasks saw themselves as more competent and rated their relationships with their parents more positively then did their counterparts who were less involved in housework. For the single-earner families, however, boys who were highly involved in housework saw themselves as less competent than their peers with fewer responsibilities. Interestingly, the boys who had the lowest scores on perceived competence were those whose level of involvement in housework was not congruent with their father's gender role attitudes or their father's own level of involvement in housework. Thus, boys in dual-earner families who performed few household chores and yet had less traditional fathers and boys in single-earner families who performed more tasks and had more traditional fathers had the lowest scores on perceived competence.

And what about girls? Perhaps because housework is such a pervasive theme in mothers' lives, we found few significant differences among girls as a function of their involvement in household chores. Our findings suggested that, regardless of family context, girls who were highly involved tended to see themselves as more competent than other girls.

The central finding in the study is that, at least for boys, the same family process (i.e., the son's level of involvement in the household economy) has quite different outcomes in single-earner and dual-earner family contexts. As we follow these families, we plan to elaborate on this theme, finding out more, for example, about the meaning fathers, mothers, and children attribute to doing household chores, including the extent to which children's involvement in housework is seen as a valued contribution to family life. We are also interested in whether children increase their involvement in housework when mothers either return to work for the first time or increase their work hours. We expect that sons' behavior will depend in part on how fathers respond to this change.

*Parental Monitoring as a Mediating Process.*     Another family process of particular importance involves parental supervision and monitoring. As mentioned earlier, several previous studies found that middle-class boys with employed mothers performed less well in school than their peers whose mothers were homemakers. Scholars have speculated that middle-class boys in dual-earner families may not receive the level of parental supervision and monitoring that they need. Bronfenbrenner and Crouter (1982), for example, suggested that:

> Sons of employed, middle-class mothers may receive less effective supervision than their peers in families in which mother remains home. The difference may be manifested in such areas as monitoring the boy's homework activities, encouraging friendships that foster social behavior, showing an interest in the child's school activities and progress, or overseeing meals, television watching, bedtime, and other routines. (p. 55)

We have explored this issue in the Family Relationships Project by elaborating on Patterson and Stouthamer-Loeber's (1984) conceptualization of "parental monitoring": The extent to which the parent is knowledgeable about the child's daily activities, companions, and whereabouts. In each of our seven evening telephone interviews, we asked parents a set of questions about the child's experiences that day that the parent could only answer correctly if he or she had been monitoring the child. Our questions addressed such commonplace issues as homework assignments, activities after school, purchases made by the child, household chores, and television watching. After our telephone conversation with the parent, the child was interviewed separately, and the match between child's and parent's answers constituted an operationalization of parental monitoring. We asked different items each evening so that parents could not "prepare" ahead of time; mothers and fathers were asked identical monitoring questions across their respective telephone interviews.

Contrary to our expectations, boys and girls from single- and dual-earner family contexts did not receive different levels of parental monitoring (Crouter et al., 1990). Nor did the distinction between full-time and part-time maternal employment make a difference. Sons and daughters received similar levels of monitoring regardless of gender and regardless of their mother's level of involvement in the labor force. We did find, not surprisingly, that mothers were better monitors than fathers. More interesting, and consistent with the person–process–context model (Bronfenbrenner & Crouter, 1983), our data indicated different patterns of association between monitoring and children's school performance, their perceptions of school competence, and conduct for boys and girls in single- and dual-earner families. Findings indicated that less well-monitored boys generally fared less well than other children and, in the case of indices of conduct, this was particularly true for less well-monitored boys from dual-earner families.

Specifically, less well-monitored boys, regardless of parental earner status, received lower school grades and felt less competent at school-related activities than other children. Analyses of separate reports of the child's conduct by mother, father, and child revealed that less well-monitored sons in dual-earner families were seen by all three respondents as having significantly more problematic conduct than other children in the sample. Interestingly, extent of parental monitoring was not linked to any of these outcomes for girls in either family context. We have not ruled out the possibility, however, that parental monitoring may have lagged effects for girls when they enter adolescence, a time when the incidence of psychological difficulties, particularly involving internalizing problems (e.g., depression), increases for girls (Eme, 1979). Our longitudinal analyses examines this possibility. We will also attempt to disentangle the causal sequence for boys: Are boys adversely affected by poor parental monitoring; are boys who are not performing well more difficult to monitor; or do parents tend to withdraw from boys who are functioning less well? It is most likely that these processes are reciprocally interrelated.

*Other Mediating Processes.*    Note that the addition of family process variables transforms maternal employment research into family research. These data begin to illuminate how the daily lives of children in contrasting family contexts may vary in ways that have developmental implications. Other evidence for the importance of including process in studies of dual-earner families comes from Moorehouse's (1991) research on cognitive and social competence in first graders. Moorehouse grouped children in her sample on the basis of stability and change in mothers' work situations over a 3-year period. Concurrent full-time employment and change to full-time employment were associated with lower scores on indices of social and cognitive competence, as rated by teachers. Most interesting, however, was the buffering role of joint mother–child activities. These negative effects of employment disappeared under conditions when mothers were highly involved with their children in such enriching activities as reading aloud, talking together, and making up stories.

One of the next steps in research on the processes linking parents' involvement in work to the development and well-being of family members should be the examination of the interrelationships among mediating processes within contexts. We have begun to do this with data from the Family Relationships Project. For example, fathers' monitoring and children's involvement in household chores are related to one another quite differently for boys and girls in dual-earner families. For boys in dual-earner families, the more housework they do, the more closely they are monitored by their fathers ($r = -.37$, $p < .05$; higher levels of monitoring represent worse monitoring). Put another way, boys in dual-earner families who do little housework tend to have fathers who know little about their activities, whereabouts, and companions. The pattern may reflect boys' level of integration into their families. Thus, the relatively lower adjustment score of dual-earner boys who do little housework and are poorly monitored may reflect that these children are on the periphery of family life in multiple ways: An insight that is only gained by examining multiple family processes. For girls, however, the more housework they do, the less closely they are monitored by their fathers

($r = .37, p < .05$; the two correlations are significantly different: $z = 3.24; p < .01$). Girls heavily involved in household tasks may be seen by their fathers as so responsible and reliable that they do not need to be as closely monitored. Again, knowing about two family processes is much more revealing than focusing simply on one. Together, the data on involvement in chores and parental monitoring begin to show why family processes have different implications for sons and daughters.

## Work as an Influence on Psychological States

The workplace has influences on the family that go far beyond simply the work status of parents. Two other types of linkages are particularly important. The first involves work as an "emotional climate" (Kanter, 1977), a setting that can influence employees' psychological states at the end of the work day, moods that in turn can be carried home where they may set in motion interactions and activities with family numbers. The second linkage, frequently overlooked but no less important, involves work as a setting for adult development, a context in which skills and perspectives are acquired that in turn affect the family system. These two types of linkages, one, by definition, transitory and the other representing more permanent change, have frequently been ignored by scholars in this area and are deserving of more systematic attention.

Anyone who has ever had an aggravating day at work will agree that it can be difficult to avoid bringing a bad mood home. Similarly, work can be a satisfying, even exhilarating experience that may influence the employee's mood at the end of the work day in a positive way. Surprisingly little research has been done on this process of work to family spillover, and much of the best research has been done very recently. Reliance on simplistic, cross-sectional research designs has often led previous researchers to interpret correlations between work and home mood as evidence of work's influence on family life. Piotrkowski and Crits-Christoph (1982), for example, correlated a measure of job mood (operationalized with a list of mood states respondents were to check off if they had experienced that mood "at any time during the last 2 days of work") and respondents' satisfaction with marital and family relations. This approach has a number of methodological limitations (see Crouter, Perry-Jenkins, Huston, & Crawford, 1989, for a critique), including the absence of a temporal sequence underlying the data on mood and behavior (e.g., data on work-induced mood preceding data on family relations), a global operationalization of mood that does not capture the ephemeral nature of psychological states, and reliance on global evaluations of family relations that, again, do not capture the short-term fluctuations in family dynamics that may be influenced by variability in mood at the end of the work day.

Several recent investigations have experimented with a variety of methodologies to capture the transitory nature of moods and the temporal sequencing of work mood and behavior in the home. Repetti (1989a), for example, focused on air traffic controllers, an occupation noted for high stress levels, exacerbated by low levels of personal control over work events. Repetti asked a sample of male air traffic controllers and their wives to complete daily surveys on 3 consecutive days. These questionnaires asked the controllers about their perceptions of the work day (i.e., the extent to which conditions were difficult) and both partners were asked to rate the controller's level of social withdrawal and anger after the work day. Repetti also utilized objective data, gathered by the National Climatic Data Center and the FAA, on weather-related visibility and traffic volume as additional perspectives on work-related stress. Repetti found that air traffic controllers returning home from demanding shifts tended to be more socially withdrawn and to exhibit less anger in marital interactions. Furthermore, this pattern was moderated by spousal support such that controllers were particularly withdrawn and unaggressive after demanding shifts when their wives had been supportive. Repetti suggested that social withdrawal is a recovery behavior that is adaptive for people in jobs that are highly stressful. She also noted that decreased anger may be a by-product of social withdrawal because spouses are less involved in conjoint activities and thus have fewer opportunities for conflict. In a related study, Repetti (1989b) examined reports of father–child interaction for a small sample of air traffic controllers who were parents of 4- to 10-year-old children. Again, difficult work conditions were associated with lower levels of emotional involvement with the child, both positive and negative.

Other researchers have examined more heterogeneous samples, using various other strategies to capture the daily work mood–family behavior dynamic. For example, Bolger, DeLongis, Kessler, and Wethington (1989) asked a sample of husbands and wives to complete short questionnaires about the day's events on each of 42 consecutive days. Respondents rated the extent to which they had experienced (a) heavy workloads, both at work and at home, and (b) interpersonal tensions, with family members or with workplace supervisors and coworkers. Bolger et al. found that when husbands experienced arguments on the job, they were more likely to quarrel with their wives when they returned home in the evening. In addition, when husbands experienced a demanding day at work they subsequently performed less work at home. In addition, their wives reported performing more housework on those days, compensating apparently for husbands' stress. In contrast, when wives experienced demanding days on the job, they subsequently did less housework but their husbands did not step in to do more. Instead, wives under stress appeared to defer housework to another day.

Similarly, Crouter et al. (1989), in the context of a larger, ongoing study of marriage, asked a small sample of husbands to complete a questionnaire about mood immediately upon return home from work. The instrument tapped stress, fatigue, arousal, and depression. Respondents and their wives were telephoned 24 hours later and asked to report on a variety of family behaviors and marital interactions that had ensued in the time since the questionnaire had been completed. High levels of stress and fatigue were associated with lower levels of subsequent involvement in housework, low levels of stress and higher levels of arousal were linked to greater subsequent involvement in active leisure activities, and higher stress was associated with wives' reports of higher levels of negative marital interactions.

Researchers interested in how moods generated at work make their mark in family interaction still face some methodological hurdles. One of these is the fact that moods are ephemeral. Thus, asking about work mood when the respondent has returned home runs the risk that the person's mood has changed during the commute home. Presumably, the longer the interval between the end of the workday and the time when mood is measured, the greater the likelihood that the individual's affect has changed. Repetti (personal communication) is currently approaching this issue in a characteristically innovative way by collecting data at work-site child-care centers when employees arrive at the end of the work day to pick up their children. Observing parent–child reunion interaction at the work-site child-care center reduces to a minimum the time interval between the end of the work day and initial involvement with a family member, enabling Repetti to examine variability in parent–child interaction across stressful and less stressful work days.

Together, these studies (e.g., Bolger et al., 1989; Crouter et al., 1989; Repetti, 1989a, 1989b) suggest that moods generated by work demands and interpersonal dynamics at work find their way into the family system where they influence the kinds of activities and interactions that occur in the family. Such data make a persuasive case that researchers should be concerned about the *nature* of the work in which employed spouses and parents are involved, not simply the fact that they are working. In addition, there is much about the relationship between moods generated at work and subsequent family behavior that remains unknown. For example, how long and under what conditions do negative (or positive) work moods linger? Is it sufficient to know the temporal order of mood and behavior, or are work moods, under some conditions, colored by the *anticipation* of a positive or negative family situation? What role do individual differences in temperament, personality, and coping style play in this relationship? Are work moods particularly powerful predictors of family behavior and interaction for individuals who are highly involved in and committed to their jobs and less so for those for whom work has less priority than other roles and interests? Do workplace interventions designed to improve workers' job satisfaction enhance employees' mood at the end of the day, and, subsequently, have positive effects on family interactions?

## Work's Impact on Adult Development

Moods, much as they may influence behavior on a short-term basis, are transitory by definition. The importance of the nature of the work that adults do is even more clear when work is conceptualized as a setting that can impede or enhance adult development. From this perspective, the roles, relationships, and activities in which employees participate at work are seen as potentially important influences on their social, cognitive, and emotional development, aspects of their psychological functioning that shape behavior not only at work, but in all contexts.

One example of work serving as a catalyst for adult development can be found in the observation by Headstart researchers that mothers who participated as volunteers in Headstart centers became more self-confident and motivated to continue their own education. Indeed, Ziegler and Freedman (1987) described the effects of this seemingly child-focused intervention as one of empowerment for many of the parents who participated.

Perhaps the best exemplar of work's influence on adult development, however, is longitudinal research conducted by Kohn and Schooler (1983). They focused on the "structural imperatives" of jobs, that is, the extent to which jobs offer workers self-direction and autonomy, as measured by (a) the routinization of work; (b) the extent to which the job is closely supervised; and (c) the substantive complexity of the tasks involved in the job. Using a large, nationally representative sample of employed men, Kohn and Schooler found that, over a 10-year period, men whose jobs permitted occupational self-direction became more "intellectually flexible," that is, better able to manipulate complex ideas. Their longitudinal data permitted them to test the alternative hypothesis, too: That men simply select themselves into jobs that reflect their level of intellectual flexibility. Their results are quite persuasive. Although both directions of effect were found, the effect of jobs on workers' subsequent psychological functioning was strong and could not be accounted for by selection effects.

Mortimer, Lorence, and Kumka (1986) expanded on these themes in longitudinal follow-up study of a sample of more than 500 men, all of whom had participated 10 years earlier in a study of attitudes and values while undergraduates at the University of Michigan. Mortimer et al.'s findings emphasized the influence of workplace autonomy showing that, over time, men in occupations that permitted autonomy and self-direction developed an increased sense of competence, work involvement, and intrinsic reward values. Moreover, work autonomy was more influential in shaping these outcomes than other indicators of work experience, including income and stability of career pattern.

Research by Kohn and Schooler and Mortimer and her colleagues makes a convincing case for the importance of work as an influence on adults' psychological functioning. These studies do not explicate, however, the possible consequences of these psychological processes for adults' involvement in nonwork settings such as the family. Nor did these studies focus on all the potential aspects of adult development that might be influenced by occupational experiences. Other dimensions of learning that may take place in some types of jobs include communication skills, interpersonal skills, responsibility and self-reliance, self-confidence, problem-solving abilities, and decision-making styles.

To examine some of these issues, I conducted an exploratory field study (Crouter, 1984a, 1984b) in a heavy manufacturing plant that was internationally known for its participative management system. In this factory, blue-collar machinists and assembly workers were organized into small teams. The teams had unusually broad responsibilities, including interviewing and selecting their own workers, providing feedback to team members on performance problems, ordering inventory, quality control, and maintaining and repairing their own equipment. From the perspective of development in an occupational context, this was a rich learning environment. In interviews with team members about their perceptions of the connections between their work and their personal life, many employees emphasized that they had learned new ways of dealing with others through the team system (see Crouter, 1984a). In particular, they stressed that they found themselves using more democratic approaches to problem solving and decision making at home. A single-parent mother said, "I say things to my daughter that I know are a result of the way things are at work. I ask her, 'What do you think about that?' or 'How would you handle this problem?' I tend to deal with her the way we deal with people at work. The logic is the same." A male team advisor summarized the same idea by saying, "It has helped in terms of dealing with my family. I'm more willing to get their opinions. We hold 'team meetings' at home to make decisions. After all, a family is kind of like a team."

But what happens when work provides psychological growth for one marital partner but not the other? To me, this is one of the most fascinating, unexplored areas in the work–family literature. I saw hints in my interviews with blue-collar women in the participative plant. Consider these quotes: "My husband got to the point where he didn't want to hear about my work. He's a little threatened by my learning new things." And another: "Somehow getting involved in inventory showed me I had ability . . . I could learn new things. It was a shock. I thought I'd be a machine operator all my life." Later she added:

> There are times I'd like to stay at work *longer* and can't because of my home obligations. My husband doesn't understand why I like it here so much and why I'd want to work later. He thinks I've become terribly independent. It bothered him at first . . . that I felt such a part of my team. He had trouble understanding and felt left out.

These interviews provide a window into a real workplace, a setting that is far more important than simply a shadowy place where people go when they are not at home. This setting has activities going on, challenges such as mastering the inventory system or working through a performance problem in the team. It has the tugs that come from relationships with and obligations to co-workers. It is a place where learning takes place, where people may develop new repertoires of interacting with others or new conceptions of themselves that they cannot help but bring home with them.

My position is a straightforward one. To really understand the interrelationship between work and family as *settings* for human development, we must think about the issue in a more thorough, systematic way. As family researchers, we have typically conceptualized work as a place that is interesting primarily because it removes parents from families for certain amounts of time. That is where the field is now. We are working hard at elaborating how families manage when both partners spend substantial amounts of time away from the family in these shadowy places. We will only fully understand work and family as settings when we pay equal attention to what is going on at work: the stresses and strains and exhilarations that shape workers' moods and get carried home, as well as the development of skills and views of self that occurs for those fortunate enough to work in settings that provide those opportunities.

## FAMILY INFLUENCES ON THE WORKPLACE

A picture of the interconnections between work and family would be incomplete without the recognition that influences operate in both directions; aspects of adults' experiences in the job affect their behavior at home, and features of adults' family lives make their mark on the workplace (Kanter, 1977). In general, however, the ways in which families influence the workplace have received little attention from researchers (Crouter, 1984b). How do problems at home influence employees' productivity at work? How do key family transitions such as the transition to parenthood or divorce influence employees' behavior on the job? Answers to these questions are important because they may provide needed evidence to convince employers and policymakers that it is in their best interest to develop and institute policies that are supportive of employees' family roles and responsibilities (Kamerman & Kahn, 1987).

Applying the same organizational structure to the literature on family influences on workplace behavior and development that was utilized to organize the research on the influence of work on behavior and development in the family reveals how little empirical work has been done in this area. Indeed, most studies have looked at the family as a social address, comparing the workplace productivity, for example, of parents versus childless adults or mothers versus fathers. For example, Fernandez (1986) surveyed more than 5,000 corporate employees about the connections between their child-care arrangements and their productivity on the job. Not surprisingly, parents of very young children were most likely to report that problems with child care increased their absenteeism and tardiness and lowered their ability to be efficient, attentive, and productive in work-related matters. Although applicable to both parents, this pattern was stronger for mothers than for fathers. Similar findings have been noted by Emlen and Koren (1984) in their book, *Hard to Find and Difficult to Manage: The Effects of Child Care on the Workplace*.

Studies of this genre rely exclusively on self-report data, which may be difficult to interpret in this context. Do workers accurately report on the links between their home lives and their behavior on the job, or are their responses colored in part by the hope that the survey will be used to improve their work situation (Crouter & MacDermid, 1990)?

There is virtually no persuasive research on other important familial conditions that may influence employees' functioning at work, such as marital distress, separation or divorce, providing care for an elderly parent, or coping with a family member's chronic illness. To be persuasive, such research would need to include objective reports of productivity, performance, and relationships at work and to carefully monitor selective attrition, as those experiencing the most stress would be most likely to leave their jobs or reduce their job involvement.

To my knowledge, little research has explored the processes within the workplace that mediate the effects of family status. Several recent studies, however, identify what some of those processes might be. Repetti (1987), for example, in a study of the relationship between the work environment and the mental health of female bank personnel, emphasized the importance of having a supportive supervisor. Even in environments generally perceived as stressful, employees fared better when they perceived their supervisor to be supportive. Given the well-documented strains that dual-earner mothers experience, particularly those with young children, a logical extension of Repetti's research would examine whether employed mothers with young children are particularly likely to benefit from a supportive relationship with a supervisor, and are particularly likely to be "at risk" for mental health problems if they have an unsupportive supervisor.

The work organization's formal policies on issues such as flexible scheduling, child care, and parental leave are important, too. Survey data collected by Greenberger, Goldberg, Hamill, O'Neil, and Payne (1989) indicated that satisfaction with the formal work–family policies and benefits of the workplace as well as social support from co-workers and supervisor accounted for a substantial portion of the variance in married women's sense of commitment to the work organization. To a lesser extent, the workplace supports were linked to enhanced job satisfaction and lower role strain for married women as well. Although Greenberger et al. found no significant relationships between formal workplace supports and married men's work-related attitudes, they did find modest associations between increased informal workplace support and higher organizational commitment, lower role strain, and fewer health problems for married men. Thus, for both men and women, the extent to which the workplace is supportive of them as individuals and family members appears to have consequences for their work-related attitudes.

There is some evidence that moods generated at home are brought to work. Bolger et al.'s (1989) daily diary study found temporal sequences of interpersonal interactions suggestive of mood spillover from family to work for husbands: Arguments at home with wife or with child increased the probability of arguments with co-workers and supervisors the subsequent day. Wives reported domestic disputes, too, but no relationship was found between arguments at home and subsequent arguments on the job for wives. More research is needed to elaborate on these issues. For example, do fathers of young children in dual-earner families who are drafted somewhat involuntarily into involvement in child care (see Crouter, Perry-Jenkins, McHale, & Huston, 1987) generalize their feelings of role strain to their interactions at work? Under what conditions, if any, do husbands and wives generalize *positive* emotional affect from family to work?

The issue of gender differences in the permeability of the work setting to family influence is also interesting and merits further study. Bolger et al.'s (1989) findings run counter to previous theoretical work (Pleck, 1977) and qualitative research (Crouter, 1984b) that suggested that women at work are more influenced by their family roles and responsibilities than are men because the traditional division of labor has assigned responsibility for the domestic sphere (housework, childrearing) to women. Future research should explore the reasons why men are more likely than women to generalize negative affect from family to work. One possibility has to do with gender differences in work-based friendships and confidantes that may buffer women from generalizing negative feelings brought to work from the family.

For the sake of symmetry, this chapter should conclude by reviewing the research on the family as a context for adult development, particularly developmental outcomes that, by their nature, should make their mark on the individual's behavior at work. This body of research would include studies on how the experience of raising children instills interpersonal skills that adults generalize to the workplace and research on how the communication and negotiation patterns, learned in the marital relationship, are translated into workplace interactions. These issues, however, remain neglected by researchers, who have consistently conceptualized the family as a context for child development, but not for adult development. Although we know a little bit about adult personality change across the transition to parenthood (e.g., Feldman & Aschenbrenner, 1983; Hawkins & Belsky, 1989), extant studies have not taken a long-term view, and no study has examined the implications of these personality changes for parents' behavior in nonfamilial settings such as work. Do men, for example, who become more emotionally expressive when they become fathers extend that interpersonal style into their relations with co-workers? Feminist philosopher Sara Ruddick (1982) argued that through the intensive "practice" of raising children, mothers develop new values and ways of looking at the world, "conceptions of abilities and virtues, according to which they measure themselves and interpret their actions" (p. 83). The next step is to attempt to document empirically that this developmental process indeed takes place and then to explore whether it has implications for relationships and behavior outside the family, including the workplace. This set of issues, at the heart of the ecology of adult development, remains to be explored.

# CONCLUSION

To summarize, we know more about work's impacts on families than we know about the family's impact on work settings. The development of knowledge in both areas of inquiry, however, has proceeded quite similarly. In both areas, the "social address" literature has long predominated—such investigations search for differential or family outcomes as a function, for example, of single- versus dual-earner status. Next, there is increasing research attention—and rightly so—to the processes within the family that link earner situations to the psychological well-being of parents and children. In contrast, however, there is very little research on the processes within the workplace that link family status to employees' functioning on the job. Possibilities for interesting studies abound. As mentioned, an interesting body of research has been initiated focusing on how moods acquired in one setting influence subsequent behavior in the other. Finally, the very promising question of how adult development—stimulated by experiences in one setting—makes its mark on the other has received very little attention from researchers.

To make this body of knowledge more coherent and complete, more family researchers must venture into the actual work settings in which employed parents spend so much of their time. As researchers focused on families and children, we tend to take the same approach when designing a study. We first identify the children or adolescents in which we are interested, identifying them through day-care centers, pediatricians, or schools. Then we reach out to the children's parents. Finally, with varying degrees of detail, we ask those parents about their work situations. Thus, our samples often have as many work settings represented as employed parents. Is it any wonder that work appears in so much "work and family research" as a status, or, at best, as a shadowy source of perceived stress or satisfaction? More family researchers need to begin at the other end by locating a workplace that is interesting for theoretical reasons. Repetti's (1989a, 1989b) research on air traffic controllers exemplifies this approach to designing a study on the interconnections between work and family. Other examples include my exploratory research in a participatively managed heavy manufacturing plant (Crouter, 1984a, 1984b) and Hareven's (1982) classic historical study of a New England textile mill and the families associated with it. Such studies locate people via their jobs and then work backward to family and children. By immersing ourselves in another section of the work–family system, we will develop a richer picture of the ways in which these two central contexts of adult life are interconnected.

# ACKNOWLEDGMENT

This chapter is based on a presentation at the Family Research Consortium Fourth Annual Summer Institute, Cape Cod, Massachusetts, May 1989. The

Family Relationships Project is funded by the National Institute for Child Health and Human Development (R01 HD 21050), Ann Crouter and Susan McHale, co-principal investigators.

## REFERENCES

Banducci, R. (1967). The effects of mother's employment on the achievement, aspirations, and expectations of the child. *Personnel and Guidance Journal, 46,* 263–267.

Bolger, N., DeLongis, A., Kessler, R. C., & Wethington, E. (1989). The contagion of stress across multiple roles. *Journal of Marriage and the Family, 51,* 175–183.

Bronfenbrenner, U. (1979). *The ecology of human development: Experiments by nature and design.* Cambridge, MA: Harvard University Press.

Bronfenbrenner, U. (1989). Ecology systems theory. In G. J. Whitehurst (Ed.), *Annals of child development* (Vol. 6, pp. 185–246). New York: JAI Press.

Bronfenbrenner, U., & Crouter, A. C. (1982). Work and family through time and space. In S. Kamerman & C. Hayes (Eds.), *Families that work: Children in a changing world* (pp. 39–83). Washington, DC: National Academy Press.

Bronfenbrenner, U., & Crouter, A. C. (1983). The evolution of environmental models in developmental research. In P. Mussen (Ed.), *Handbook of child psychology* (pp. 357–414). New York: Wiley.

Crouter, A. C. (1984a). Participative work as an influence on human development. *Journal of Applied Developmental Psychology, 5,* 71–90.

Crouter, A. C. (1984b). Spillover from family to work: The neglected side of the work-family interface. *Human Relations, 37,* 425–442.

Crouter, A. C., & MacDermid, S. M. (1990). Into the lion's den: Methodological issues for work-family research inside the corporation. *Marriage and Family Review, 15,* 59–74.

Crouter, A. C., MacDermid, S., McHale, S. M., & Perry-Jenkins, M. (1990). Parental monitoring and perceptions of children's school performance and conduct in dual- and single-earner families. *Developmental Psychology, 26,* 649–657.

Crouter, A. C., Perry-Jenkins, M., Huston, T. L., & Crawford, D. (1989). The influence of work-induced psychological states on behavior at home. *Basic and Applied Social Psychology, 10*(3), 273–292.

Crouter, A. C., Perry-Jenkins, M., Huston, T. L., & McHale, S. M. (1987). Processes underlying father involvement in dual-earner and single-earner families. *Developmental Psychology, 23,* 431–440.

Davis, K. (1984). Wives and work: The sex role revolution and its consequences. *Population and Development Review, 10,* 397–417.

Elder, G. H. (1974). *Children of the great depression.* Chicago: University of Chicago Press.

Elder, G. H. (1981). History and the family: The discovery of complexity. *Journal of Marriage and the Family, 43,* 489–519.

Eme, R. E. (1979). Sex differences in childhood psychopathology: A review. *Psychological Bulletin, 86,* 574–596.

Emlen, A. C., & Koren, P. E. (1984). *Hard to find and difficult to manage: The effects of childcare on the workplace.* Portland, OR: The Workplace Partnership.

Feldman, S. S., & Aschenbrenner, B. (1983). Impact of parenthood on various aspects of masculinity and femininity: A short-term longitudinal study. *Development Psychology, 19*(2), 278–289.

Fernandez, J. P. (1986). *Child care and corporate productivity: Resolving family/work conflicts.* Lexington, MA: Lexington Books.

Gerson, K. (1985). *Hard choices: How women decide about work, career, and motherhood.* Berkeley: University of California Press.

Gold, D., & Andres, D. (1978). Developmental comparisons between ten-year-old children with employed and nonemployed mothers. *Child Development, 49,* 75–84.

Greenberger, E., Goldberg, W. A., Hamill, S., O'Neil, R., & Payne, C. (1989). Contributions of a supportive work environment to parents' well-being and orientation to work. *American Journal of Community Psychology, 17,* 755–783.

Hareven, T. K. (1982). *Family time and industrial time.* New York: Cambridge University Press.

Hawkins, A., & Belsky, J. (1989). The role of father involvement in personality change in men across the transition to parenthood. *Family Relations, 38,* 378–384.

Hayghe, H. (1986, February). Rise in mothers' labor force activity includes those with infants. *Monthly Labor Review,* 43–45.

Hedges, J. N., & Barnett, J. K. (1972). Working women and the division of household tasks. *Monthly Labor Review, 95,* 9–14.

Hoffman, L. W. (1989). Effects of maternal employment in the two-parent family. *American Psychologist, 44*(2), 283–292.

Huston, A. C. (1983). Sex-typing. In P. Mussen (Ed.), *Handbook of child psychology* (pp. 387–467). New York: Wiley.

Kamerman, S. B., & Kahn, A. J. (1987). *The responsive workplace: Employers and a changing labor force.* New York: Columbia University Press.

Kanter, R. M. (1977). *Work and family in the United States: A critical review and agenda for research and policy.* New York: Russell Sage.

Kline, M., & Cowan, P. A. (1989). Re-thinking the connections among "work" and "family" and "well-being." *Journal of Social Behavior and Personality, 3,* 61–90.

Kohn, M. L., & Schooler, C. (1983). *Work and personality: An inquiry into the impact of social stratification.* Norwood, NJ: Ablex.

McHale, S. M., Bartko, W. T., Crouter, A. C., & Perry-Jenkins, M. (1990). Children's housework and psychosocial functioning: The mediating effects of parents' sex role behaviors and attitudes. *Child Development, 61,* 1413–1426.

Moorehouse, M. (1991). Linking maternal employment patterns to mother-child activities and children's school competence. *Developmental Psychology, 27,* 295–303.

Mortimer, J. T., Lorence, J., & Kumka, D. S. (1986). *Work, family, and personality.* Norwood, NJ: Ablex.

Patterson, G. R., & Stouthamer-Loeber, M. (1984). The correlation of family management practices and delinquency. *Child Development, 55,* 1299–1307.

Piotrkowski, C. S., & Crits-Christoph, P. (1982). Women's jobs and family adjustment. In J. Aldous (Ed.), *Two paychecks: Life in dual-earner families* (pp. 105–127). Beverly Hills, CA: Sage.

Pleck, J. (1977). The work-family role system. *Social Problems, 24,* 417–427.

Propper, A. M. (1972). The relationship of maternal employment to adolescent roles, activities, and parental relationships. *Journal of Marriage and the Family, 34,* 417–421.

Repetti, R. L. (1987). Individual and common components of the social environment of work and psychological well-being. *Journal of Personality and Social Psychology, 52,* 710–720.

Repetti, R. L. (1989a). Effects of daily workload on subsequent behavior during marital interaction: The roles of social withdrawal and spouse support. *Journal of Personality and Social Psychology, 57,* 651–659.

Repetti, R. L. (1989b). *Daily job stress and father–child interaction.* Paper presented at the biennial meeting of the society for Research in Child Development, Kansas City, MO.

Ruddick, S. (1982). Maternal thinking. In B. Thorne (Ed.), *Rethinking the family: Some feminist questions* (pp. 76–94). New York: Longman.

Zelizer, V. (1985). *Pricing the priceless child.* New York: Basic.

Ziegler, E. F., & Freedman, J. (1987). Head start: A pioneer of family support. In S. Kagan, D. Powell, B. Weissbourd, & E. F. Zigler (Eds.), *American's family support programs* (pp. 57–76). New Haven: Yale.

# 2 Families and Maternal Employment During Infancy: New Linkages

P. Lindsay Chase-Lansdale
*Harris Graduate School of Public Policy Studies, and Chapin Hall Center for Children, University of Chicago*

The links between family life and the world of work have long been of research interest (Bronfenbrenner & Crouter, 1982). However, examining these links when infants are concerned represents a recent focus, involving considerable controversy. Employed mothers of infants became a majority only since the late 1980s. Specifically, the percentages of employed women with children under 1 year of age were 51% in 1987, 43% in 1982, and 32% in 1977 (U.S. Bureau of the Census, 1988).

Controversy about this issue has been fueled by four main factors: (a) a paucity of research; (b) conflicting findings as to negative short- and long-term consequences for children; (c) relevant knowledge that has developed in disparate, unconnected literatures; and (d) recent policy decisions to require low-income mothers of infants to be employed (Chase-Lansdale & Brooks-Gunn, in press; Chase-Lansdale, Michael, & Desai, 1991).

A clear message that emerges from the controversy is the need to develop a more substantive integration of the related knowledge that does exist. The goal of this volume—exploring family relationships with other contexts—provides a useful conceptual framework for synthesizing what we know about maternal employment during infancy. Toward that end, this chapter defines and examines work–family linkages within three relevant literatures: maternal employment, child care, and intervention. These literatures are briefly reviewed, and suggestions for future work are indicated. In each case, it is evident that specifying what is meant by work–family linkages improves our understanding of the phenomenon. The final section of the chapter introduces the recent data set, Children of the National Longitudinal Survey of Youth (NLSY). Findings from studies using this unusual data set are presented with the goal of illustrating new opportunities for pursuing work–family linkages.

## MATERNAL EMPLOYMENT LITERATURE

### Research Review

*Socioemotional Development.* The primary focus of the maternal employment literature pertaining to infants has been on socioemotional development, in particular the infant's attachment to the mother. A secondary focus has been on cognitive development. Concerns have developed regarding the negative effects of daily mother–child separation, one argument being that infants are more vulnerable to separation than are preschoolers. Several recent studies of primarily White middle-class families have shown that when mothers work full time during their children's infancy, their infants are more likely to develop insecure attachment relationships by 1 year of age. The Strange Situation (Ainsworth, Blehar, Waters, & Wall, 1978) has been used in these studies to assess attachment behavior in the laboratory setting, by means of a series of mother–child separations and reunions. During reunions in this assessment, infants of full-time employed mothers are more likely to avoid their mothers rather than reunite happily (Barglow, Vaughn, & Molitor, 1987; Schwartz, 1983). Other studies indicate that boys of employed mothers are more likely to develop insecure attachment relationships to both mothers and fathers (Belsky & Rovine; 1988; Chase-Lansdale & Owen, 1987). These studies have all raised cautions regarding the risks of early maternal employment.

Yet, there is currently no consensus regarding the meaning of avoidant behavior, the central outcome measure in these studies. Although it has been shown to relate to antecedent and subsequent maladaptive behavior in children of homemaker mothers, avoidant behavior could be adaptive on the part of infants who are used to separating from their mothers every day due to employment. Such behavior may reflect a healthy independence (Clarke-Stewart, 1989). One way to test this question would be to examine developmental trajectories (after the first year) of avoidant infants of employed and nonemployed mothers to see if different patterns of socioemotional adjustment emerge. Unfortunately, no such long-term data are currently available.[1]

*Cognitive Development.* In contrast to the research attention devoted to the socioemotional domain, only a few studies have examined effects of early maternal employment on cognitive development (Gottfried, 1991). In terms of short-

---

[1] A recent study conducted in Great Britain by Melhuish, Hennessy, Martin, and Moss (1990) found no long-term negative effects of early maternal employment on children's socioemotional adjustment at age 6 years, although attachment per se was not assessed at age 1 year.

term effects, the findings are contradictory. Two studies report no relation between early resumption of employment and cognitive development in 1-year-olds
(Hock, 1980; Pedersen, Cain, Zaslow, & Anderson, 1982), whereas two other
studies show a decrement in Stanford Binet or Bayley scores among 2-year-olds
whose mothers were employed during their child's first year of life (Cohen,
1978; Schacter, 1981).[2]

Regarding long-term effects (7 to 8 years) on cognitive development of maternal employment during infancy, three studies using self-selected samples have
addressed this topic. Two studies find positive effects of mothers' employment on
cognitive development and grade performance of 7- and 8-year-olds, one study
involving an impoverished sample of African-American families in the Southern
United States (Cherry & Eaton, 1977), and the second study involving families
of various income levels in Sweden (Andersson, 1989). Vandell and Corasaniti,
(1991) report deleterious consequences of mothers' early employment on IQ tests
and study habits in a sample of third graders in Dallas, Texas. Each investigator
poses that the timing of mothers' employment (i.e., return during infancy), has
an important influence on children's developmental trajectories, but cautions are
also raised because the quality of the child-care settings was not assessed; (more
detail on this issue is presented in the child-care section; Chase-Lansdale, Michael, & Desai, 1991).

## Work–Family Linkages

The maternal employment studies have defined work–family linkages from the
standpoint of the mother's work status or employment history. The link that is
examined is the effect on child outcome, with little embellishment in design
involving mediating or moderating factors—Bronfenbrenner's social address
model (1988). Children of employed mothers are compared with children of
nonemployed mothers. Although this has been a logical place to start in a nascent
literature, work–family linkages as defined by the mother's employment can be
better specified and more systematically explored by considering five additional
issues: (a) sampling, (b) selectivity, (c) family context, (d) job characteristics,
and (e) design issues. Because Crouter's chapter in this volume addresses the
family context and job characteristics, I do not focus on them here.

*Sampling.*    Most of the studies on mother's employment during infancy have
utilized small, self-selected, White, two-parent middle-class families (but see
Vaughn, Gove, & Egeland, 1980, as an exception). Clearly, this poses problems
regarding generalizability to other groups, such as low-income families, single-
mother households, or Hispanic and African-American families. For low-income

---

[2] This former study has been strongly criticized for confounding low birth weight and single
parenthood with mothers' employment (Hoffman, 1984).

families, maternal employment may represent a life line out of poverty with positive outcomes for infants. Cultural differences also exist regarding maternal employment. For example, it is more widely accepted and has a longer history among African-American than White families (Heyns, 1982; Washington, 1988). Our understanding of the effects of maternal employment during infancy will be greatly improved if larger, more varied, and preferably nationally representative samples can be obtained (Chase-Lansdale, Mott, Brooks-Gunn, & Phillips, 1991).

*Selectivity.*    Failure to address preexisting differences between mothers who resume employment early and those who do not is another problem in current studies. For example, studies have shown that mothers who return to work early in their infants' first year of life are more likely to have higher levels of ability and education, and to have fewer and more widely spaced children (Desai & Waite, 1991; Eggebeen, 1988). Other between-group differences include higher levels of maternal separation anxiety among homemaker mothers (DeMeis, Hock, & McBride, 1986), higher levels of achievement aspirations among employed mothers (Furstenberg, Brooks-Gunn, & Morgan, 1987), and greater likelihood of good health on the part of the infants of employed mothers (Brooks-Gunn, 1991). Such differences need to be accounted for when examining work–family linkages, and clearly require larger and more varied samples.

*Design Issues.*    A third challenge to examining work–family linkages in infancy has been the difficulty in executing prospective designs. This is particularly problematic in studies evaluating long-term effects of early employment. Following a sample from birth to 7–8 years of age is expensive and time consuming. Yet, the long-term questions are the most pressing. Do the problems in attachment identified at 1 year of age persist into the preschool years? Such trajectories have been primarily studied in samples of nonemployed mother families. The long-term studies reviewed here have all had to rely on retrospective accounts of employment history. This introduces problems of reliability as well as selection bias, the latter involving the risk that certain families either with particular employment histories or particular child outcomes will systematically refuse to participate (cf. Chase-Lansdale & Owen, 1987). The NICHD Study of Early Child Care and the National Longitudinal Survey of Youth (discussed later) both offer opportunities to address the issues of sampling, selectivity, and retrospective designs.

## CHILD-CARE LITERATURE

### Research Review

Until recently, the child-care literature has had a distinct or encapsulated orientation, focusing specifically on links between the quality of the child-care environment and children's development, without taking into account links to the family. The emphasis has been primarily on center care and more recently on family day-care homes (Hayes, Palmer, & Zaslow, 1990). A sizable body of literature has shown that certain structural aspects of child-care settings (i.e., those that can more readily be regulated from a policy standpoint) are important correlates of the emotional and cognitive development of children in care. These child-care characteristics include the following: ratio of adults to infants, stability of care-givers and care arrangements, group size, training of caregivers, and the physical space and safety of the environment (Hayes et al., 1990; Phillips, 1987; Phillips, Howes, & Whitebook, 1992).

Other studies within the child-care literature have focused more on the qualita-tive aspects of interaction in the care setting. These include the responsivity of the caregivers, the extent of individual attention they devote to the infants, the complexity of language used, and the emotional atmosphere of the setting, (e.g., cheerful tones of voice, engaged and active but calm children; McCartney, 1984; Owen, Cross, Henderson, & Cox, 1990; Phillips, 1987).

As mentioned earlier, one of the major limitations of the maternal employ-ment and infancy studies is that the quality of child care was not measured. The negative findings that have emerged in some studies may be due to the infants' experience in poor quality child-care settings. Without observations of the in-fants in these alternate care settings, we are limited in our understanding of why higher rates of avoidance occur in the attachment studies or why contradictory findings emerge regarding effects on cognitive development. Indeed, in some of the studies the investigators speculate that the findings may be due to un-measured quality of child care. For example, Andersson (1989) pointed out that positive effects on cognitive development may be due to the fact that in Sweden, day care is of high quality, publicly funded, and widely accepted. In contrast, the Vandell and Corasaniti study took place in Texas, where child-care standards are among the lowest in the United States.

## Work–Family Linkages

*Interdependence of Systems.*    A recent turning point in the child-care litera-ture is the explicit acknowledgment in research designs that the child participates in two systems—the child-care system and the family system—and that he or she actively constructs a view of the social world based on experiences in both contexts. Furthermore, research has now developed demonstrating that the two systems are interdependent and that considerable insights may be gleaned by exploring the links between the two systems (Zaslow, 1991). The complexity of the question, "How does maternal employment during infancy affect develop-ment?" can be more fully addressed not only by examining the child in the family and child-care settings, but also by asking, "How does one system affect the other?"

This orientation is evident in several recent studies. Howes and Olenick (1986) showed that certain families choose certain types of child care. For example, families who are more stressed, experience less social support, and engage in restrictive parenting, are more likely to select poor quality child care. Howes and Olenick suggested a pattern of interdependence where a cycle of deterioration develops due to difficulties compounded by both settings. This is similar to the pattern of linkages that Patterson (1986) proposed in his studies of older children with antisocial behavior. In these studies, stress and other factors negatively impact parenting that leads to coercive cycles of interaction at home and antisocial behavior on the part of the child. When the child is in his or her other important social context—the school—he or she experiences poor peer relations, negative evaluations by teachers, and poor self-esteem. The child's antisocial behavior is exacerbated, which in turn has stronger negative effects on the parents, and coercive cycles become worse at home.

In contrast to these negative links, other work has examined positive connections between family dynamics and child-care quality. For example, families with high-quality parenting as measured in infancy or with secure infant–mother attachments choose better quality child care for their children (Howes, Rodning, Galluzzo, & Myers, 1988; Owen et al., 1990). The latter study also indicates that an infant's strong, secure attachments with parents can buffer the child against experiences in poor quality child care.

*NICHD Study of Early Child Care.*    Taking into account the quality of the child's experience in the family and child-care setting and the interdependence of these two contexts is one of the central goals of the NICHD Study of Early Child Care. This is a multisite consortium funded specifically to examine short- and long-term outcomes of full-time maternal employment during the child's infancy as well as the processes leading to these outcomes. There is a shared protocol across 10 sites, resulting in a sample of approximately 1,200 infants and their families followed from early infancy through 3 years of age (NICHD Early Child Care Network, 1993).

*Clinical Intervention in the Child-Care Setting.*    To take the work–family link in the child-care literature one step further, one may ask the question, "Can intervention to improve a child's socioemotional adjustment in the child-care setting affect the family system?" Typically, when infants and young children develop emotional problems, pediatricians or preschool caregivers refer families to mental health specialists who then deal directly with the family in an office or home setting. With the widespread increases in early maternal employment, some mental health professionals and researchers are responding to the viewpoint that the infant and preschool child construct a view of the self and the social world based on experiences in the two systems—child-care setting and family. For example, a new type of clinical consultation has been developed at the

Infant–Parent Program at the University of California at San Francisco, where child-care providers—either centers or family day-care homes—can request clinical consultation on behalf of a child having problems within the child-care setting (Johnston, 1989). Clinical work is undertaken with the child-care providers and the child in that setting, not with the family as is usually the case. The consultation is designed to promote a more sensitive, effective caregiving environment and to enable the child with emotional problems to function more healthily in the child-care setting.

Case study reports by Johnston (1989) indicate that such intervention is successful, as indicated by the child's improved behavior in the child-care setting. The question remains, however, as to whether the family system changes and/or whether positive experiences in the child-care setting buffer the child from negative experiences at home. A study by Howes (1989) lends support for the latter hypothesis. Infants who are insecurely attached to their mothers but securely attached to their child-care providers are more socially competent than infants who are insecurely attached to both mother and caregiver.

Thus, the work–family linkage within the child-care literature necessitates measurement of processes within the child-care and family systems as well as an examination of the paths of mutual influence that one system may have on the other. Other linkages between the family and child-care context that remain to be explored are the ways in which families learn about different child-care settings in the community and the reasons why families choose different types of child care (i.e., center, relative, father, day-care home). The impact of these different types of care is also a new area of inquiry; findings from the NLSY along these lines are presented in the last section of this chapter.

## INTERVENTION LITERATURE

### Research Review

*Early Childhood Education.*    Two components of the intervention literature are relevant here. The first involves early childhood education programs which attempt to counteract the ravages of poverty by providing enriching experiences for young children whose development may be in jeopardy (Zigler & Muenchow, 1984). In some programs, enrolling children during infancy has been a primary goal in order to maximize the impact of the curricula (in some cases as early as 6 weeks of age; cf. Burchinal, Lee, & Ramey, 1989). Measurement of the mothers' employment status has not been a high priority in studies of these programs, nor has concern about mother–child separation been a central issue as it has in the maternal employment studies. Rather, the focus has been on the child's experience in an enriching and cognitively stimulating environment.

The conclusion from this considerable body of research is that well-designed early intervention programs of this nature have significant positive effects on children's intellectual development and school achievement (Brooks-Gunn, 1990; Burchinal et al., 1989; Clarke-Stewart & Fein, 1983; Infant Health and Development Program, 1990; Lazar, Darlington, Murray, Royce, & Snipper, 1982; Ramey & Campbell, 1987). The possible effects of mother–infant separation on emotional development due to enrollment in these programs have often not been examined, yet clearly the same questions that have emerged from the attachment literature apply here as well.

*Employment Training Programs for Mothers.*    Interventions to improve the economic standing of impoverished mothers by means of educational and employment training programs are also relevant to the issue of employment effects on infants. The United States has a long history of requiring impoverished mothers of young children to work (Chase-Lansdale & Vinovskis, in press) dating back to the post-Civil War era. The Chapin Hall Center for Children,[3] for example, was originally a "half orphanage" so that widows of Civil War soldiers could place their children in residential care, thus freeing these women to work 6 days per week, visiting their children on Sundays.

In the past decade, there have been renewed efforts to develop employment training programs for impoverished mothers of young children. These have included (a) the Work Incentive (WIN) demonstration programs, established by Congress in 1981 to stimulate such initiatives at the state level for welfare recipients; and (b) large-scale experimental programs (e.g., Project Redirection), primarily for adolescent mothers at multiple sites across the country, designed and evaluated by nonprofit research firms such as the Manpower Demonstration Research Corporation (MDRC) and Mathematica Policy Research, Inc. (Chase-Lansdale, Brooks-Gunn, & Paikoff, 1991).

The WIN demonstration programs and the other experimental comprehensive training programs such as Project Redirection have had moderately positive effects on promoting maternal employment and economic self-sufficiency (Nightingale, Wissoker, Burbridge, Bawden, & Jeffries, 1990; Polit, 1989). These results (in the context of broad political support), contributed to a significant reform in our nation's welfare system—the Family Support Act of 1988.

The Family Support Act of 1988 reflects policymakers' intent to change the U.S. welfare system from one of income maintenance for poor families to a system of transitional assistance to financial self-sufficiency (Chase-Lansdale & Vinovskis, in press). Mothers' responsibility toward their children has been reconceptualized; whereas the Aid to Dependent Children Program (AFDC) once had the goal of enabling poor mothers to stay home to raise their children, the goal of the Family Support Act is to facilitate mothers' financial responsibility to

---

[3] In 1985, the board of directors voted to establish the Chapin Hall Center for Children as an independent children's policy research center at the University of Chicago. The center's goal is to improve the lives of children through knowledge, and it has a diverse, multidisciplinary research program.

their children through employment. The demographic changes cited at the beginning of this chapter also influenced the formulation of this policy. As Senator Daniel Moynihan stated when introducing the bill to the Senate, "It is now the *normal* experience for women to work, at least part-time. This accounts for the expectation and desire that AFDC mothers should do likewise" (U.S. Senate, 1987, p. 5).

Under the Family Support Act of 1988, mothers who wish to receive AFDC must participate in educational and employment training programs and seek employment. Under previous law, this was expected of mothers whose youngest child was 6 years of age. The Family Support Act requires this of mothers of children age 3 years and older; states have the option of requiring mothers of infants to participate. Mothers without a high school diploma or GED are required to stay in school or to undergo educational services, regardless of the ages of the children involved. Thus, increasing proportions of mothers of infants will seek child care. States cover the majority of child-care costs while the mother is on AFDC and for 12 months after she leaves the system for employment. No provision is made to ensure the quality of the child care beyond the enforcement of existing state standards; mothers choose from what is available in the community (Chase-Lansdale & Vinovskis, in press; Cherlin, in press).

## Work–Family Linkages

The assumptions of the employment training programs, including those under the Family Support Act, are that mothers' exit from the welfare system (attaining economic self-sufficiency) will have positive implications for herself and her child. A concern that has been raised is that infants' experiences during mothers' efforts to improve her economic status have been given short shrift. Child care available in the community for these mothers is at best variable in quality, and in all likelihood, of low quality. An issue that must be addressed is the relative power of indirect effects on the child of mother's improved financial status versus the direct effects on the child of the experience in child care. Assuming that mothers' exit from the welfare system has positive effects on the family, will these outweigh the possible negative impacts of poor quality child care or mother–infant separation?

Interestingly, interventions have been directed at either impoverished mothers or children, but rarely both simultaneously (Clewell, Brooks-Gunn, & Benasich, 1989). Recently, goals to develop two-generation programs have become more explicit (Chase-Lansdale, Brooks-Gunn, & Paikoff, 1991; Smith, in press), the logical argument being that improvement in mothers' lives (i.e., employment vs. welfare) combined with improvement in children's lives (i.e., high-quality vs. low-quality child care) would have additive or multiplicative positive effects on children's development.

These assumptions are largely untested (see Field, Widmayer, Greenberg, &

Stoller, 1982, as an exception) and represent one of the most compelling work–family linkages to consider. Hypotheses along these lines will be assessed in two new intervention programs—New Chance, administered and evaluated by MDRC, and ECCO (Expanded Child Care Options), developed and evaluated by Mathematica Policy Research, Inc. (Chase-Lansdale, Brooks-Gunn, & Paikoff, 1991). In the latter demonstration, children and mothers will be randomly assigned to three groups: basic Family Support Act services (reimbursement of 1 year of child care as available in the community); extended Family Support Act services (available child care reimbursed until the child enters kindergarten); and enriched child care (high-quality child care identified and reimbursed until kindergarten). The mothers will receive the education and employment training services required by the Family Support Act for mothers on AFDC. This design will permit researchers to test which changes affect child development and whether positive changes in mothers' lives and childrens' lives have additive or multiplicative effects.

The mechanisms by which changes in child outcomes occur will also be examined in this study. In other words, why would positive effects on child development occur as a result of mothers' leaving AFDC and becoming employed? Mechanisms could include mothers' change in economic status, moves to better housing or schooling, mothers' behavior toward the child at home (e.g., being more verbally responsive and stimulating), mothers' aspirations for herself, or a combination of these (Brooks-Gunn, in press; Chase-Lansdale, Brooks-Gunn, & Paikoff, 1991). Studies such as ECCO will shed considerable insight on the impact of employment on infants among low-income families.

## CHILDREN OF THE NATIONAL LONGITUDINAL SURVEY OF YOUTH (NLSY)

The Children of the NLSY is a relatively new data set comprised of more than 7,000 children and their parents. The NLSY itself was begun in 1979 with the collection of a nationally representative sample of more than 6,000 youth 14–21 years old and a supplementary sample of approximately 5,000, representing Black, Hispanic, and impoverished White youths (Chase-Lansdale, Mott, Brooks-Gunn, & Phillips, 1991). Through annual personal interviews, extensive information has been obtained from these youths on their life trajectories, including educational, marital, employment pathways as well as information on their families of origin, their psychological well-being and intellectual abilities (see Baker & Mott, 1989, for more detail).

Due to a partnership with child development scholars, the children of the youth in the NLSY were assessed for the first time in 1986 (when the original youth were 21–29 years of age). The children were reassessed in 1988, 1990, and 1992, and any new children born to the parent sample were also evaluated.

Multiple measures of cognitive and socioemotional development were included in all three waves. Plans are underway to continue following all children every 2 years.

The Children of the NLSY is thus an unprecedented data set due to its large sample, longitudinal design, and considerable information on mothers, families, and children. It has been in the public domain since 1988, and increasing numbers of developmentalists are using it for the first time to address a variety of issues (in contrast to sociologists, economists, and demographers who have conducted thousands of studies on the original NLSY panel; Chase-Lansdale, Mott, Brooks-Gunn, & Phillips, 1991).

The disciplinary heritage of the NLSY is labor force economics, and a significant sponsor has been the Department of Labor, which has funded the NLSY in order to understand the causes and consequences of labor force participation in the United States. With the addition of child outcome and child-care variables, funded by NICHD, the data set is thus particularly suitable for studies of maternal employment and child development. In the following section, new studies and the potential for others using Children of the NLSY are presented to illustrate advances in work–family linkages as discussed in the three literatures here.

## Maternal Employment

Several teams of investigators are using the Children of the NLSY to address the impact of employment during infancy. The three main studies that have examined the effects on 3- to 6-year-olds all report negative consequences of employment during the first year of life (Baydar & Brooks-Gunn, 1991; Belsky & Eggebeen, 1991; Desai, Chase-Lansdale, & Michael, 1989). Among children of mothers employed since infancy, Belsky and Eggebeen found higher rates of noncompliance among 4- to 6-year-old boys and girls, Baydar and Brooks-Gunn reported higher levels of behavior problems and lower Peabody Picture Vocabulary Test (PPVT) scores among 3- to 4-year-olds, and Desai et al. found lower PPVT scores among 4-year-old boys from middle-income families, but not for boys of low-income families, or for girls from either income group (each study contrasts employment histories).

The Children of the NLSY has enabled researchers to respond to the criticisms regarding sampling, selectivity, and retrospective designs of the smaller scale studies of maternal employment and infancy. With sample sizes ranging from 500 to 1,200 children, striking variability in family background factors, and maternal employment histories constructed from annual longitudinal data, these studies thus improve the specification of work–family linkages. Each study has found preexisting differences between employed and nonemployed mothers, and has developed statistical models that control for these influences because of the strengths of the data set.

It should be noted, however, that the Children of the NLSY is not a nationally representative sample of all children in the United States, because it is comprised of younger childbearers (whereas the NLSY is indeed nationally representative of a cohort of youth as they transition into adulthood and middle age). At the time of the first child assessment in 1986, children ranged in age from infancy to 12 years, whereas mothers' ages were 21 to 29 years. Despite this limitation, however, the results of the studies discussed here can be generalized with confidence to the population of young families with children in the United States.

The Desai et al. study, however, stands in contrast to the other two, in reporting differential effects of maternal employment by child gender as well as family income. That study drew upon Bronfenbrenner's (1988) person–process–context theory, which poses that in different social contexts (e.g., socioeconomic status), the same phenomenon (e.g., maternal employment) may affect different subgroups (e.g., boys and girls) in different ways. Desai et al. hypothesized that among middle-income families, mothers' employment might have a negative effect on children, due to the loss of resources the mother provides at home in combination with child care that is not as adequate as maternal care. In contrast, maternal employment was hypothesized as a positive influence within the ecological context of low-income families, with any negative effects of mother's employment (such as separation, poor quality care) more than overshadowed by the positive influence of moving out of poverty (Desai et al., 1989). That study also hypothesized that boys would be more negatively affected than girls. Both of these hypotheses find support in related studies of maternal employment (Chase-Lansdale & Owen, 1987; Hoffman, 1989), and both are supported by the findings from the Children of the NLSY based on 4-year-olds (Desai et al., 1989, Table 4).

There were no effects of intermittent employment, defined as employed on and off during the children's life, primarily after the first year. Controlling for several other important family background characteristics (such as family size, structure, race/ethnicity, mothers' schooling level), as well as other aspects of mother's employment, (e.g., earnings), the effects of early and continuous employment on boys' PPVT scores were negative in middle-income but not in low-income families and not for girls. Further analyses suggested that the negative effects on boys in middle-income families are largely accounted for by mothers' employment during the first year of life. (Desai et al., 1989, Table 4).

Differences among the findings from the Desai et al. study and those of the other two investigations may be due to differences in the investigators' choice of sample size, outcome variables, ways of splitting the sample into different income groups, and the details of variable definitions. For example, Baydar and Brooks-Gunn examined 3- to 4-year-olds, while the Desai, Chase-Lansdale and Michael study examined only 4-year-olds. The former tested income effects by splitting the sample into poverty/nonpoverty groups, while the latter split the sample into two income groups based on family income, with the top one-third of the sample representing the middle class, and the lower two-thirds representing low-income and impoverished families. These are examples of how the same data set can be used by different investigators asking the same substantive question. When conflicting findings arise as in this instance, steps may be taken with the same data set to pursue reasons why.

In a second study designed to pursue these differences, Desai, Michael and Chase-Lansdale (1990) used a larger sample of the Children of the NLSY dataset—all 3-, 4-, and 5-year-olds. This second study, with a larger sample size of 1,222 (compared to the 503 4-year-olds in earlier study), confirmed an overall negative effect of early and continuous maternal employment on PPVT scores for all boys, but not girls. Once again, when the effects of maternal employment were tested separately for middle- versus low-income families, the negative impact of mother's employment history was evident only for boys in middle-income families and not for the other groups.

We thus conclude from these two studies that it is extremely important to examine work–family linkages separately by differences in socioeconomic status and gender. It does appear that maternal employment operates differently within middle and low socioeconomic groups for the reasons discussed here. In addition, we have argued that boys seem to be more vulnerable to the psychosocial stress related to maternal employment (e.g., separation or poor quality child care) and that parents in employed mother families may treat boys more harshly than girls (Chase-Lansdale, Michael, & Desai, 1991). These hypotheses need to be tested in studies using observational methodology.

## Child Care

The Children of the NLSY also has extensive data on child care use for the first 3 years of the children's lives. Although other national data sets contain considerably more information on families' use of child care, the Children of the NLSY is the first to include measures of child outcome as well (Chase-Lansdale, Mott, Brooks-Gunn, & Phillips, 1991). Thus, it has been possible to describe the different types of care (e.g., center, family day care, grandmother) chosen by different types of families (e.g., Hispanic, two-parent) and the proportions of different aged children in each. However, only the Children of the NLSY permits the development of dynamic measures of child-care experience (e.g., mini child-care histories, such as "Grandmother care in the first 2 years, center care in the third year" and an assessment of their impact on child development). In a study of such child-care histories, for example, Baydar, Paikoff, and Brooks-Gunn (1990) found that the most optimal pattern of child care for socioemotional and cognitive development of impoverished White 3- to 4-year-olds in the NLSY was mother or grandmother care in the first year of life, followed by center-based care in the second and third years.

In a separate study of types of child care used by employed mothers during their children's infancy, Baydar and Brooks-Gunn (1991) reported that boys may be more sensitive to types of child care than are girls. At ages 3 and 4 years, boys of employed mothers had higher PPVT scores if they had been cared for in infancy by grandmothers or other relatives (not fathers), rather than in centers or family day-care homes. Baydar and Brooks-Gunn suggested that negative effects of early maternal employment on boys in other studies may be due to boys' vulnerability to aspects of the child-care setting. In their study, the child-care setting (i.e., grandmothers and relatives) may not have caused problems due to the probability that such care is more stable and individualized than other types of care. Unfortunately, the Children of the NLSY does not contain adequate measures of the quality of the child-care settings along the dimensions described in the review of the child-care literature. Conclusions as to why these different effects occur must await new observational studies.

## Intervention

The Children of the NLSY is a promising data set for pursuing intervention effects. These include issues raised by the implementation of Family Support Act of 1988. Mothers' entry into and exit from the nation's welfare (AFDC) program and the corresponding consequences for children's development may be assessed. Mothers' participation in job training programs and subsequent outcomes for children may also be examined. This data set takes on greater importance for research with policy implications as children have been followed from preschool into early adolescence.

## CONCLUSION

This chapter has illustrated what is meant by work–family linkages in three separate literatures—maternal employment, child care, and intervention—toward the goal of integrating diverse and at times conflicting findings regarding the impact of mother's employment during infancy on child development. Definitive conclusions have been hindered in the past by studies with retrospective designs and self-selected samples representing only two-parent middle-class White families. Recent investigations using the Children of the NLSY provide new evidence that mothers' employment in the first year of life may indeed be problematic for certain subgroups of children. These findings carry more weight, because they emerge from studies whose design improvements include larger sample size, prospective measures of employment patterns, and models that either control for or test the effects of variation in important family characteristics. However, caution is in order, given that the Children of the NLSY is not representative of all U.S. children, but rather of those in young families. In addition, conflicting findings remain from the NLSY research as to which groups of children are negatively affected by mothers' early return to work. Some studies (e.g., Desai et al., 1989) point to special vulnerability of boys in middle-income families. Others (Baydar & Brooks-Gunn, 1991; Belsky & Eggebeen, 1990) find that both boys and girls of all incomes are negatively affected. Interestingly, Baydar and Brooks-Gunn also find that boys are more vulnerable to certain types of child-care settings (e.g., center care) in the first year of life, whereas girls are not, lending support for considering work–family linkages separately by child gender.

Still missing in this debate is extensive observational data on (a) how families handle the ups and downs of maternal employment at home at the end of the day and on weekends; (b) how infants and preschoolers are affected by their various child-care settings; and (c) how these two systems affect one another. We have indications from small samples and case studies that certain subsets of infants experience a double-edged vulnerability because their experiences at home are stressed and punitive, and their families choose child-care settings that are inadequate. Yet, there are also indications that positive experiences in one setting may protect children from negative experiences in the other. The NICHD Study of Early Child Care will go a long way toward identifying which subgroups of children are affected and why, based on children's experiences in both the family and the child-care setting.

Finally, the intervention literature reveals how a focus just on children or a focus just on mothers leaves untested too many assumptions as to how families respond to programmatic efforts to change individual members' lives. The controversial issue of mother–infant separation and attachment outcomes in studies of middle-class families has not figured prominently in enrichment programs for low-income infants. Similarly, policies such as the Family Support Act of 1988 that require AFDC mothers of infants to be employed, get job training, or complete a high school degree have assumed that improvements in mothers' lives will benefit children. This assumption is not straightforward, and the positive and negative aspects of policies on maternal employment need to be extensively unpackaged. Evaluations of such policies have the potential of contributing significantly to our understanding of when and why maternal employment may benefit infants and young children.

## REFERENCES

Ainsworth, M. D. S., Blehar, M. C., Waters, E., & Wall, S. (1978). *Patterns of attachment.* Hillsdale, NJ: Lawrence Erlbaum Associates.

Andersson, B. E. (1989). Effects of public day-care: A longitudinal study. *Child Development, 60,* 857–866.

Baker, P. C., & Mott, F. L. (1989). *NLSY child handbook.* Columbus, OH: Center for Human Resource Research, Ohio State University.

Barglow, P., Vaughn, B., & Molitor, N. (1987). Effects of maternal absence due to employment on the quality of infant-mother attachment in a low-risk sample. *Child Development, 58,* 945–954.

Baydar, N., & Brooks-Gunn, J. (1991). *Effects of maternal employment and child-care arrangements in infancy on preschoolers' cognitive and behavioral outcomes: Evidence from the Children of the NLSY. Developmental Psychology, 27,* 932–945.

Baydar, N., Paikoff, R., & Brooks-Gunn, J. (1990). *Effects of child care arrangements on cognitive and behavioral outcomes in 3 to 4 year olds: Evidence from the children of the NLSY.* Unpublished manuscript.

Belsky, J., & Eggebeen, D. (1991). Early and extensive maternal employment and young children's socioemotional development: Children of the National Longitudinal Survey of Youth. *Journal of Marriage and the Family, 53,* 1083–1110.

Belsky, J., & Rovine, M. J. (1988). Nonmaternal care in the first year of life and the security of infant-parent attachment. *Child Development, 59,* 157–167.

Bradley, R. H., Caldwell, B. M., Rock, S. L., Ramey, C. T., Barnard, K. E., Gray, C., Hammond, M. A., Mitchell, S., Gottfried, A. W., Siegel, L., & Johnson, D. (1989). Home environment and cognitive development in the first 3 years of life: A collaborative study involving six sites and three ethnic groups in North America. *Developmental Psychology, 25,* 217–235.

Bronfenbrenner, V. (1988). Interacting systems in human development: Research paradigms: Present and future. In N. Bolger, A. Caspi, G. Downey, & M. Moorehouse (Eds.), *Persons in context: Developmental processes* (pp. 25–49). New York: Cambridge University Press.

Bronfenbrenner, U., & Crouter, A. C. (1982). Work and family through time and space. In S. B. Kamerman & C. D. Hayes (Eds.), *Families that work: children in a changing world* (pp. 39–83). Washington, DC: National Academy Press.

Brooks-Gunn, J. (1990). Identifying the vulnerable young child. In D. E. Rogers & E. Ginsberg (Eds.), *Improving the life chances of children at risk* (pp. 104–124). Boulder, CO: Westview Press.

Brooks-Gunn, J. (1991, February). *Enhancing the development of young children and their parents: New directions in family and intervention research.* Colloquium presented to Teachers College, Columbia University, New York.

Brooks-Gunn, J. (in press). Strategies for altering the outcomes of poor children and their families. In P. L. Chase-Lansdale & Jeanne Brooks-Gunn (Eds.), *Escape from poverty: What makes a difference for poor children?* New York: Cambridge University Press.

Burchinal, M., Lee, M., & Ramey, C. (1989). Type of day-care and preschool intellectual development in disadvantaged children. *Child Development, 60,* 128–137.

Caldwell, B. M., & Bradley, R. H. (1984). *Home observation for measurement of the environment.* Little Rock, AK: University of Arkansas at Little Rock. Unpublished manuscript.

Chase-Lansdale, P. L., & Brooks-Gunn, J. (Eds.). (in press). *Escape from poverty: What makes a difference for poor children?* New York: Cambridge University Press.

Chase-Lansdale, P. L., Michael, R. T., & Desai, S. (1991). Maternal employment during infancy: An analysis of "Children of the National Longitudinal Survey of Youth (NLSY)." In J. V. Lerner & N. L. Galambos (Eds.), *Employed mothers and their children.* (pp. 37–61). New York: Garland Publishing Company.

Chase-Lansdale, P. L., Mott, F. L., Brooks-Gunn, J., & Phillips, D. A. (1991). Children of the NLSY: A unique research opportunity. *Developmental Psychology, 27,* 918–931.

Chase-Lansdale, P. L., & Owen, M. T. (1987). Maternal employment in a family context: Effects on infant-mother and infant-father attachments. *Child Development, 58,* 1505–1512.

Chase-Lansdale, P. L., Brooks-Gunn, J., & Paikoff, R. (1991). Research and programs for adolescent mothers: Missing links and future promises. *Family Relations, 40,* 396–404.

Chase-Lansdale, P. L., & Vinovskis, M. A. (in press). Whose responsibility? An historical analysis of the changing roles of mothers, fathers, and society in assuming responsibility for U.S. children. In P. L. Chase-Lansdale & J. Brooks-Gunn (Eds.), *Escape from poverty: What makes a difference for poor children?* New York: Cambridge University Press.

Cherlin, A. J. (in press). Child care and the Family Support Act: Policy issues. In P. L. Chase-

Lansdale & J. Brooks-Gunn (Eds.), *Escape from poverty: What makes a difference for poor children?* New York: Cambridge University Press.

Cherry, F. F., & Eaton, E. G. (1977). Physical and cognitive development in children of low-income mothers working in the child's early years. *Child Development, 48,* 158–166.

Clarke-Stewart, K. A. (1989). Infant day care: Maligned or malignant? *American Psychologist, 44,* 266–273.

Clarke-Stewart, K. A., & Fein, G. (1983). Early childhood programs. In P. H. Mussen (Series Ed.) & H. Haith & J. J. Campos (Vol. Ed.), *Handbook of child psychology (Vol. 2): Infancy and developmental psychobiology* (pp. 917–1000). New York: Wiley.

Clewell, B. C., Brooks-Gunn, J., & Benasich, A. A. (1989). Evaluating child-related outcomes of teenage parenting programs. *Family Relations,* 201–209.

Cohen, S. E. (1978). Maternal employment and mother-child interaction. *Merrill-Palmer Quarterly, 24,* 189–197.

DeMeis, D. K., Hock, E., & McBride, S. L. (1986). The balance of employment and motherhood: Longitudinal study of mothers' feelings about separation from their first-born infants. *Developmental Psychology, 22,* 627–632.

Desai, S., Chase-Lansdale, P. L., & Michael, R. T. (1989). Mother or market: Effects of maternal employment on the intellectual ability of 4-year old children. *Demography, 26,* 545–561.

Desai, S., Michael, R. T., & Chase-Lansdale, P. L. (1990). *The home environment: A mechanism through which maternal employment affects child development. Population Research Center Discussion Paper Series.* Chicago, IL: NORC/The University of Chicago.

Desai, S., & Waite, L. (1991). Women's employment during pregnancy and after first birth: Occupational characteristics and work commitment. *American Sociological Review, 56,* 551–566.

Eggebeen, D. J. (1988). Determinants of maternal employment for white preschool children: 1960–1980. *Journal of Marriage and the Family, 50,* 149–159.

Field, T. M., Widmayer, S., Greenberg, R., & Stoller, S. (1982). Effects of parent training of teenage mothers and their infants. *Pediatrics, 69*(6), 703–707.

Furstenberg, F. F., Jr., Brooks-Gunn, J., & Morgan, S. P. (1987). *Adolescent mothers in later life.* New York: Cambridge University Press.

Gottfried, A. E. (1991). Maternal employment in the family setting: Developmental and environmental issues. In J. V. Lerner & N. L. Galambos (Eds.), *Employed mothers and their children* (pp. 63–84). New York: Garland Publishing Company.

Hayes, C., Palmer, J., & Zaslow, M. (1990). *Who cares for America's children: Child care for the 1990s.* Washington, DC: National Academy of Sciences.

Heyns, B. (1982). The influence of parents' work on children's school achievement. In S. B. Kamerman & C. D. Hayes (Eds.), *Families that work: Children in a changing world* (pp. 229–267). Washington, DC: National Academy Press.

Hock, E. (1980). Working and nonworking mothers and their infants: A comparative study of maternal caregiving characteristics and infant social behavior. *Merrill-Palmer Quarterly, 26,* 79–101.

Hoffman, L. W. (1984). Maternal employment and the young child. In M. Perlmutter (Ed.), *Minnesota symposium in child psychology* (Vol. 17, pp. 101–127). Hillsdale, NJ: Lawrence Erlbaum Associates.

Hoffman, L. W. (1989). Effects of maternal employment in the two-parent family. *American Psychologist, 44,* 283–292.

Howes, C. (1989, April). *Social relationships with adults and peers within child care and families.* Paper presented in the symposium, "New directions in research on infant day care," at the biennial meeting of the Society for Research in Child Development, Kansas City.

Howes, C., & Olenick, M. (1986). Family and child care influences on toddler compliance. *Child Development, 57,* 202–216.

Howes, C., Rodning, C., Galluzzo, D., & Myers, L. (Eds.). (1988). Relationships with mother and caregiver. *Early Childhood Research Quarterly, 3*(403–416).

Infant Health and Development Program. (1990). Enhancing the outcomes of low birth weight, premature infants: A multi site randomized trial. *Journal of the American Medical Association, 263*(22), 3035–3042.

Johnston, K. (1989, May). *Promoting infant mental health: The day care question.* Paper presented at the conference "Day care: Who's minding our children?" Sponsored by The Texas Association for Infant Mental Health, Dallas.

Lazar, I., Darlington, R. B., Murray, H., Royce, J., & Snipper, A. (1982). Lasting effects of early education: A report from the Consortium for Longitudinal Studies. *Monographs of the Society for Research in Child Development, 47*(Nos. 2–3, Serial No. 195).

McCartney, K. (1984). The effect of quality of day care environment upon children's language development. *Developmental Psychology, 20,* 244–260.

Melhuish, E., Hennessy, E., Martin, S., & Moss, P. (1990, September). *Social development at 6 years as a function of type and amount of early child care.* Paper presented at the conference, "Child Care in the Early Years," Lausanne, Switzerland.

NICHD Early Child Care Network (1993). Child-care debate: Transformed or distorted? *American Psychologists, 48,* 692–693.

Nightingale, D. S., Wissoker, D. A., Burbridge, L. C., Bawden, D. L., & Jeffries, N. (1990). *Evaluation of the Massachusetts Employment and Training* (ET) *Choices Program.* Washington, DC: The Urban Institute Press.

Owen, M. T., Cross, D. R., Henderson, K. V., & Cox, M. J. (1990). *Relations between child care quality and child behavior at age 4: The significance of family dynamics.* Unpublished manuscript.

Patterson, G. R. (1986). Performance models for antisocial boys. *American Psychologist, 41,* 432–444.

Pedersen, F. A., Cain, R. A., Zaslow, M. J., & Anderson, B. J. (1982). Variation in infant experience associated with alternative family roles. In L. Loasa & I. Sigel (Eds.), *Families as learning environments for children* (pp. 203–221). New York: Plenum Press.

Phillips, D. A. (Ed.). (1987). *Quality in child care: What does the research tell us?* Washington, DC: National Association for the Education of Young Children.

Phillips, D. A., Howes, C., Whitebook, M. (1992). The social policy context of child care: Effects on quality. *American Journal of Community Psychology, 20,* 25–51.

Polit, D. F. (1989). Effects of comprehensive program for teenage parents: Five years after Project Redirection. *Family Planning Perspectives, 21*(4), 164–169.

Ramey, C. T., & Campbell, F. (1987). The Carolina Abcedarian Project: An educational experiment concerning human malleability. In J. J. Gallagher & C. T. Ramey (Eds.), *The malleability of children* (pp. 127–139). Baltimore: Brooks.

Schachter, F. F. (1981). Toddlers with employed mothers. *Child Development, 59,* 958–964.

Schwartz, P., (1983). Length of day-care attendance and attachment behavior in eighteen-month old infants. *Child Development, 54,* 1073–1078.

Smith, S. (in press). (Ed.). *Two-generation programs for children in poverty.* Norwood, NJ: Ablex Publishing Corporation.

U.S. Bureau of the Census. (1988). Fertility of American Women: June 1987. *Current Population Reports* (Series P-20, No. 427). Washington, DC: U.S. Government Printing Office.

U.S. Senate. (1987). *Welfare: Reform or replacement? (Work and Welfare).* Hearing before the Subcommittee on Social Security and Family Policy, February 23. S. Hrg. 100-320. Washington, DC: U.S. Government Printing Office.

Vandell, D. L., & Corasaniti, M. A. (1990). Child care and the family: Complex contributors to child development. In K. McCartney (Ed.), *New directions in child development research* (pp. 23–37). San Francisco: Jossey-Bass.

Vaughn, B. E., Gove, F. L., & Egeland, B. (1980). The relationship between out-of-home care and the quality of infant-mother attachment in an economically disadvantaged population. *Child Development, 51,* 1203–1214.

Washington, V. (1988). The black mother in the United States: History, theory, research, and issues. In B. Birns & D. Hay (Eds.), *The different faces of motherhood* (pp. 185–214). New York: Plenum Press.

Zaslow, M. T. (1991). Variation in child care quality and its implications for children. *Journal of Social Issues, 47,* 125–138.

Zigler, E., & Muenchow, S. (1984). How to influence social policy affecting children and families. *American Psychologist, 39,* 415–420.

# 3

# Patterns of Marital Interaction and Children's Emotional Development

Lynn Fainsilber Katz
John M. Gottman
*University of Washington*

Current research findings suggest that marital distress is the best familial predictor of childhood behavior problems (for a review, see Emery, 1982). However, the precise nature of this effect is not understood. Much of the effort of the past three decades has been directed toward identifying the parameters of the effect. Questions about whether boys are differentially affected by marital distress than are girls, and whether marital discord is more detrimental to younger than to older children have received some attention. This focus on the "status" characteristics of the child has been at the expense of understanding the *processes* by which characteristics of the marital relationship come to affect the child's socioemotional development. As a result, there are no theories to describe exactly how distress within one family subsystem (i.e., the couple) comes to affect the functioning of another family subsystem (i.e., the child).

As a first step in theory development, what is needed is greater precision in the description of both the characteristics of the marital and parent–child relationship that may be most detrimental to the child, as well as greater precision in the description of child outcomes. In this chapter, we discuss our current thinking about the specific characteristics of the marital relationship that may affect the way couples parent their children, and how these marital interaction and parenting styles predict risk factors in the development of psychopathology. The focus of our laboratory has been on studying the nature of affective communication within the family, with the goal of using highly specific means of describing the processes that occur during marital and parent–child interaction that lead to detrimental child outcomes.

There are two questions we have been pursuing most recently. First, we have been interested in understanding whether children are differentially affected by the affective style that their parents use when they are resolving marital conflict. We have noticed that couples use different emotional styles when trying to resolve a marital dispute. Some couples are very angry and argumentative, freely expressing their outrage at their spouse's behavior and attitudes. These couples use what might be called "hot" emotions when expressing their feelings. Other couples seem quite withdrawn from each other when working out their differences, showing little eye contact and expressing such "cool" and distance-inducing emotions as contempt and disgust. One question we raise in this chapter is whether angry and hot marital interaction is associated with more negative child outcomes than withdrawn marital interaction. We think of couples who have hot marriages as couples who are willing to express a great deal of negative affect with their partners and do not avoid conflict. They are angry and argumentative when they conflict, and make clear and direct statements about their negative feelings, yet are still able to use small amounts of positive affect (i.e., humor) during conflict resolution. Essentially, these couples have marriages that are very lively, and that can tolerate the expression of a wide range of emotion.

A second related problem is to identify the outcomes associated with different marital styles. Given our interest in affective communication, we have been examining the effect of different marital interaction styles on children's ability to express and regulate emotion. Do children from homes in which the couple express hot marital interaction use different emotional styles than those from withdrawn marriages? According to a modeling hypothesis, we would expect the affective nature of the marital relationship to be mirrored in the child's predominant emotional style. For example, couples who use an argumentative and angry style during conflict resolution should have children who express a great deal of anger. However, a modeling hypothesis may be inadequate to describe such linkages. For example, it is conceivable that cold and withdrawn parents may produce angry children. These children might use their anger to elicit a response from a detached and unavailable parent.

We have also been examining whether couples marital conflict-resolution style is related to their child's social skills with peers. Evidence of a link between family experience and peer relationships is beginning to emerge (e.g., Cohn, Patterson, & Christopoulos, 1991; Parke & Ladd, 1992). In general, parents who are inconsistent, affectively negative, controlling, and punitive with their children are more likely to have children who are actively disliked and rejected by peers (Attili, 1989; Dishion, 1990; Kolvin et al., 1977; Putallaz, 1987). However, most of the research on the family and children's peer relations has focused primarily on the parent–child relationship, even though evidence suggests that the nature of the marital relationship is associated with both characteristics of the parent–child relationship (Goldberg & Easterbrooks, 1984; Hetherington, Cox, & Cox, 1982) and with behavior problems in children (Emery, 1982). There is a need for greater understanding of how the functioning of other family subsystems, such as the marital relationship, are related to children's behavior with their peers. Conflict-resolution patterns within the marital relationship may be a particularly fruitful avenue to explore, particularly because the marital relationship is one of the child's primary models of close interpersonal relationships.

This chapter explores whether there is any evidence to link specific marital conflict resolution styles to specific child emotions and to children's peer relations. Preliminary data on the link between conflict patterns in marriage and children's emotions are presented. In an effort to build theory, we examine the parent–child interactive context as the mediating link between marital conflict resolution styles and children's expression of emotion. We explore whether couples who display what we call hot marital interaction also tend to express anger and other hot emotions toward their child, and similarly whether withdrawn and distant couples are withdrawn and distant parents. We also speculate about the link between marital conflict patterns and children's peer relations using case example families in which couples use hot or withdrawn behavior patterns during marital conflict resolution. We begin by exploring the effects of different marital interaction styles on children's socioemotional development.

## MARITAL INTERACTION

The conceptualization of the marital relationship in the literature on the transfer of marital discord has begun with a simple unidimensional view. Marriages have generally been characterized as falling on a continuum of marital satisfaction, ranging from satisfied to dissatisfied to divorced couples. Although there is a great deal of validity to the concept of marital satisfaction (Gottman, 1979; Jacobsen & Margolin, 1979; Revenstorf, Vogel, Wegener, Hahlweg, & Schindler, 1980), much of the recent thrust in marital research has been to break down this global concept of marital satisfaction into the specific ways in which couples display marital conflict and disagreement (e.g., Gottman & Levenson, in preparation-a; Margolin, 1988; Howes & Markman, 1989). In her paper entitled, "Marital Conflict is Not Marital Conflict is Not Marital Conflict," Margolin argued that marital conflict is not a unitary entity and that couples differ in the way they experience and exhibit conflict. For example, Margolin suggested that some couples are highly expressive and display their conflict in a very visible way, whereas for others the conflict is more silent and hidden.

The main attempt to go beyond the general concept of marital satisfaction has been to examine the degree of conflict in the marital relationship. Although this concept has not been established to be orthogonal to marital satisfaction, research findings have consistently suggested that high levels of marital conflict may be associated with childhood behavior problems. This has been found to be the case both among divorced couples (e.g., Enos & Handal, 1986; Forehand, Brody, Long, Slotkin, & Fauber, 1986; Hetherington et al., 1982; Long, Forehand,

Fauber, & Brody, 1987) as well as in intact marriages (Amato, 1986; Peterson & Zill, 1986; Porter & O'Leary, 1980).

One common feature of many of these studies is that measures of "conflict" have almost entirely been based on self-report. The consequence of the predominance of self-report methods has been that it is often difficult to assess exactly what it is that is being measured. For example, it has been found in several studies that children whose parents reported having high levels of "conflict" or postseparation "acrimony" had the highest levels of internalizing and/or externalizing difficulties (e.g., Peterson & Zill, 1986; Shaw & Emery, 1987). These studies are difficult to interpret because it is unclear exactly what interactive behaviors are leading couples to describe their relationship as "acrimonious" or "conflictual." It is conceivable that many different kinds of couples might consider their relationship to be conflictual or acrimonious, including couples who are withdrawn and emotionally detached from each other, as well as those who adopt an angry interactive style. By combining these different styles of marital interaction into a single category, the concept of *marital conflict* has become amorphous and nondescriptive.

This lack of precision is also characteristic of studies using clinical interview methods. In one of the few attempts to break apart the concept of marital conflict, Rutter et al. (1974) conducted interviews with mothers about their "feelings about family life and other family members." These interviews were then rated by the interviewers who classified the marriages into those that were "quarrelsome" and those that were "apathetic." They found a stronger relation with child behavior problems in unhappy marriages characterized by "quarrelsomeness" than in those characterized by "apathy." However, again it is difficult to draw conclusions from this study because like self-report methods, clinical interviews at best obtain the couple's perception of their behavior rather than their actual behavior. Asking interviewers or independent raters to then classify or rate couples according to such dimensions as quarrelsomeness or apathy then adds another layer of inference and perception onto the assessment, making it highly indirect.

In order to build theory, a greater precision in the description of the different types of behaviors that occur during marital conflict is needed. Clarity in the description of the marital relationship may also lead to more order in the linkages between marital, parent–child, and child outcomes. Currently, the results are quite global in that negativity in the marital relationship predicts negative behaviors in the child. A wide range of negative child outcomes have been linked to maritally distressed families, including such different difficulties as depression (Peterson & Zill, 1986); withdrawal (Hetherington et al., 1982); poor social competence (Forehand et al., 1986; Gottman & Katz, 1989); insecure attachment classification (Belsky & Isabella, 1988; Goldberg & Easterbrooks, 1984); worse health problems (Gottman & Katz, 1989); poor academic performance (Cowan & Cowan, 1987); and such conduct-related problems as antisocial behavior

(Rutter, 1971), hostility (Whitehead, 1979), delinquency (Emery & O'Leary, 1982; Porter & O'Leary, 1980), noncompliance (Easterbrooks, 1987), and aggression (Hetherington et al., 1982). It has been assumed that these outcomes are associated with the same stressor—marital distress. If there were greater precision in the definitions of marital conflict, perhaps we might find a more direct mapping between specific marital interaction patterns and specific forms of childhood behavior problems.

What might we see? Following a modeling theory, we might see a one-to-one mapping between marital conflict resolution style and child outcomes. For example, couples who express a great deal of anger might have angry children. If this were true, anger in the marital relationship may be related to externalizing behaviors in the child. Similarly, sadness in the marital relationship may be associated with sadness in the child. Looking at the parent–child context, Zahn-Waxler (1988) reported that depressed mothers have children who "take on" their mother's depressive symptomatology as a way of being close to the mothers. Alternatively, rather than model the parent's anger, we might see the child react to it. Children of angry couples may be highly fearful, not knowing when the anger will be directed at them. They may appear to be withdrawn, tense, and cowering children.

To summarize, the use of imprecise self-report methods has seriously compromised the goal of describing the kinds of marital and parent–child patterns that are most detrimental to the child. This lack of precision has made it difficult to specify the exact forms of marital conflict that contribute to childhood behavior problems. Direct observations of marital and parent–child interaction styles might better accomplish the goal of describing patterns of interaction that may have deleterious consequences for the child.

A step in this direction has been taken by Cummings and his colleagues, who have used direct observation to assess children's reactions to anger. This body of research represents the closest we have come to linking specific interaction patterns with child outcomes.

## THE ANGRY ENVIRONMENT

In a series of investigations, Cummings and his colleagues have been exploring children's reactions to observing anger between adults (e.g., Cummings, 1987; Cummings, Iannotti, & Zahn-Waxler, 1985; Cummings, Zahn-Waxler, & Radke-Yarrow, 1981, 1984). The studies have used children varying in age and in the context within which the children have been observed.

The early studies examined 1- to 2½-year-old children's reactions to expressions of anger by family members in the home environment. In a series of sessions with the experimenters, mothers were trained in techniques of observing and reporting incidents of naturally occurring and simulated anger in the home.

For each incident that occurred, mothers provided a narrative description of the emotional event, the child's response to it, and the consequences of the child's reaction, if any. They were told to taperecord their observations as soon as possible after the emotional incident. Thus, this procedure trained mothers to act as observers, noticing particular behaviors, rather than to rely on their own ideas of what to observe and report, differentiating it from many self-report measures. Cummings et al. (1981) found that distress was the most common child response to naturally occurring anger in adults (46.5% of responses), with anger as the next most common response (24.3% of responses). This finding challenges a simple modeling theory. Looking at developmental changes in response to anger, Cummings, Zahn-Waxler, and Radke-Yarrow (1984) found that older, rather than younger, children appear to act in a more controlled manner with angry adults, either taking on the role of mediator and acting toward resolution of the conflict, or comforting their parents.

Cummings et al. (1985) and Cummings (1987) arranged an ingenious ruse in which they exposed dyads of familiar peers to angry adults in a laboratory setting. Dyads of children and their mothers were invited into an apartmentlike laboratory and exposed to two experimenters who first talked in a warm and friendly fashion (positive emotion), then interacted angrily toward each other, with one complaining loudly about the other experimenter's laziness around the laboratory. This was then followed by a friendly interaction as the adults reconciled their differences. Cummings (1987) and Cummings et al. (1985) were interested in children's distress reactions during the display of anger, as well as any aggression that might be displayed following exposure to anger. They found that in 2 year olds, greater distress was induced by background anger than by displays of positive emotion. In addition, there was evidence of increased displays of intense physical aggression (i.e., potentially dangerous aggression that elicited a desire in adults to intervene) subsequent to exposure to anger. Among preschoolers, increases in verbal aggression following anger were also found, but no increases in physical aggression (Cummings, 1987). Thus, by the preschool period, physical aggression seems to be replaced by verbal aggression as a way of responding to anger between adults.

Cummings and colleagues have also examined the role of marital distress and parental history of verbal or physical aggression on children's responses to anger. Cummings et al. (1981) found that the more interparent fights that were reported by the mother, the more likely children were to respond to anger in the home with anger, distress, or with affectionate/prosocial behavior. Cummings, Pellegrini, Notarius, and Cummings (1989) reported that children from maritally distressed homes showed increased social support-seeking and increased preoccupation with the angry adults. In addition, the form of the marital conflict interacted with age in predicting children's response to anger. That is, children whose parents reported engaging in physical aggressiveness showed increased preoccupation, concern and support-seeking, and social responsibility (i.e., providing physical or verbal comfort to the mother; staying near mother, inquiring about mother's feelings) with increasing age. Thus, this study suggests that in maritally distressed homes, children tend to respond to adults' anger with greater distress and interruption of on-going activity than do children from maritally satisfied homes.

If one argues that a child's reactions to anger between unfamiliar adults may apply to their reactions to their parent's expressions of anger toward each other, then Cummings' results support the hypothesis that families in which the marriage is full of anger and hostility (what we have described earlier as hot marriages) have children who are distressed, angry, and engage in physical aggression. Taken together with Rutter et al.'s (1974) report that quarrelsome marriages were associated with more behavior problems in children than those that were apathetic, we would expect to see more negative child outcomes associated with hot marital interaction than with withdrawn or "cool" marital interaction.

However, recent work in the area of marital interaction suggests that anger during marital interaction predicts improvement in marital satisfaction longitudinally. In two 3-year longitudinal studies, Gottman and Krokoff (1989) found that anger (particularly by the wife) predicted an increase in marital satisfaction over a 3-year period, but a constellation of behaviors including compliance, whining, stubbornness, defensiveness, and withdrawal from interaction predicted a decrease in marital satisfaction over time. Markman (1988) found that conflict avoidance predicted deterioration in marital satisfaction longitudinally. Assuming that what is good for the marriage may also be good for the child, anger in the marriage may instead be associated with positive (or at least, fewer negative) child outcomes.

There is also reason to hypothesize that those children whose parents' marriages are heading toward dissolution may be at heightened risk for the development of psychopathological coping styles. Gottman and Levenson (in preparation-a) have recently identified styles of marital interaction that are predictive of separation and divorce. They have been able to predict each spouse's considerations of separation, divorce, and their actual separation or divorce from observations of marital interaction, physiological data and questionnaires obtained 4 years earlier. The pattern of results suggested that at Time 1, emotional detachment in the marriage was characteristic of those couples who would separate or consider divorce or separation. Behaviorally, both spouses were defensive, the wives were complaining and criticizing, husbands were conflict-engaging and high on stonewalling, wives expressed disgust facially, husbands expressed fear facially, both spouses were high on expressing non-"Duchenne" smiles (Ekman & Friesen, 1982), and wives reported that the couple led separate and parallel lives. Gottman and Levenson argued that these couples could be described as defensive and detached rather than hot (which might involve such affects and behaviors as sadness, anger, and stubbornness).

In summary, there is evidence to suggest that marriages that are heading toward dissolution are characterized by a pattern of behavior that can be described as detached and withdrawn. Because detached and withdrawn marriages may be on the road toward marital dissolution, it is reasonable to hypothesize that children from such marriages may be more negatively affected than children from hot marriages. This prediction is in direct contrast to the results of Rutter et al. (1974), but follows from careful and precise observation of marital interaction.

If this prediction is true, then it raises the question of the exact form of child behavior problem that might be associated with marital withdrawal and marital engagement. According to the modeling hypothesis, one might expect that if children are exposed to hot marital interaction, they may exhibit problems of aggression and acting out. On the other hand, if children are exposed to withdrawn marital interaction, they might show signs of internalizing disorders, such as anxiety and depression. In the next section, we argue that children may not only show signs of clinical or subclinical deviance when they come from maritally distressed families, but their day-to-day emotional reactions and peer relationships may also be shaped by the oppressive affective environment created in their homes.

## CRITERION VARIABLES: CHILDREN'S EMOTIONAL EXPRESSIONS AND PEER RELATIONSHIPS

Many investigations of the consequences of marital discord for the child have predominantly conceptualized child outcomes in terms of pathology. Two classes of behavior problems, those of undercontrol (e.g., aggression, acting out) and overcontrol (e.g., depression, anxiety) have been examined. Gender differences in the form in which the behavior problem is manifested have also been studied, with some evidence that boys display more antisocial, aggressive behaviors and girls demonstrate more anxiety, depression, and withdrawal (e.g., Block, Block, & Morrison, 1981). Very little attention has been paid to more subtle aspects of the child's development, such as their peer relationships or the everyday emotional reactions that children express with their parents or siblings.

In our research, we have been considering that there may be many other aspects of child functioning that are disrupted when parents are experiencing marital distress. One of these are children's daily emotional reactions. For example, we have noticed that some children react to the daily stresses and frustrations in their lives with anger, others with sadness, and yet others use humor and laugh their way through uncomfortable experiences. These emotional reactions may be an important link in predicting positive outcomes or the development of more extreme forms of emotional disturbances.

In our research we are using two theoretical constructs to make the link from children's expression of emotion to the prediction of potential risk and psychopathology. One is Ekman's (1984) concept of *flooding*. Ekman suggested the concept of flooding as a way of straightening out the confusion that exists in emotion words between emotions (such as sadness), to longer lasting moods (such as dysphoria), and pathological states such as depression. He argued that flooding was a mechanism for describing the transition from one state (e.g., sadness) to another state (e.g., depression). Ekman suggested that for some people almost any negative experience will invoke the same negative affect. For example, for some people almost any negative situation will evoke sadness. As a result, such people will tend to be sad quite often because eventually many different situations will give rise to sadness. The same concept has been used in the spouse abuse literature, but has been called *funneling* (Dutton, 1988). Thus, the concept of flooding helps explain the pervasiveness of negative affective reactions in psychopathology.

The second theoretical construct that links everyday emotion to either positive or negative child outcomes is the child's ability to regulate emotion. The ability to regulate emotional experience and expression has often been described as an important developmental milestone (e.g., Kagan, Rosman, Day, Albert, & Phillips, 1964; Kopp, 1982; Redl & Wineman, 1951). There seems to be a particular developmental period that is most important in the development of emotional regulation. Maccoby (1980) targeted young childhood as the period most important to the development of emotional control and regulation. She noted that the *inhibition of action* is the basis for the organization of behavior. We believe that when a child is flooded by affect and is unable to regulate his or her emotions, the flooded affect is disorganizing to the child in terms of disrupting the child's ability to focus attention and to become organized for coordinated action in the service of an objective. The resulting deficits in attentional processes and the disorganization of goal-related activity in the child who cannot regulate his or her emotions may be an important step in the development of more severe behavior problems.

The ability to regulate emotion is also important in the area of peer relations. Gottman (1983) found that being able to coordinate play and manage conflict with an unacquainted peer predicted a child's ability to make friends. The management of fantasy play in existing friendships also appears to be affected by children's ability to regulate emotion. In fantasy play there is continual discussion and negotiation that takes place, interspersed with acting out the roles. Agreement-to-disagreement ratios during fantasy play for friends are about 5.0. This level of agreement compared to disagreement requires children to regulate their own affect and negotiate the play, because they rarely exactly get their own way. Children who are not able to regulate their emotions and remain upset about disagreements and not getting their way often keep restating their wishes more and more emphatically until they get their way or the play requires adult intervention and external regulation of emotion. Thus, the ability to regulate emotion may be important both to the establishment of new friendships as well as to the ability to engage in the high levels of engagement necessary to sustain fantasy play among existing friends.

To summarize, we have highlighted the importance of examining normative events such as children's emotional reactions and peer relationships as outcome measures in studies of marital discord, and have provided some theoretical constructs that may function to link normative developmental processes with more pathological outcomes. We have also argued that children's emotional reactions and peer relations may be shaped by the way in which their parents resolve marital conflict. If children learn the rules of interpersonal behavior by modeling the affects their parents display when they disagree, then children whose parents have hot marriages will show a great deal of anger, whereas children whose parents are more withdrawn during conflict resolution may be more sad or fearful. We have some preliminary data to address some of these issues.

## LINKAGES BETWEEN MARITAL CONFLICT PATTERN AND CHILDREN'S EMOTIONAL EXPRESSIONS

In the Family Psychophysiology Laboratory at the University of Washington, we have been engaged in research on the link between marital discord, parent–child interaction, and child outcomes. The goal of our research has been to develop theoretical models of the processes by which marital discord affects the child's socioemotional development. Self-report, observational, and physiological measures were obtained within a naturalistic social interactive context to examine the marital and parent-child processes predictive of risk and psychopathology. This chapter focuses on the findings from observational and self-report data.

Fifty-six families were recruited for this study. Couples were married, living together, and had a 4- to 5-year-old child. Couples were screened for marital satisfaction using a telephone version of the Locke–Wallace Marital Inventory (developed in our laboratory by Krokoff, 1984) in an attempt to obtain a wide range of families.

### Procedures

Because fantasy play is such a prominent activity of preschool children, it seemed advisable to design a laboratory that would be built around a fantasy play theme the children would enjoy and that would preserve a naturalistic quality of behavior. In our pilot observational study of games and rides at a Chuck-E-Cheese Pizza House, we found that the most popular children's ride of children in this age group was an Apollo space capsule. The most popular games were video games. On the basis of these data, we constructed a full-scale mock-up of the Apollo space capsule, and made astronaut space suits for the children. Children were seated in the space capsule throughout all the laboratory procedures.

### Laboratory Sessions

Procedures consisted of laboratory sessions for both parents and children. A combination of naturalistic interaction, highly structured tasks, and semi-structured interviews were used. Observational data were obtained during all laboratory sessions. The procedures described here are a portion of a larger study examining the effects of marital discord on children's emotional development, peer relationships, and physical health. Interested readers are referred to Gottman and Katz (1989) and Katz and Gottman (1991) for details about additional procedures.

*Marital Laboratory Visit.*   Couples were seen in a lab session whose main function was to obtain a naturalistic sample of the couple's interaction style during a high-conflict task. The high-conflict task consisted of a 15-minute discussion of two self-defined problem areas in the marriage (Gottman, 1979). Observational data was obtained on both spouses.

*Parent–Child Laboratory Session.*   The parent–child interaction task consisted of a modification of two procedures used by Cowan and Cowan (1987). In the first task, parents were asked to obtain information from their child. The parents were informed that the child had heard a story and that they were to find out as much of the story as possible. The story that the children heard was difficult to remember because it did not follow normal story grammar (Glenn, 1978) and was read in a monotone voice. The story used by the Cowans was rewritten for our use by the original author so that it was more suited for 4- to 5-year-old children (Pratt, personal communication July 15, 1985). The parents' second task involved teaching the child how to play an Atari game ("Plaque Attack") that the parents had learned to play while the child was hearing the story.

The parent–child interaction task was designed by the Cowans to be difficult, with a potential for the escalation of negative affect in the parent–child interaction. There was approximately 20 minutes between the time the child heard the story and the time the parents asked about the story, and during this time the child engaged in an exciting pretend "blast-off." As a result, children typically did not remember the story. To make the parents' task even more difficult, we turned on the video game so that the child was able to watch the game play by itself. The children found the video game a much more attractive activity, creating a situation in which parents and children had competing goals: The children wanted to play the video game and the parents wanted to find out about the story. Observational data were collected on the parents and child throughout the entire session. The interaction lasted 10 minutes.

## Characterizing Marital Interaction as Hot or Withdrawn

One of our main challenges was operationalizing the concepts of hot or withdrawn marital interaction in a precise and clear way. We began with two summary variables from the MICS-III coding system (Weiss & Summers, 1983). Because Gottman and Krokoff (1989) found that stubbornness predicted a decline in marital satisfaction over a 3-year period, husband stubbornness was our first variable. This variable also displayed as pattern of correlations that suggested its usefulness as an index of hot marital interaction. Husband stubbornness was related to wife stubbornness, as well as both husband and wife conflict engagement. Thus, this constellation of correlations seems to portray a relationship that is highly engaged and angry.

Hot marital interaction was also operationalized using sequential analysis. A number of different indices of sequential connection can be used to identify important sequences of behavior (see Bakeman & Gottman, 1986). For this study, $z$ scores of sequential connection were utilized to assess the number of times a consequent event occurred following an antecedent event, correcting for differences in the base rates of the antecedent event. The index of hot marital interaction consisted of several $z$ scores of sequential connection. Couples who were hot during their marital interaction tended to be stubborn and conflict engaging for longer periods of time. Yet, these couples were also capable of positive interaction (e.g., the wife tended to shift from a state of compliance to one in which she made positive verbal comments). This variable might thus better be called "hot and positive" marital interaction.

Detached or withdrawn marital interaction was indexed by the wife withdrawal variable. Gottman and Krokoff (1989) also found that withdrawal predicted deterioration in marital satisfaction longitudinally. In addition, it showed a pattern of correlations suggestive of detachment. In the present study, couples who were withdrawn had wives who did not respond to their husbands' comments, did not make eye contact when their husbands spoke, made irrelevant comments, and made nonverbal gestures of displeasure, disgust, or disapproval. Wife withdrawal was related to low positive interaction in the relationship (low husband and wife positive verbal and nonverbal behaviors) as well as high husband withdrawal, high husband and wife conflict engagement, and high wife stubbornness. This pattern seems to be one in which the couple might vacillate from being engaged speakers to being withdrawn and detached listeners. Husband stubbornness and wife withdrawal from interaction were also found to differentiate between couples high and low in marital satisfaction [$F(1,51) = 9.56, p < .01$ for husband stubbornness; $F(1,51) = 10.28, p < .005$ for wife withdrawal]. These variables were also selected because withdrawal and stubbornness have been found to predict decreases in marital satisfaction over a 3-year period (Gottman & Krokoff, 1989).

## Characterizing the Child's Emotional Reactions

One positive and two negative affects from the Specific Affect (SPAFF; Gottman, 1986) coding system were used. The SPAFF is a microanalytic gestalt coding system that uses facial, vocal, gestural, and content cues to determine which of 10 affects and affective behaviors are being displayed by the speaker.

The SPAFF also codes listener behavior into negative, positive, and neutral affect categories. The three codes used for the present analyses were: child humor, child sadness, and child anger. The two negative affect categories were examined separately in order to differentiate between those affects that might be related to internalizing disorders (i.e., sadness) and those that might be related to externalizing disorders (i.e., anger). Child humor was selected as the positive affect because our paradigm was designed to have the potential for a great deal of fun and excitement.

## Characterizing Parenting Behavior

We reasoned that not only may there be a direct relationship between marital conflict-resolution style and children's emotional reactions toward their parents, but this relationship may also be mediated by the emotional reactions that parents display toward their child. Parenting behaviors were examined as possible mediating variables. Mothers and fathers reactions were treated separately.

*Mother's Behavior.*    Maternal behavior was obtained from both the SPAFF and the Cowan and Cowan (1987) Parenting Styles Coding System. This system, based on Baumrind's (1971) notion of authoritative parenting, uses global ratings that code parent behaviors on dimensions of warmth–coldness, presence or lack of structuring and limit-setting, parental anger and displeasure, whether parents back down when the child is noncompliant, happiness, responsiveness or unresponsiveness, and whether parents make maturity demands of their child.

Two summary variables were used to operationalize maternal behavior. One consisted of a summary index of the mother's structuring and confidence obtained from the Cowan coding system. Mothers who were high in structuring broke down the task into logical steps, provided the child with adequate information about what was to be done, and structured the situation so that the child understood the task objectives. Mothers who were confident with their children did not back down in face of child noncompliance. They acted without undue hesitation and self-doubt, and appeared to feel secure and effective in the parental role. The second summary score was derived by summing mother's anger and whining during the parent–child interaction from the SPAFF coding system. Mothers who were angry and whining were irritable and impatient when asking the child about the story and when teaching the child the video game, and showed frustration at the child's failure to perform well on the video game.

*Father's Behavior.*    Father's behavior during parent–child interaction was operationalized using variables from the SPAFF affect coding system. Father's positive affect was characterized with the humor and excitement affective blend SPAFF code. Fathers high in humor and excitement were enthusiastically involved in teaching the child how to play the video game and thoroughly enjoyed the child's efforts. Father's negative affect was operationalized using two separate SPAFF affect scores: father sadness and father anger. These were examined separately because they were thought to identify two different affective reactions fathers might have in this situation, and might differentially predict the child's emotional reactions.

*Parent's Negative Listener Behavior.*    The negative listening behavior consisted of any nonverbal index of negativity, including such different reactions as a disapproving facial expression or complete withdrawal from the interaction. The negative listening behavior of each parent on the SPAFF was summed to yield a single score.

## Results

The data were first analyzed using Pearson product-moment correlations. As indicated in Table 3.1, there were no relationships between marital satisfaction and any of the child outcome variables. However, there were some relationships between marital interaction patterns and children's emotions. Hot and positive marital interaction was positively related to humor in the child ($r = .48$, $p < .05$). Husband stubbornness, another index of an engaged marriage, was also related to humor in the child ($r = .34$, $p < .05$). There were no direct relationships between wife withdrawal and any child outcomes.

There were also some correlations between parental behavior during parent–child interaction and children's expressions of humor, anger, and sadness. Parents who engaged in negative listening behaviors had children who showed anger during the parent–child interaction ($r = .35$, $p < .05$). It was also found that father's emotional reactions, rather than those of the mother, were predictive of the children's emotions. In particular, father's sadness was strongly related to children's display of anger ($r = .54$, $p < .05$), and father's anger was correlated with children's display of sadness ($r = .26$, $p < .05$). Father who showed a great deal of humor and excitement had children who were high in humor ($r = .42$, $p < .05$).

These correlational analyses give us a picture of the direct pathways between marital interaction and child outcomes, as well as between parenting behavior and child outcomes. However, in order to test whether there were any indirect pathways from marital interaction patterns to child outcomes that were mediated by the behaviors of the parents, the data were analyzed using structural equations modeling. For our purposes, the advantage of structural equations modeling is that one can assess both direct and indirect effects. This is not possible with correlational or regression analyses. In forward regression, for example, the second variable stepped into a prediction of a criterion variable is that part of the

TABLE 3.1
Correlations Between "Hot" and Withdrawn Marital Interaction, Parenting Behaviors, and
Children's Emotional Reactions

|  | Child Humor | Child Anger | Child Sadness |
|---|---|---|---|
| Marital satisfaction | -.03 | -.01 | -.11 |
| Husband stubbornness | .34* | .09 | .02 |
| "Hot and positive" marital interaction | .48* | -.05 | .25 |
| Wife withdrawal | -.06 | .15 | -.11 |
| Father anger | -.00 | -.07 | .26* |
| Father sadness | -.00 | .54* | -.08 |
| Father humor and excitement | .42* | -.12 | -.02 |
| Mother confident and structuring | .19 | -.01 | -.05 |
| Mother angry and whining | -.08 | .20 | -.02 |
| Parents as negative listeners | -.09 | .35* | -.20 |

*$p < .05$.

second variable that is uncorrelated with the first. Thus, it is not possible to assess indirect effects in which one believes that an effect on the criterion of one variable is mediated through another variable. Path analytic techniques are conservatively employed to generate hypotheses about possible models that can organize the data, not to suggest causal structure in these correlational data.

## Results of Structural Modeling

Bentler's program EQS (Bentler & Weeks, 1980) was used for structural equations modeling. A model was developed linking specific conflict resolution styles in the marital relationship with parenting behaviors and specific emotions displayed by the child. Only selected pathways in the model are discussed here.[1]

We found that husbands who were stubborn during marital interaction were from hot and positive marriages (path coefficient = .67), validating our thinking that stubbornness is an index of hot marital interaction. Hot and positive marital interaction was related to high levels of humor in the child during parent–child interaction (path coefficient = .49; see Fig. 3.1).

What appeared to be associated with more negative child reactions were marriages in which the wives were withdrawn. When wives were withdrawn during marital interaction, both parents were negative listeners during the parent–child interaction (path coefficient = .29). This in turn predicted anger in

---

[1] The reader should note that select pathways are discussed here for illustrative purposes only. Because structural equations modeling requires solving simultaneous equations, all path coefficients are a function of the entire model and select pathways must be understood within the context of the greater model. The reader is referred to Katz (1990) for a discussion and presentation of the entire model.

FIG. 3.1. Child outcomes related to hot and positive marital interaction.

the child (path coefficient = .35; see Fig. 3.2). Parents who were negative listeners made negative facial expressions (such as showing disappointment in their child or disgust) or withdrew from the interaction entirely. It is possible that parents who are withdrawn during marital conflict may also be displaying withdrawal toward their child during what many families find to be an enjoyable game. A more direct measure of parental withdrawal is necessary to test this hypothesis. Children who were angry usually refused to comply with their parent's suggestions, shouted at their parents in frustration when they could not remember the story, and demanded that their parents turn on the video game and stop asking them questions about the story. Essentially, these were children who "ruled the roost." To the extent that parental negative listening behavior reflects an affective withdrawal from the child, children's anger may be their way of recruiting attention or assistance from a sullen and uninvolved parent. Children's anger may also be a reaction to parents who are affectively negative, albeit in a nonverbal manner.

To better illustrate how these linkages between marital interaction style and children's emotional reactions function, we examine two case examples. One is a family in which the couple display a hot form of conflict resolution and the other is a family in which the couple is withdrawn during conflict resolution. Both of these couples initially scored in the maritally distressed range on the telephone version of the Locke–Wallace Marital Satisfaction Inventory (Locke & Wallace, 1959; adapted by Krokoff, 1984). Interestingly, when given the paper-and-pencil version of the Locke–Wallace approximately 2 to 4 weeks later, the hot couple then scored within the maritally satisfied range. Perhaps the hot behavior pattern also has a perceptual component that results in a quickly changing evaluation of their marital relationship. These couples may account for the less than perfect test–retest reliability of self-report instruments of marital satisfaction (typically $r$ = .80).

FIG. 3.2. Child outcomes related to withdrawn marital interaction.

# SPECULATIONS ABOUT LINKAGES BETWEEN MARITAL CONFLICT PATTERNS, CHILDREN'S EMOTIONAL EXPRESSIONS, AND PEER RELATIONSHIPS: SOME CASE STUDIES

In this section, we describe the marital and parent–child interaction sessions of a hot and withdrawn couple. We also illustrate and speculate about how the style of conflict used in the marital relationship may be affecting the child's peer relations.

## Case 1: A Hot Couple

Debbie and Ron's conflict-resolution style was confrontive and direct. There was a great deal of eye contact between them, even when they expressed anger toward each other. They were clear about their feelings and about the compromises or inconveniences they were willing to tolerate. Yet despite any negativity they expressed, they also validated each other's feelings, even when they did not agree with the content of what their spouse was saying. Moreover, they were able to retain some sense of humor about their predicament, laughing about how Ron could probably make more money blowing a tuba at the side of the street than he was making as a staff sergeant in the Air Force. The following excerpt from their conversation about Ron's desire to leave the military highlights the confrontive quality of their conflict resolution style:

| Debbie (D): | [Laughs] I thought so. Ya, but you wanted to come here. You said it would be better for your career. You'd love being an instructor. Now you tell me you hate being an instructor. |
| Ron (R): | I like being an instructor. I just don't like being here. |
| D: | Well, where else can you go and be an instructor? |
| R: | Here. |
| D: | [Laughs] Oh, you're stuck here. |
| R: | No, I might be able to get into an F.T.D. after I've been here 2 years. |
| D: | Well, then why don't you do that? I don't mind if you want to go somewhere else. You know? I'm not telling you not to do what you want. I just think you're going to make a big mistake if you get out. |
| R: | How big of a mistake? |
| D: | Big enough to lose me. That's how big. |
| R: | You think so? |

| D: | Yes sir. |
|---|---|
| R: | Why? |
| D: | Because I'm not going to be out there have to be hustling for a job for the rest of my life. I won't do that. And I know you don't want to be doing that for yourself either. I'm not saying you've got to be in the service 20 years either. Just long enough to find something else that's going to be good for you. [Long pause]. Understand? [Pause]. Don't look at me like that! |
| R: | I understand what you're saying. |
| D: | Alright! |
| R: | But whether I agree with it or not is a different story. |

Our marital interaction task asks couples to resolve an on-going marital disagreement. It is unusual to see both the amount of confrontation and humor and lightheartedness we see in Debbie and Ron's interaction. This sense of humor and positivity was also evident in the parent–child interaction. Amy and her parents approached the video game as an opportunity for the family to engage in an enjoyable shared activity. Although Amy did not remember much of the story she had previously heard, her parents were not bothered by her inability to remember. Instead they joked about her having forgotten the story and easily moved on to the task of teaching Amy how to play the video game.

The video game play was full of fun and laughter. Debbie and Ron praised Amy continuously about how well she was doing and were especially supportive when Amy seemed disappointed with her performance, recognizing that she needed a little extra encouragement at those times. There was also a great deal of humor and laughter between parents and child.

The positive affective climate was balanced by the parents' ability to regulate Amy's tendency to become affectively out of control. At times, Amy's positive affect turned into an out-of-control tendency to use the joystick without purpose, and her parents were able to help her focus attention and calm down at those times. Amy responded well to her parents' structuring and her video game performance successively improved over time. When discipline was needed, it was given promptly and clearly, and then the focus of the interaction swiftly moved back to the video game. Amy was given the direction she required and then the family turned back to the task of having fun. It was interesting that the parent–child interaction did not mirror any of the negative affect seen in the marital relationship.

Amy's interaction with her best friend Katie showed a striking resemblance to her parent's volatile marital interaction. Amy and Katie's play had an interesting quality of rapidly shifting from negative to positive engagement. One moment they were bickering about what to play with and the next moment they were laughing with glee and being silly together.

They began their play with a moderate amount of negative affect. Amy was bossy and angry, commanding Katie not to play with certain prized possessions. Although they attempted to cycle out of their negative affective engagement by using humor and silliness, they were initially unsuccessful and their negativity rapidly deteriorated into bouts of conflict. This eventually resulted in a need for parental intervention.

Despite this negativity, their play was among the highest in our sample in the amount of positive affect expressed. They eventually got involved in a high energy fantasy play about monsters in the kitchen and spent a great deal of their interaction enjoying this activity. They laughed and shrieked in fear of the monster, made witty comments, gently teased each other with affection and good humor, and were sympathetic toward each other's fear of the dark and the monster.

It is interesting to note that the quality of the peer interaction more closely resembles that of the marital interaction than the parent–child interaction. This observation suggests the possibility that there may be a direct pathway from the marital to the peer system that is independent of parent–child interaction. This would suggest that children learn about interpersonal relationships from the way their parents behave toward each other rather than the way they behave toward the child. Another possibility is that hot couples may be better able to buffer their child from any negativity within the marital relationship. This may be because they have not lost the positivity within the marriage and are better able to be positive with their child than parents whose marriage is devoid of positive interaction. Further research is needed to explore these possibilities.

We have described one type of marital conflict-resolution style and speculated about how it may be related to child outcomes. It may be interesting to contrast this pattern with a very different style of marital conflict resolution, that of a withdrawn couple.

## Case 2: A Withdrawn Couple

Chuck and Maggy seemed to be novices at discussing problem areas in their relationship. They were quite anxious at the beginning of their conversation and giggled childishly, unable to gain control of their laughter for several minutes. When they eventually began their discussion, it was awkward and disjointed. There was very little eye contact between them and many long silences.

Maggy raised the issue of wanting Chuck to go to church with the rest of the family. She has been taking their children, Jenny and Chuck Jr. to church regularly and wanted Chuck to participate in what was now becoming an important part of her life. Chuck evaded the problem by refusing to make a commitment: "I ain't saying yes, I ain't saying no," he responded. When Maggy tried to determine whether he refused to go to church because he didn't know how to communicate with the people who attended the church, Chuck again answered the question in a very general way, stating that he doesn't "know how to communicate with *no* people."

Chuck's use of vague, one line answers provided little basis for continued discussion and functioned to shut down their conversation. Maggy became sullen and frustrated, recognizing the futility in her attempts to change Chuck's attitude toward church. She quickly gave up on the conversation about church, and switched to their second chosen topic of friends. This conversation was a replay of the first. Their discussion was vague and general, never getting down to the source of their differences. As soon as the conversation began to touch on the specific ways in which they differed, the tension between Chuck and Maggy would rise and they would stop the conversation and become silent. Their conversation consisted of brief exchanges followed by longer silences.

Chuck and Maggy's behavior during the parent–child interaction similarly lacked structure and specificity. When their 5-year-old daughter Jenny couldn't remember the story she had heard, her parents simply restated their request to hear the story. They did not help facilitate her recall by breaking down the task into components. For example, because children's stories often have animals as the main protagonist, many parents typically ask whether the story was about an animal, and then follow up with questions about what the animal was doing, or where the animal was located. This form of structuring would often jar the child's memory of the story. Instead, Chuck and Maggy simply reiterated that they would like to hear the story. After repeated requests, Jenny became frustrated and angry and eventually made up a story simply to satisfy her parents and to get them to let her play the video game.

Jenny seemed to enjoy playing the video game, although she was not given much of an opportunity to do so by her parents. Chuck and Maggy were critical of how she was playing the game and kept taking the joystick from Jenny's hands to show her how to play the game. Chuck and Maggy also argued continuously throughout the teaching task. When Chuck intruded on Jenny's playing, Maggy scolded Chuck, instructing him to let Jenny play the game by herself, and then later, when Maggy intruded on Jenny's game, Chuck would retort that Jenny should be playing the game rather than Maggy.

Jenny's peer play with her friend Chrissy was virtually devoid of positive affect and fun. The children engaged in parallel play and used basic conversational skills, such as clarifying messages and exchanging information, to maintain this minimum level of interaction. They each played with their own kitten, provided running narratives of all the things their kitten was doing, and discussed what they liked about kittens. However, they were not able to establish any common ground activity or fantasy play. When Chrissy made a bid to increase their level of interaction by taking some toys that belonged to Jenny and her younger brother out of a bag, Jenny objected to Chrissy's efforts, became angry and bossy, and the interaction deteriorated into a squabble. Their inability to establish a minimal amount of engagement resulted in their play requiring a great deal of adult intervention and external regulation of emotion. They quickly became bored with the kittens and their play lacked focus and involvement. Being at a loss for what to do next, they kept making excuses to leave the room to talk to Jenny's dad. When Jenny's dad reprimanded her for leaving the room, she came back to the room upset and took her frustrations out on Chrissy. In one instance, Jenny came back in the room crying because she thought her father was going to take her kittens away. She then got mad at Chrissy and wouldn't allow Chrissy to read any of the books in her room.

The resemblance between the quality of the marital and peer interactions is once again apparent. In this family, the child's inability to establish a common ground activity with their best friend mirrors the couple's withdrawal and inability to specify and articulate the differences that exist in their marriage. The parents' inability to cooperate on a common activity is also seen in the parent–child interaction, when their teaching of how to play the video game deteriorated into childish squabbling. One possible explanation for Jenny's tendency to play in parallel with her friend rather than establish a common activity is that her parents do not provide her with a model of cooperative interaction.

It is interesting that Chuck and Maggy readily expose their child to marital conflict. This may suggest that, unlike the hot couple we described earlier, couples who are withdrawn are unable to buffer their children from the negativity in their marital relationship. This may also be related to Jenny's free expression of anger toward her parents during the parent–child interaction. This pattern of exposing children to negative affect between their parents may communicate that the uncontrolled expression of anger is an acceptable form of interpersonal interaction.

## CONCLUSION

We are beginning to see that marriages come in different shapes and sizes. From the complexity and uniqueness inherent in the different ways couples go about the task of expressing their negative feelings and resolving conflict, we have identified two sets of marital behaviors that may have consequences for the child. We have by no means exhausted the marital conflict-resolution strategies that couples use. If the conflict-resolution strategies that parents use teach their children ways of handling interpersonal relationships, then each of these different strategies may be associated with different outcomes.

Our preliminary data suggest that in intact marriages, it is better for children if their parents engage in conflict when working out their marital differences than if they withdraw from each other. When parents are withdrawn from each other, the child shows heightened expressions of anger. Why might this be the case? Perhaps hot marital interaction reflects the active problem solving of a couple that is trying to work out the problems that naturally come up throughout the course of a long-term relationship. This may also be a marriage in which conflict is resolved when it arises, and the child has the opportunity to observe its healthy resolution. Our conceptualization of hot and positive marital interaction may be different from those used by Cummings et al. (1981, 1984) and Rutter et al. (1974), in which anger, tension, and hostility seem to be the sole ingredients. Child whose parents have marriages in which only hostility, tension, and anger are expressed without any corrective balancing from the presence of positive affect may not fare as well as children whose parents are still able to retain some amount of positive affect in their relationship.

On the other hand, a disengaged and withdrawn marriage might be one that is on the road to marital dissolution (Gottman & Levenson, in preparation-a). In such a marriage, spouses have distanced themselves from each other. These couples may be so psychologically disengaged from the relationship that they no longer care enough about it to invest any energy into working out their disagreements. This might be a later stage of marital conflict that may be more detrimental to the child.

Rather than ask how children respond to discrete instance of a negative affect such as anger between their parents, what may be more telling is the *context* within which the affect occurs. When anger is expressed between parents who are working toward a common solution, and use anger to express their outrage as well as positive affect to reduce the harshness of the anger's impact, children may learn that anger is normal and not to be feared. These children may be developing within a family in which the free expression of a wide range of emotions is encouraged, and they themselves may feel comfortable expressing a range of emotions, both positive and negative. On the other hand, if children live in an environment in which their parents are emotionally withdrawn from each other, then seeing their parents express anger may be very frightening to the child. If, as we suspect, children can sense the fragility of their parents' marriage, then children of withdrawn couples may experience their parent's anger as a confirming sign of an impending marital break-up. In addition, when parents are withdrawn, they may not provide the child with sufficient structure, and the child may become angry and noncompliant both as a way of expressing their fears as well as to demand more structure.

Another possibility for the connection between withdrawal and negative child emotion may have to do with a more general problem-solving style characteristic of some marriages. Gottman and Levenson (in preparation-b) have reported that withdrawal in marital interaction is related to a conflict-avoiding style in which couples do not share their emotions when they are upset, and do not use each other as resources to get over bad moods. Perhaps these couples use denial as a way of coping with negative affect. From a family systems perspective, their children may sense the existence of unspoken and unresolved negative affect, and may be acting out the anger that remains unspoken between parents.

There are many questions that we have not addressed. For example, we do not know the effects of direct exposure to hot marital interaction. In a replication study currently being conducted in which parents were interviewed about their philosophy about exposing children to marital disagreement, the vast majority of parents report that they cannot help but disagree in the child's presence. It is possible, however, that parents monitor the intensity of their disagreements and only voice relatively minor disagreements in front of their child, saving the more substantive arguments for the hours after the child's bedtime. Further research studying the effects of direct exposure to hot and withdrawn marital interaction styles would be useful to clarify the parameters of the relationship between these forms of marital conflict and child outcomes.

We have examined relatively normative behaviors—the child's emotional reactions with their parents and their peer relations—as outcome variables. However, the use of such normative reactions is only important if they can be shown to be early risk factors predictive of negative child outcomes. Although there is evidence linking poor childhood peer relationships to a variety of negative mental health outcomes (Parker & Asher, 1987), the long-term predictors of children's daily emotional reactions have yet to be established. We are currently conducting a longitudinal follow-up of this sample at school entry. If it can be shown that the use of certain emotional reactions at the preschool age can predict whether the child will be identified by "natural raters" such as teachers, camp counsellors, or other important adults in the child's environment (Kellam, personal communication May 30, 1989) as showing troublesome behaviors at school entry, then the use of these subtle emotional reactions can be validated.

In this chapter, we have tried to illustrate the theoretical gain that can come from greater precision in the description of marital distress and conflict. Our preliminary data suggests that there are patterns linking specific forms of marital conflict with specific child reactions. This may be a first step in disentangling the web of confusion that exists in identifying the child outcomes associated with marital distress. Perhaps we have been framing our questions too simplistically. Instead of asking *whether* there are detrimental effects of marital distress on children, perhaps the time has come to ask more specifically "What types of marital difficulties are associated with what types of child outcomes?"

## REFERENCES

Amato, P. R. (1986). Marital conflict, the parent-child relationship and child self-esteem. *Family Relations: Journal of Applied Family and Child Studies, 35,* 403–410.

Attili, G. (1989). Social competence versus emotional security: The link between home relationships and behavior problems at school. In B. H. Schneider, G. Attili, J. Nadel, & R. P. Weissberg, (Eds.), *Social competence in developmental perspective* (pp. 293–311). London: Kluwer Academic Publishers.

Bakeman, R., & Gottman, J. M. (1986). *Observing interaction: An introduction to sequential analysis.* New York: Cambridge University Press.

Baumrind, D. (1971). Current patterns of parental authority. *Developmental Psychology, 4,* 1–103.

Baumrind, D. (1971). Current patterns of parental authority. *Developmental Psychology, 4,* 1–103.

Belsky, J., & Rovine, M. (1981). Pennsylvania Infant and Family Development Project IV: Marriage, personality and temperament as determinants of personality.

Belsky, J., & Isabella, R. (1988). Maternal, infant and social contextual determinants of attachment security. In J. Belsky & T. Nezworski (Eds.), *Clinical implications of attachment* (pp. 41–94). Hillsdale, NJ: Lawrence Erlbaum Associates.

Bentler, P. M., & Weeks, G. D. (1980). Linear structural equations with latent variables. *Psychometrika, 45,* 289–308.

Block, J. H., Block, J., & Morrison, A. (1981). Parental agreement-disagreement on child-rearing orientations and gender-related personality correlates in children. *Child Development, 52,* 965–974.

Cohn, D. A., Patterson, C. J., & Christopoulos, C. (1991). The family and children's peer relations. *Journal of Social and Personal Relationships, 8,* 315–346.

Cowan, P. A., & Cowan, C. P. (1987, April). *Couple's relationships, parenting styles and the child's development at three.* Paper presented at the Society for Research in Child Development. Baltimore, MD.

Cummings, E. M. (1987). Coping with background anger in early childhood. *Child Development, 58,* 976–984.

Cummings, E. M., Iannotti, R. J., & Zahn-Waxler, C. (1985). Influence of conflict between adults on the emotions and aggression of young children. *Developmental Psychology, 21,* 495–507.

Cummings, E. M., Zahn-Waxler, C., & Radke-Yarrow, M. (1981). Young children's responses to expressions of anger and affection by others in the family. *Child Development, 52,* 1274–1282.

Cummings, E. M., Zahn-Waxler, C., & Radke-Yarrow, M. (1984). Developmental changes in children's reactions to anger in the home. *Journal of Child Psychology and Psychiatry, 25,* 63–74.

Cummings, J. S., Pellegrini, D. S., Notarius, C. I., & Cummings, E. M. (1989). Children's responses to angry adult behavior as a function of marital distress and history of interparent hostility. *Child Development, 60,* 1035–1043.

Dishion, T. J. (1990). The family ecology of boys' peer relations in middle school. *Child Development, 61,* 874–892.

Dutton, D. G. (1988). *The domestic assault of women: Psychological and criminal justice perspectives.* Boston: Allyn & Bacon.

Easterbrooks, M. A. (1987, April). *Early family development: Longitudinal impact of marital quality.* Paper presented at the Meeting of the Society for Research in Child Development. Baltimore, MD.

Ekman, P. (1984). Expression and the nature of emotion. In K. P. Scherer & P. Ekman (Eds.), *Approaches to emotion* (pp. 319–344). Hillsdale, NJ: Lawrence Erlbaum Associates.

Ekman, P., & Friesen, W. V. (1982). Felt, false and miserable smiles. *Journal of Nonverbal Behavior, 6,* 238–252.

Emery, R. E. (1982). Interparental conflict and the children of discord and divorce. *Psychological Bulletin, 92,* 310–330.

Emery, R. E., & O'Leary, K. D. (1982). Children's perceptions of marital discord and behavior problems of boys and girls. *Journal of Abnormal Child Psychology, 10,* 11–24.

Enos, D. M., & Handal, P. J. (1986). The relation of parental marital status and perceived family conflict to adjustment in white adolescents. *Journal of Consulting and Clinical Psychology, 54,* 820–824.

Forehand, R., Brody, G., Long, N., Slotkin, J., & Fauber, R. (1986). Divorce/divorce potential and interparental conflict: The relationship to early adolescent social and cognitive functioning. *Journal of Adolescent Research, 1,* 389–397.

Glenn, C. G. (1978). The role of episodic structure and of story length in children's recall of simple stories. *Journal of Verbal Learning and Verbal Behavior, 17,* 229–247.

Goldberg, W. A., & Easterbrooks, M. A. (1984). Role of marital quality in toddler development. *Developmental Psychology, 20,* 504–514.

Gottman, J. M. (1979). *Marital interaction: Experimental investigations.* New York: Academic Press.

Gottman, J. M. (1983). How children become friends. *Monographs of the Society for Research in Child Development, (2, Serial No. 201).*

Gottman, J. M. (1986). *Specific Affect Coding Manual.* Unpublished manuscript. University of Washington.

Gottman, J. M., & Katz, L. (1989). Effects of marital discord on young children's peer interaction and health. *Developmental Psychology, 25*(3), 373–381.

Gottman, J. M., & Krokoff, L. (1989). Marital interaction and marital satisfaction: A longitudinal view. *Journal of Consulting and Clinical Psychology, 57,* 47–52.

Gottman, J. M., & Levenson, R. W. (in preparation-a). *The social psychophysiology of marriage.*

Gottman, J. M., & Levenson, R. W. (in preparation-b). *Male withdrawal from marital interaction.* University of Washington.

Hetherington, E. M., Cox, M., & Cox, R. (1982). Effects of divorce on parents and children. In M. Lamb (Ed.), *Nontraditional families* (pp. 233–288). Hillsdale, NJ: Lawrence Erlbaum Associates.

Howes, P., & Markman, H. J. (1989). Marital quality and child functioning: a longitudinal investigation. *Child Development, 60,* 1044–1051.

Jacobson, N. S., & Margolin, G. (1979). *Marital therapy: Strategies based on ed on social learning and behavior exchange principles.* New York: Brunner/Mazel.

Kagan, J., Rosman, B. L., Day, D., Albert, J., & Phillips, W. (1964). Information processing in the child: Significance of analytic and reflective attitudes. *Psychological Monographs, 78*(1, Whole No. 578).

Katz, L. F. (1990). *Marital interaction patterns and child outcomes.* Unpublished doctoral dissertation, University of Illinois at Urbana-Champaign, IL.

Katz, L. F., & Gottman, J. M. (1991). Marital discord and child outcomes: A social-psychophysiological approach. In K. Dodge & J. Garber (Eds.), *The development of affect regulation.* Cambridge: Cambridge University Press.

Kolvin, I., Garside, R., Nicol, A., MacMillan, A., Wolstenholme, F., & Leitch, I. (1977). Familial and sociological correlates of behavioral and sociological deviance in 8-year-old children. In P. Graham (Ed.), *Epidemiology of childhood disorders* (pp. 195–222). New York: Academic Press.

Kopp, C. B. (1982). Antecedents of self-regulation: A developmental perspective. *Developmental Psychology, 18,* 199–214.

Krokoff, L. (1984). Anatomy of negative affect in working class marriages. *Dissertation Abstracts International, 45,7A.* (University Microfilms no. 84-22 109).

Long, N., Forehand, R., Fauber, R., & Brody, G. H. (1987). Self-perceived and independently observed competence of young adolescents as a function of parental marital conflict and recent divorce. *Journal of Abnormal Child Psychology, 15,* 15–27.

Maccoby, E. E. (1980). *Social development.* New York: Harcourt, Brace & Jovanovitch.

Margolin, G. (1988). Marital conflict is not marital conflict is not marital conflict. In R. DeV. Peters & R. J. MacMahon (Eds.), *Social learning and systems approaches to marriage and the family* (pp. 193–216). New York: Brunner/Mazel.

Markman, H. J., Floyd, F. J., & Stanley, S. M. (1988). Prevention of marital distress: A longitudinal investigation. *Journal of Consulting and Clinical Psychology, 56,* 210–217.

Parke, R. D., & Ladd, G. W. (1992). *Family-peer relationships: Modes of linkage.* Hillsdale, NJ: Lawrence Erlbaum Associates.

Parker, J. G., & Asher, S. R. (1987). Peer relations and later personal adjustment: Are low-accepted children "at risk"? *Psychological Bulletin, 102,* 357–389.

Peterson, J. L., & Zill, N. (1986). Marital disruption, parent-child relationships, and behavior problems in children. *Journal of Marriage and the Family, 48,* 295–307.

Porter, B., & O'Leary, K. D. (1980). Marital discord and childhood behavior problems. *Journal of Abnormal Child Psychology, 8*(3), 287–295.

Putallaz, M. (1987). Maternal behavior and children's sociometric status. *Child Development, 58,* 324–340.

Redl, F., & Wineman, D. (1951). *Children who hate.* Glencoe, IL: The Free Press.

Revenstorf, D., Vogel, B., Wegener, C., Hahlweg, K., & Schindler, L. (1980). Escalation phenomena in interaction sequences: An empirical comparison of distressed and non-distressed couples, *Behavioral Analysis and Modification, 4,* 97–115.

Rutter, M. (1971). Parent–child separation: Psychological effects on the children. *Journal of Child Psychology and Psychiatry, 12,* 233–260.                              ,

Rutter, M., Yule, B., Quinton, D., Rowlands, O., Yule, W., & Berger, M. (1974). Attainment and adjustment in two geographic areas: Some factors accounting for area differences. *British Journal of Psychiatry, 126,* 520–533.

Shaw, D. S., & Emery, R. E. (1987). Parental conflict and other correlates of the adjustment of school-age children whose parents have separated. *Journal of Abnormal Child Psychology, 15,* 269–281.

Weiss, R. L., & Summers, K. J. (1983). Marital interaction coding system III. In E. E. Filsinger (Ed.), *Marriage and family assessment* (pp. 85–120). Beverly Hills, CA: Sage.

Whitehead, L. (1979). Sex differences in children's responses to family stress. *Journal of Child Psychology and Psychiatry, 20,* 247–254.

Zahn-Waxler, C. (1988, May). *Maternal depression and children's empathy.* Paper presented at the Emotion Regulation Consortium, sponsored by the Society for Research in Child Development. Nashville, TN.

# 4 Prebirth to Preschool Family Factors in Children's Adaptation to Kindergarten

Philip A. Cowan
Carolyn Pape Cowan
Marc S. Schulz
Gertrude Heming
*University of California, Berkeley*

Teddy is a shy little boy who celebrated his fifth birthday in the middle of August. It is now Tuesday morning, the day after Labor day, and the family is getting ready for Teddy's first day of kindergarten. He awakens his mother, Barbara, with what he describes as a tummy ache and a sore throat. Normally able to wolf down a big breakfast, Teddy pushes away his cereal, toast, and eggs. He barely responds to his father's familiar attempts to make jokes. Barbara, believing that Teddy just needs some quiet time, says nothing.

In the car on the way to school Teddy remains silent. Barbara lets him be. As they approach the school, she mentions the classroom visit they made together several months ago, and reminds Teddy how much he liked the toys in the kindergarten room, and the teacher, Mrs. Stewart. Barbara parks the car, gets out, and offers Teddy her hand. With a quick look at the other children and parents walking toward the school, he declines emphatically. In the yard by the kindergarten door Teddy notices a friend from his preschool class, but he makes no move in his direction. Barbara, wanting desperately to give Teddy a hug but taking care not to embarrass him, crouches down, gives his cheek a pat, and tells him that she will be back at lunch time when school lets out. She turns and slowly walks away. From her car she watches her son, who stays rooted to the spot, trying unsuccessfully to look casual. When the school bell rings, Teddy draws himself together, hitches up his shoulders, and marches slowly toward the kindergarten door.

Teddy's transition to elementary school is not made in one morning. Many events in his young life and in the life of his family have led to this moment, and many will follow before we can say that he has completed his transition from preschool to kindergarten. We present this vignette, described by a mother in our study of the early years of family life (C. Cowan & P. Cowan, 1992; P. Cowan & C.

Cowan, 1990) to remind readers about the giant steps children must make when they enter elementary school for the first time.

To a child who has spent 5 years at home with his or her parents or a baby-sitter, the first months of kindergarten may come as something of a shock. Even for children who have spent time in a small preschool classroom or a child-care setting, as Teddy has, kindergarten presents exciting but anxiety-provoking new challenges. Elementary schools are usually larger than preschools or day-care facilities, with more children and fewer adults in each room. The new kinder-gartners may know a few of their classmates, but they must spend much of their time and emotional effort figuring out how get along with strangers. They don't know the school rules, where to put their jackets, or what the teacher expects. They must learn to sit quietly and do what they are told. Days that used to be spent in play are now filled with work. Ready or not, they must grapple with learning the skills to prepare them for reading, writing, and arithmetic.

Different groups of researchers have been trying to identify the factors in children's social environments that facilitate or interfere with their cognitive development and their relationships with friends. Some have focused primarily on the family system, others on the school system, and still others on the peer system in an attempt to explain the wide range of variations in children's adaptation. We believe that to create a more differentiated and integrated contextual model of children's development, we must bring together these various lines of research. This daunting task feels even more formidable because of the many gaps in our knowledge about how family, school, and peer systems are interrelated and about whether linkages among these systems change from middle childhood through adolescence. But given heightened concerns about children's academic and social difficulties in schools, we feel the need to press on toward more integrative approaches despite the lack of extensive background information.

Using the rich ecological framework outlined by Bronfenbrenner (1979, 1986; Bronfenbrenner & Crouter, 1983) as a general guide, we construct and test a beginning version of a model intended to understand the connections between family functioning and children's adaptation to school. Bronfenbrenner sug-gested that a fully contextual approach to the study of children's development would encompass four levels of analysis. First, we must examine the micro-system in which family interaction processes have a direct effect on the child. Second, we need to take into account the mesosystem—the combined impact of the multiple social systems of which the child is a member (extended families, peer groups, day-care settings, schools). Third is the exosystem, the societal arrangements that have both direct and indirect effects on family life (the work-place, external social supports, community institutions, the socioeconomic con-text of family life). Finally, systematic changes that occur over the life course and over historical time—the chronosytem—cannot be ignored. A "full" explanatory model of family–school linkage, then, would provide a longitudinal study of the bidirectional interactions among family, school, and peer environments, with some attention to other important psychosocial settings whose cumulative effects unfold over time and shape children's development.

In this chapter we limit our focus primarily to the microsystem—the environment and processes in the family that function as a context for the child's adaptation to kindergarten. We begin with a discussion of why the preschool to kindergarten transition is a particularly important time to examine the connecting links between family and school, and to discover how the family environment contributes differentially to children's academic and social adaptation. A brief review of family–school research suggests that we need more information about family processes in the preschool years if we are to identify the mechanisms affecting children's adaptation to kindergarten. We turn to the data from the Becoming a Family Project, our longitudinal study following couples and families from their first pregnancy through the child's kindergarten year (C. Cowan & P. Cowan, 1992; P. Cowan & C. Cowan, 1990). Using path analytic techniques we show that information obtained in pregnancy about the parents' families of origin and marital quality, in combination with indices assessing individual, marital, and family functioning from 6 months to $3\frac{1}{2}$ years postpartum, enables us to predict about one quarter of the variation in the child's aggressive or shy and withdrawn behavior with peers in kindergarten. A second path model containing identical information about early family adaptation allows us to predict slightly more than half of the variation in the children's academic achievement test scores in the summer following their completion of kindergarten.

Although we are pleased with the predictive power of our conceptual model, it is far from providing a complete picture of the bidirectional effects of family and school system variables on children's early development. We describe some of the important conceptual and empirical work that will be necessary to reach this challenging and elusive goal in a final section of the chapter.

## THE TRANSITION TO ELEMENTARY SCHOOL AS A "CRITICAL PERIOD"

In ethological studies, a critical period refers to a narrow window of time in which, if conditions are right, the organism is responsive to specific stimuli that influence the development of essential adaptive behaviors (Lorenz, 1943; Scott, Fredericson, & Fuller, 1951; Tinbergen, 1951). We do not argue that the transition to kindergarten is a critical period for a child's school adaptation in the strict sense of an irreversible, make-or-break time in his or her intellectual and social life. Alexander and Entwisle (1988) suggested that children in kindergarten and first grade are "launched into achievement trajectories that they follow the rest of their school years" (p. 1). We focus on children's adaptation during their transition into elementary school because we believe that it is pivotal to our understanding of the pathways that their educational development will take.

Follow-forward studies of high-risk samples have provided clear evidence supporting Alexander and Entwisle's trajectory hypothesis: Adolescents with problematic educational and mental health outcomes are more likely to have experienced earlier academic difficulties and to have been rejected by their peers during the first few years of elementary school (Ginsberg, Gottman, & Parker 1986; Kellam, Simon, & Ensminger, 1982; Kupersmidt, Coie, & Dodge, 1990; Lambert, 1988; Werner & Smith, 1982). Furthermore, indicators of risk or vulnerability to later problems and disorders can be identified during the child's first year or two of elementary school in relatively advantaged, low-risk samples as well (Baumrind, 1991; Block, Block, & Keyes, 1988). As children enter kindergarten, then, assessments of their adjustment can provide centrally important information about both their present level of functioning and their developmental risk status for the next 10 to 12 years.

We are referring here to a substantial proportion of the school population. Almost one third of the students entering kindergarten are at risk for developing serious academic and personal problems before they finish high school, including dropping out of school, attempting suicide, experiencing clinical depression, running away, becoming pregnant, displaying antisocial behavior, becoming delinquent, drinking heavily or abusing other substances, and experiencing attention deficit disorders (Lambert, 1988). Kindergarten provides an ideal beginning platform from which to survey children's educational trajectories. We can project ahead to make long-term predictions about their academic and social adaptation and look back to identify the risk factors that have a negative impact at the start of their educational careers. Information from both vantage points may point the way to helpful interventions addressed to children's academic and social relationship success.

Transition periods are particularly good times to study connections between family processes and children's development (Bronfenbrenner, 1986; Caspi & Moffitt, 1991; P. Cowan, 1991). Major life changes may precipitate reorganizations of family roles and intimate relationships in ways that challenge family members' existing cognitive, social, and emotional coping skills. As individuals and families attempt to meet these new challenges, their intrapsychic and interpersonal coping mechanisms and processes are brought into sharp relief. Alexander and Entwisle (1988) described how the mechanisms linking family adaptation and children's academic competence are highlighted during the child's transition to elementary school as variability among individuals increases: "As in a bicycle race, people cluster together along the straightaway but pull apart when they go up a hill. Transitions, like hills, pose challenges; they test the competitors' mettle and, in so doing, reveal both weak and strong points" (p. 99). As the "cyclists" begin to spread out along both academic and social pathways, we can see more clearly that some maintain their speed with ease, whereas others lose momentum and begin to fall further and further behind the pack.

Three questions are central to the issue of understanding the links between family environments and children's school adaptation: (a) *Which* family variables contribute to explanations of the variance in children's adaptation to school? (b) *How much* of the variance in school adjustment can be explained by a combination of family variables? and (c) What can we learn about the *mechanisms or processes* through which the risks in the family environment have their effects on children's developmental outcomes (Cowan, Cowan, & Schulz, in press; Rutter, 1987)? If we can identify the risk conditions, determine the strength of their impact, and discover how they operate to affect children's development, we can plan more effective interventions specifically targeted to facilitate school-children's academic and social competence in the early years of elementary school.

## FAMILY CORRELATES OF CHILDREN'S ADAPTATION TO KINDERGARTEN

Our aim here is not provide an exhaustive review of the large and scattered research on family–school correlations, but rather to provide some examples of what is known and what is not yet known about this topic. In the search for correlations between the child's family environment and competence at school, most researchers focus on one or two of five aspects of the family environment: (a) the family's sociocultural background (e.g., education, income, occupation; ethnicity); (b) family structure (e.g., number of children, married or divorced); (c) each parent's level of functioning (e.g., IQ, personality, psychopathology); (d) parents' cognitions (e.g., values, beliefs, expectations, aspirations); and (e) parents' behaviors (e.g., as socialization agents, tutors, and "gatekeepers" controlling children's access to people and institutions in the world outside the nuclear family).

### Family Correlates of Academic Achievement

Because studies of academic competence rarely include kindergarten children or pre-kindergarten family data, ideas about what constitute family factors important to school achievement must come primarily from studies of children 7 years of age and older. A large body of evidence documents consistent, low to moderate correlations between a number of parental characteristics and children's achievement. Children tend to receive lower grades, lower scores on achievement tests, and lower teacher ratings of intellectual performance when their parents have lower socioeconomic status (SES; Scott-Jones, 1984), fewer years of schooling (Laosa, 1982), recently divorced (Guidubaldi & Perry, 1984; Hetherington, Cox, & Cox, 1982; Kaye, 1989), lower IQs (Majoribanks 1979), diagnoses of schizophrenia or clinical depression (Baldwin, Cole, & Baldwin, 1982; Sameroff, Seifer, & Zax, 1982), and lower expectations for their children's ultimate achievement in life (Alexander & Entwisle, 1988; Seginer, 1983).

These correlational findings provide a relatively static view of family to school connections in that they fail to account for the mechanisms that link family environments with school performance (Kalinowsky & Sloane, 1981). There is emerging empirical support for the hypothesis that parents' beliefs, personality characteristics, and symptom patterns influence children through their impact on parenting behavior, which in turn, affects the quality of the parent–child relationship (Belsky, Rovine, & Fish, 1992; Brunquell, Crichton, & Egeland, 1981; Susman et al., 1985).

The quality of parents' interactions with their children, either in the laboratory or at home, is a consistent concurrent and predictive correlate of children's cognitive progress (Baumrind, 1979; Block & Block, 1980; Clarke-Stewart, 1977; Maccoby & Martin, 1983). A number of studies of young children report correlations between the clarity and complexity of mothers' verbal communication in the home and children's school achievement (see Hess & Holloway, 1984). Looking at more global aspects of parenting style, Baumrind (1979) identified two orthogonal dimensions: one involving warmth and responsiveness, the other including structure, limit-setting, and maturity demands. Parents who are high on both dimensions (i.e., both responsive and demanding) are described as having an *authoritative parenting style*. In contrast with parents who show other styles (e.g., low responsive and high demanding), authoritative parents tend to have children who are more cognitively and socially competent at ages 3, 8, and 14, as assessed both on psychological tests (Baumrind, 1979, 1991) and in the school environment (Hess & Holloway, 1984). Steinberg, Elmen, and Mounts (1989) have shown in a longitudinal study of 10- to 16-year-olds that authoritative parenting is not only correlated with school success, but also plays a role in facilitating academic performance.

How parents deal with specific school-related tasks at home is correlated with their children's academic achievement. For example, Pratt and his colleagues (Pratt, Green, MacVicar, & Bountrogianni, 1992) reported that parents of Grade 5 children who are classified as authoritative are more sensitive to their children's level of performance while assisting them on homework tasks, and the children, in turn, show better homework performance and better mathematics achievement at school.

The studies we have been summarizing link data about parents' beliefs, expectations, aspirations, or behavior and their children's achievement at the same point in time. We were able to find only three studies that used preschool measures of family functioning as predictors of children's academic competence and only one of them focused on kindergarten performance. Schaefer and Hunter (1983), observing mothers' interaction with their 12-month-olds, found that when mothers were more demanding, stimulating, interactive, and responsive with their infants, the children were rated as more intelligent and curious/creative by their kindergarten teachers more than 4 years later. In their impressive cross-national study of contexts of achievement, Stevenson and Lee

(1990) attributed some of the academic superiority of Japanese children to the families' pre-elementary school focus on academic rather than social activities. Another excellent cross-national study (McDevitt et al., 1987) found that when American and Japanese mothers were more accurate in their referential communication with their 4-year-olds, the American children had greater vocabulary skills at age 12, and the Japanese children had greater mathematics skills at age 12, than did children of mothers with low referential communication skills.

There is little doubt, then, that current social status, family structure, parents' beliefs and level of adaptation, and especially parents' behavior toward their children, show significant correlations with some aspects of academic achievement in children of varying ages, but the question remains: *What are the mechanisms* linking preschool family patterns with future academic competence? We present some of our own data on this point later in this chapter.

## Family Correlates of Social Competence

Studies of family risk factors in children's social development tend to examine most of the variables previously described as linked to academic achievement, with an even stronger emphasis on the consequences of patterns of parenting and intrafamily processes. Studies of elementary school children using concurrent family and school measures suggest that intrafamily stress, distress, aggression, and conflict are associated with children's aggression and peer rejection at school (e.g., Asher & Coie, 1990; Loeber & Dishion, 1984; Masten et al., 1988; G. Patterson, 1982). Researchers have begun to explore preschool family predictors of children's social competence in kindergarten and the early elementary grades. Schaefer and Hunter (1983) found that when mothers were described by observers as more demanding, stimulating, interactive, and showing greater pleasure in parenting their 1-year-olds, their children were rated 4 years later in kindergarten as more socially independent. Children who were subject to early physical abuse by parents were rated by their kindergarten teachers as more aggressive than children with no history of abuse (Dodge, Bates, & Pettit, 1990). The early abuse was likely to be followed by coercive and intrusive parenting in the preschool years and by the pre-kindergarten child's tendency to overinterpret aggressive intent in their accounts of videotaped peer interactions (Pettit, Harris, Bates, & Dodge, 1991). That is, ineffective parenting and cognitive information-processing style may be mechanisms linking early abuse with children's later difficulties in forming peer relationships. In another shorter term predictive study (Barth & Parke, 1993), parent–child relationships during the summer before kindergarten entrance were implicated in children's hostility toward peers in the early weeks of kindergarten and in the decline in quality of their peer relationships over the school year.

Additional evidence supports links between children's preschool family environments and their socioemotional adjustment at school. Easterbrooks and Goldberg (1990) found that toddlers who tended to avoid their parents upon reunion in the Strange Situation procedure (Ainsworth & Wittig, 1969), and toddlers who resisted parent contact, were more likely than securely attached toddlers to display over control of impulses and emotions 3 years later as kindergartners. Campbell, March, Pierce, and Ewing (1991) reported that boys who are hard to manage in preschool tend to have negatively controlling mothers, and more family life stress; these boys are more likely to be described by parents and teachers as externalizing one year later. Data from the Minnesota Mother–Child Project (Renken, Egeland, Marvinney, Mangelsdorf, & Sroufe, 1989) show that a combination of (a) the child's developmental history of insecure attachment and poor adjustment (12, 18, and 42 months), (b) inadequate or hostile parent care (42 months), and (c) stressful family life circumstances, predicts up to one third of the variance in teachers' ratings of children's aggression and passive withdrawal in elementary school (averaged over Grades 1 to 3). It is clear that the presence of family violence in the home, early attachment difficulties, and ineffective parenting of preschool children are associated with higher levels of externalizing behavior in the classroom. It is less clear how family processes are related to social relationship problems on the internalizing (e.g., shy/withdrawn) end of the continuum.

## What's Missing From Current Family–School Research?

Most family–school studies use one of three types of measures of children's adaptation to school: academic achievement, social competence (usually "peer status" as accepted, rejected, or ignored), and the presence or absence of behavior problems. Although there is ample evidence that these three outcomes overlap, especially in middle childhood and adolescence (cf. Wentzel, 1991), their intercorrelations are far from perfect (e.g., Asher & Coie, 1990). We need to know a great deal more about the specificity of family–school connections. Does the overlap change systematically with age? Are the same family patterns associated with children's achievement in reading and mathematics, with social competence, and with conduct-disordered behavior? We will not know the answers until studies include a variety of outcome measures obtained from parents and children, with both longitudinal and cross-sectional examinations of developmental changes in the patterns of results.

Until the most recent family–school studies cited here, conclusions about family processes were not buttressed with direct observational information about the quality of the relationships between parents and their children. Furthermore, self-reports from mothers, the usual informants, provide only one point of view about the nature of family life; fathers' perspectives and behavior may contribute unique information and unique explanatory power to our understanding of their children's adaptation.

Although there has been growing interest in the question of how parents' marital relationships affect children's development (Belsky, Lang, & Rovine, 1985; C. Cowan, P. Cowan, Heming, & Miller, 1991), the impact of marital conflict on the child's coping with school has largely been ignored except, ironically, in the case of marital dissolution (Crockenberg & Covey, 1991). Children and adolescents whose parents have been divorced tend to show increases in behavior problems, decreases in academic achievement, and disruptions in peer relationships (see Hetherington, Stanley-Hagan, & Anderson, 1989). The children's difficulties in school are associated with ongoing conflict between the divorced spouses (McCombs & Forehand, 1989), and with disruptions in the effectiveness of parenting (Hetherington et al., 1989; G. Patterson & Capaldi, 1991).

Recent evidence from studies of "nonclinical" families indicates that the quality of the parents' marriage plays a central role in the child's early development in intact families too. Impressive correlations between prebirth marital quality and parenting behavior with infants have been documented in several samples (Grossman, Eichler, & Winickoff, 1980; Heinicke, Diskin, Ramsay-Klee, & Oates, 1986; Lewis, Tresch-Owen, & Cox, 1988). More harmonious marriages have also been linked with developmental progress in infants and toddlers (Dickie, 1987; Easterbrooks, 1987; Goldberg & Easterbrooks, 1984; Heinicke & Guthrie, 1991; Howes & Markman, 1989), and in the early school years (Brody, Pellegrini, & Sigel, 1986; Gottman & Fainsilber, 1989). We located only two studies that showed direct links between the state of the parents' marriage and the children's school adaptation in a nondivorced population (Feldman, Wentzel, Weinberger, & Munson, 1990; Long, Forehand, Fauber, & Brody, 1987). Both of these reports focus on adolescents (Feldman looking at male adolescents only) and the correlations were moderate at best. More comprehensive studies of the links between marital functioning and school adaptation are needed for children beginning their educational trajectories, when they may be particularly vulnerable to conflict between their parents.

Especially when academic competence is the outcome of interest, most studies have reported concurrent correlations between family variables and children's school outcomes (see reviews by Hess & Holloway, 1984; Scott-Jones, 1984). In any single-time assessment design, it is impossible to evaluate the direction of effects—to know whether family processes are affecting the child's behavior at school (e.g., harsh parental discipline contributing to the child's aggression on the playground) or whether aspects of the school environment are influencing the child's behavior and the parents' response in the home. These two possibilities are usually considered in separate studies. One recent extreme example was the publication of two books on literacy acquisition, one focusing on school influences (Chall, Jacobs, & Baldwin, 1990), the other on home influences (Snow, Barnes, Chandler, Goodman, & Hemphill, 1991), with both sets of researchers using the same subjects and data set.

An important first step in untangling the direction of effects in family–school research requires an assessment of family processes and children's competence before as well as after the children enter school, although this procedure does not fully resolve the issue of causality or direction of effects. If we find that the degree of warmth and structuring of parents' interactions with their preschooler predicts the child's academic competence 2 years later, it could still be argued that parents are reacting to the (earlier) temperament of their child. However, if we can obtain data concerning the parents' characteristics before their children are born, we will be able to address more directly the question of what comes first, although even with this design, we cannot make strong causal inferences on the basis of antecedent-consequent relations between variables.

Almost all of our criticisms of previous research circle around one central point. Very few studies of school children gather the kind of family or school data that allow us to make inferences about the mechanisms linking children's social contexts and specific developmental outcomes. In an attempt to fill in some of the missing connections, we turn now to some data from our longitudinal study of new families.

## DESCRIPTION OF THE STUDY

In the Becoming a Family Project, we assessed 72 couples in late pregnancy with interviews, observations, and a battery of questionnaires. We followed each family again when the children were 6 months, $1\frac{1}{2}$, $3\frac{1}{2}$, and $5\frac{1}{2}$ years old. In the last two assessments we added to the repeated assessments of both parents as individuals and as a couple, videotaped assessments of the individual child, of each parent with the child, and of the whole family working and playing together in our laboratory. The kindergarten year assessment added teachers' ratings and an individually administered standardized test of academic achievement.

Of the original 72 children born during the study, we were able to assess 87% 18 months after birth, 70% at $3\frac{1}{2}$, and nearly 80% at the kindergarten follow-up. Although we have data from 56 of the children, we have complete family data from only 44 families because 9 of the couples had divorced by the $3\frac{1}{2}$-year follow-ups, and 3 of the fathers from intact families did not return for the videotaped assessments.

The total sample ranges in ethnic background and socioeconomic circumstances. When they joined the study, the parents lived in 28 communities in the greater San Francisco Bay Area, and ranged in age from 21 to 48 years, with a mean of approximately 30 years for the expectant fathers and 29 for the expectant mothers. At the beginning of the study, the partners had been together for an average of 4 years, with a range extending from 8 months to 12 years. At the $3\frac{1}{2}$-year follow-up, 90% of the participants were Caucasian and 10% were Black,

Asian-American, or Hispanic, a decline of 5% in the proportion of ethnic minority participants since the beginning of the study.

Attempting to synthesize previous theoretical descriptions of important dimensions of family life (e.g., Belsky, 1984; Heinicke, 1984; Parke & Tinsley, 1982), we have developed a five-domain model, arguing that to predict and understand family adaptation during major transitions, we must examine five aspects of family functioning:

1. the inner life of each individual in the family (each parent and the child at the kindergarten follow-up), with special emphasis on each person's sense of self, view of the world, and emotional well-being or distress,
2. the quality of the relationship between the husband and wife, with special emphasis on their division of marital roles and communication patterns,
3. the quality of relationships the parents recall in their families of origin and the ongoing relationships they describe among grandparents, parents, and grandchildren,
4. the quality of relationship between each parent and child, and
5. the relationships between nuclear family members and key individuals or institutions outside the family (e.g., friends, work, child care, school), with emphasis on the sources of stress and support from outside the nuclear family.

These five domains form the elements of a structural model of marital and family adaptation in two ways. First, each domain describes a different level of system organization: individual, peer dyad (marital), hierarchical parent–child dyads, three-generational extended family, and the relation between the nuclear family and social systems in the larger society. Second, the focus of the model is not only on the content within the domains but also on their patterns of interconnection. The impact of a life transition on the individual is not the simple result of adding together positive and negative changes in each domain, but a product of the synergistic way in which these changes reverberate throughout the system. Our working hypothesis throughout the study is that a combination of data from all five domains will help us to understand variation in both parents' and children's adaptation and dysfunction when the family system or any of the individuals within it goes through a major life change (cf. Heming, 1987).

We have shown that in all of these domains, couples in transition to parenthood experience more change, and more negative change, than comparable couples who have not yet decided about having children (C. Cowan & P. Cowan, 1992; C. Cowan et al., 1985). As in almost every study of this transition (e.g., Belsky, Lang, & Rovine, 1985), couples becoming families in our study show small but consistent statistically significant declines in satisfaction with marriage from pregnancy through their child's entrance to kindergarten. We have shown that this decline in satisfaction is not correlated with change per se but with the widening gap between husbands and wives in roles, experiences, and perceptions in each of the family domains as partners become parents (C. Cowan & P. Cowan, 1992; C. Cowan et al., 1985).

A focus on change during major life transitions sometimes obscures the continuity of adaptation in individuals and in the family (Belsky, Lang, et al., 1985; Caspi & Moffitt, 1991). Despite clear shifts in every domain during the transition to parenthood, there is impressive consistency of pre- to postbirth measures of satisfaction and adaptation (C. Cowan et al., 1991). Even though the stresses involved in parenting make an additional contribution to men's and women's feelings about themselves and their marriages (Kline, P. Cowan, & C. Cowan, 1991), negative and positive outcomes of the transition to parenthood appear to be predictable from prebaby levels of distress and adaptation (Heming, 1987). That is, although a moderate downward slide in parents' satisfaction and well-being after the birth of the baby is normative, couples tend to remain consistent (i.e., in the same rank order) over time. Husbands and wives tend to react in their characteristic fashion—only more so. These findings suggest that it is possible to identify individuals and couples who are at risk for distress during the early period of family formation from information obtained before the baby is born. If the continuity hypothesis holds from one transition to another, we should find that individuals and families who navigate life changes successfully at earlier points are more competent in dealing with subsequent life transitions (P. Cowan, 1991).

## PREDICTING CHILDREN'S ACADEMIC AND SOCIAL ADAPTATION TO KINDERGARTEN

We expected to find that the couple's transition to parenthood and the child's transition to school would be linked by a set of family processes assessed during the preschool period. We tested the hypothesis that husbands and wives who coped well with becoming a family would show less conflictful and more positive responses toward one another in the presence of their $3^1/_2$-year-old child, and that they would combine warmth and structure in their behavior toward their child during the preschool period. We then predicted that children whose parents showed more positive marital interaction and more effective parenting styles when they were $3^1/_2$ would, in turn, have more positive relationships with their classmates and attain higher scores on a standardized achievement test 2 years later at the end of kindergarten.

We used the Latent Variable Path Analysis with Partial Least Squares estimation procedure (LVPLS or "soft modeling"; Falk, 1987; Lohmoeller, 1989; Wold, 1982) to examine the relationships among the variables over time. From single measures (manifest variables), we constructed multiple indicators of nine theoretically important constructs (latent variables), in which the variance shared by the measures is taken as a single index of the central construct.

We chose structural modeling as our analytic technique because it enabled us to describe both direct and indirect paths linking parents' and children's adaptation.[1] The LVPLS "soft modeling" procedure allows us to explore hypothesized relationships among the latent variables without imposing certain restrictive statistical and structural assumptions that underlie the widely used LISREL structural modeling programs (Joreskog & Sorbom, 1985). For example, in soft modeling, the error terms of the variables may be correlated, and small numbers of subjects may be used in the analysis without violating the statistical assumptions of the model.[2] For more detailed descriptions of this approach, see Falk and Miller (1991, 1992), and for an application to data from families of preschoolers and preadolescents, see Miller, P. Cowan, C. Cowan, Hetherington, and Clingempeel (1993).

In the LVPLS estimation of each latent variable, scores from manifest variables are combined, with the contribution of each score based on weights derived from a principal components analysis using partial least squares estimates. The relationships among the latent variables are determined by a set of multiple regression equations in which the path weights are adjusted to provide the optimal linear coefficients between predictor and predicted latent variables in the model.

Three principles governed our choice of latent variable constructs and manifest measures. First, we constructed separate structural models to examine the pathways from family environments to children's academic achievement and to the quality of their peer relationships. Second, because we believe that marital adaptation plays a central role in both parents' and children's adaptation, we included latent variables representing marital quality at three different time periods—pregnancy, and 18 and 36 months postpartum. Finally, we selected other indices of individual and family functioning that included at least one construct from each of the five domains of our family model. Because there was a relatively limited number of subjects for this analysis (44 families), and because we were reporting data from five different assessment points, we could not measure adaptation in every domain at every point.

We began with the assumption that each of the latent variables describing parents' adaptation or behavior would include two measures obtained from moth-

---

[1] Simple multiple regression equations reveal how much variance in the dependent variable is accounted for by a cluster of independent variables, but they do not describe the network of relationships among the independent variables. That is they assess the direct relationships between variables, without informing us about the indirect pathways through which one variable is associated with another.

[2] Although the model is very flexible, the program will not run when the number of manifest variables approaches the number of subjects. In data sets like ours with a high ratio of measures to subjects, choices concerning which measures to include in a latent variable must still be made.

ers and two from fathers. However, when preliminary data analyses informed us that in several cases one of the measures did not "fit," that is, it did not load highly on a particular latent variable construct,[3] it was not included in the final structural models. The final set of latent variables always contained at least one measure from both partners, based on our assumption that the couple was the appropriate unit of analysis in this study. The loadings of each manifest variable on the latent variables in the academic competence model and the social competence model are presented in Table 4.1.

## Measures of Adaptation to Parenthood

In describing the manifest measures included in each latent variable we have provided a brief description and citation for previously created scales. Additional details concerning the psychometric properties of the measures we created are included in the appendix. The numbering of the latent variables corresponds to Figures 4.1 and 4.2.

*Parents' Family of Origin (LV 1).*    Previous research has demonstrated that family patterns of behavior and dysfunction tend to be repeated across generations (cf. Caspi & Elder, 1988; Main & Goldwyn, 1984). Using the Family Environment Scale (Moos, 1974), participants were asked to describe their family relationships as they remembered them when they were young children. Because family conflict appears to be an important risk factor for children's subsequent development (e.g., Caspi & Elder, 1988), we focused on scales describing family conflict and cohesion. Included in the final test of the structural models were two scales measuring conflict and cohesion in the husband's family of origin and one scale measuring conflict in the wife's family of origin. Although we do not expect that these scales necessarily paint an accurate picture of parents' early childhood experience, we do assume that parents' current memories of the past affect their expectations, feelings, and behavior in the family they have created to rear their child.

*Marital Quality in Pregnancy (LV 2).*    Husbands' and wives' marital satisfaction scores on the widely used Locke–Wallace Brief Marital Adjustment Test (1959) were included in the latent variable measuring marital quality in pregnancy. Because it loaded highly on this latent variable, wives' but not husbands' satisfaction with the couple's division of family labor was used in the final models. The high loading may reflect the fact that role satisfaction is a more important ingredient of women's than of men's feelings about the state of the marriage during the transition to parenthood (C. Cowan & P. Cowan, 1988) and later in family life as well (Hochschild, 1989).

---

[3] The concept of loading here is similar to that of factor analysis. When a measure loads highly on a latent variable construct, it correlates strongly with the shared variance among all the measures included in that construct.

TABLE 4.1
LVPLS Component Loadings on Manifest Variables With Academic Competence and Social
Competence as Outcomes

| | Academic Competence | Social Competence |
|---|---|---|
| LV 1: Family of Origin | | |
| Fa   Cohesion | -.83 | -.88 |
| Fa   Conflict | .90 | .84 |
| Mo   Conflict | .41 | .55 |
| | | |
| LV 2: Marital Quality | | |
| Fa   Marital Satisfaction | .72 | .76 |
| Mo   Marital Satisfaction | .92 | .88 |
| Mo   Role Satisfaction | .67 | .63 |
| | | |
| LV 3: Stressors | | |
| Fa   Parenting Stress | .66 | .73 |
| Fa   Life Stress Events | .76 | .83 |
| Mo   Life Stress Events | .75 | .77 |
| | | |
| LV 4: Marital Quality | | |
| Fa   Cohesion | .81 | .86 |
| Mo   Cohesion | .75 | .74 |
| Mo   Role Satisfaction | .54 | .62 |
| | | |
| LV 5: Marital Interaction | | |
| Positive Interaction | .81 | .84 |
| Negative Interaction | .86 | .82 |
| | | |
| LV 6: Parenting Style | | |
| Mo   Warmth | .60 | .61 |
| Fa   Warmth | .86 | .88 |
| Fa   Structure | .49 | .64 |
| | | |
| LV 7: Academic Achievement | | |
| Reading Comprehension | .76 | |
| Reading Recognition | .80 | |
| Spelling | .82 | |
| Information | .50 | |
| Mathematics | .77 | |
| | | |
| LV 8: Aggressive Behavior | | |
| Antisocial | | .83 |
| Hostile | | .94 |
| Negative | | .97 |
| | | |
| LV 9: Shy/Withdrawn | | |
| Introversive | | .90 |
| Extraversive | | -.87 |
| Tense | | .71 |

*Stressors and Perceived Stress (LV 3).* We have found that stressful life
events for new mothers and fathers are highest in the early postpartum period, 6
months after the birth of a first child (C. Cowan et al., 1985). We selected
measures of stress to create an index of how couples were adapting as individuals
at an early point in their transition to parenthood. Men's and women's total life
stress scores at 6 months postpartum were assessed by the Horowitz, Schaefer,

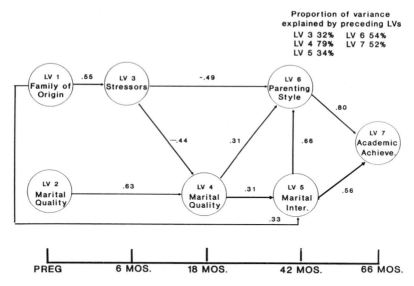

FIG. 4.1.   From pregnancy to kindergarten: Path model with academic competence as outcome.

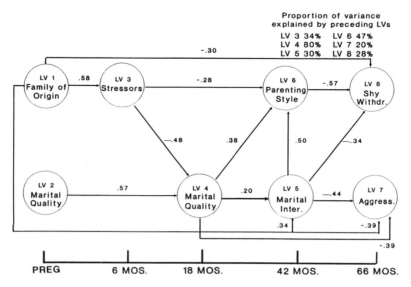

FIG. 4.2.   From pregnancy to kindergarten: Path model with social competence as outcome.

Hiroto, Wilner, and Levin (1977) adaptation of the Holmes and Rahe (1967) Recent Life Events scale. The final latent variable also included new fathers' perceptions of stress in their role as parents, as measured by Abidin's Parenting Stress Index (1983). Because mothers' perceptions of parenting stress did not load highly on LV 3, they were not included in the final path analysis.

*Marital Quality at 1½ Years Postpartum (LV 4).*    This latent variable included both husbands' and wives' descriptions of the degree of cohesion in their current family (conflict, warmth, expressiveness) using the Family Environment Scale (Moos, 1974). A different measure of marital quality from the one used in pregnancy was selected so as not to inflate the level of consistency in marital functioning across time. Because we did not have an alternate measure of satisfaction with the division of labor, we repeated the wives' measure of role satisfaction on the Who Does What? questionnaire at 1½ years postpartum.

## Measures of Marital Interaction and Parenting Behavior in the Preschool Period

*Marital Interaction (LV 5).*    In one 40-minute visit to our laboratory, mothers and fathers together spent time working and playing with their 3½ year old child. The children were presented with some challenging tasks and the parents were invited to help them as they would typically. In the first task, the parents were asked to elicit a story that had been told to the child outside the playroom (see Pratt, Kerig, P. Cowan, & C. Cowan, 1988, for details). In the second task, the child was asked to replicate a complicated model of a "train" using tinker-toy materials. In the last 10 minutes of each visit, the parents and the child were invited to "build a world together in the sand" using miniature figures and a sand tray. From a set of 12 rating scales, two factors were identified and included in LV 5 as indexing the quality of the marital relationship in the presence of the child—negative interaction (anger, coldness, and competition) and positive interaction (warmth, responsiveness, and cooperation) between the spouses.

*Parenting Style (LV 6).*    We assessed parenting style with observers' ratings of the interaction between mother and preschool-aged child and between father and child as each parent–child dyad worked and played together in two additional 40-minute sessions in our laboratory. The story task, as described earlier, was repeated with a different story in each session. Following the story, the parent presented a series of structured tasks adapted from Block and Block (1980), in which the child matched a model with wood blocks or shapes, traversed a maze taped on an etch-a-sketch board, and completed a two-dimensional matrix on a game board. Finally, the parent and child were asked to build a world in the sand. A number of factors emerged from an analysis of 15 rating scales (see the appendix). For LV 6 we selected mothers' and fathers' scores on the factors

Warmth and Structure to represent the construct of authoritative parenting (Baumrind, 1979). Fathers with high scores on this construct were warm, showed little anger, coldness, and displeasure, communicated about the tasks clearly, and tended to present them in an organized way that helped their children to manage them. Because of low loadings, mothers' warmth but not their structuring behavior was included in the final path models.

## Measures of Children's Adaptation to School

*Academic Achievement (LV 7).* Our measure of academic achievement was derived from the Peabody Individual Achievement Test (PIAT), administered individually to each child at home in the summer after the completion of kindergarten year. The PIAT has five subscales with standardized scores measuring reading recognition, reading comprehension, mathematics, spelling, and general information, all of which were included in LV 7.

*Social Adaptation in the Classroom (LVs 8 and 9).* In 1986, when we were looking for an instrument that parents could complete to describe their child at home and that teachers could use to describe the child at school, we were concerned that the Child Behavior Checklist (Achenbach & Edelbrock, 1981) contained too few items assessing social and academic competence (only 20 of 138 items), that it was too pathologically oriented, and that it was too long to ask teachers to fill out on every child in the classroom. The Child Adaptive Behavior Inventory (CABI) developed by Schaefer and Hunter (1983) focused more on competence than on problematic behavior. We chose to begin with Schaefer's 60-item scale and added 30 items from the downward extension of the Quay–Peterson Behavior Problem Checklist (O'Donnell & VanTuinen, 1979) and from Achenbach and Edelbrock's instrument to cover the behavior problem end of the scale. Teachers agreed to use this modified CABI to describe every child in their class in late fall and late spring, without knowing which child was in our study. Scores on each scale were converted to *z* scores representing the behavior of the child in the study compared with that of the other children in the classroom. In this way we hoped to control both for teachers' general positive or negative rating bias and for the fact that classrooms have different atmospheres for the development of peer relationships. The data reported here are from the late spring ratings, obtained closest in time to the Academic Achievement measures.

Children high in *Aggression* (LV 8) were rated by their teachers as high on three scales: antisocial behavior, hostility, and negative engagement. More than their classmates, these children were seen by teachers as disobeying, breaking rules, arguing, lying, being uncooperative, and getting into fights. Children rated low on these scales were cooperative and not aggressive with their peers.

Children who were *Shy/withdrawn* (LV 9) were described as high on two scales—introversion and tension—and low on an extroversion scale. According to the teachers they were shy or bashful, preferred solitary activities, did not make friends easily, and were nervous or high strung. Children low on these scales tended to be outgoing and gregarious.

## The Couple's Transition to Parenthood as a Predictor of Family Interaction

To simplify the presentation of our structural models, we examine the results in two temporal segments—from pregnancy to preschool, and from preschool to kindergarten. The path weights and patterns linking the latent variables in the pregnancy to preschool period were similar but not identical, regardless of whether academic achievement (Fig. 4.1) or social competence (Fig. 4.2) was chosen as the ultimate outcome (see Table 4.1). Slight differences in path weights result from the fact that the LVPLS program provides the best fit among all of the latent variables in the model.

Time is represented on the horizontal axis of Fig. 4.1 and 4.2, beginning on the left with pregnancy. As we move farther to the right, the couple begins the transition to parenthood, copes with the first 6 months of becoming a family, settles into the issues raised by toddlerhood, and works and plays with their 3½-year-old preschooler separately and then together as a family. This takes us past the horizontal midpoint of the diagram. The four latent variables assessing husbands' and wives' well-being during the transition to parenthood (LVs 1–4) are all constructed from self-report questionnaire data. The two latent variables assessing marital interaction (LV 5) and parenting style (LV 6) when the child is 3½ are derived from observations in our laboratory playroom. The continuities that we find over time, then, are revealed across independent methods and sources of data.

Latent variables measured at later points in family life account for variation over and above that explained by earlier variables. For example, marital quality at 1½ years postpartum (LV 4), can be interpreted as a measure of change, typically a decline, in level of marital adjustment since pregnancy (LV 1). This change accounts for variation in subsequent latent variables (e.g., in both marital interaction [LV 5] and parents' behavior toward the child in the laboratory playroom [LV 6]).

We tested a fully recursive structural model in which each latent variable is assumed to predict all other latent variables in the domains to the right of it. This clearly exploratory approach was necessary because we had no a priori information to formulate specific hypotheses about which variables were likely to produce sizable direct paths, and which paths were more likely to be indirect. Paths with weights that represented less than 10% of the variance linking one latent variable with another are not represented in Fig. 4.1 and 4.2.

Because the connections among the first six latent variables are very similar in Fig 4.1 and 4.2, we can interpret the results in Fig. 4.1 as representative of the

pregnancy to preschool family trends. Our long-term interest in preventive intervention to reduce or alleviate family difficulties (cf. C. Cowan, 1978) influenced
our decision to focus the presentation of results on the problematic end of the
continuum. That is, we describe the findings in terms of links between negative
feelings or maladaptive behavior in one domain as they predict negative or
maladaptive behavior in another domain. We can, of course, read the same
diagrams and focus on predictors of well-being and positive relationship qualities.

We find three major pathways extending from parents' adaptation during
pregnancy to family interaction in the preschool period, with both direct and
indirect statistical associations among parents' family of origin experiences,
marital quality, life stress, and the quality of parent–child relationships.

*Family of Origin as a Context of Marital Interaction and Parenting Style.*
There is a direct path from conflict in the family of origin, assessed in pregnancy
by the Family Environment Scale (LV 1), to marital conflict between the parents
almost 4 years later (LV 5). Parents who remember the atmosphere in the families they grew up in as high in conflict are rated by our staff team as more angry,
cold, and competitive, and less warm, responsive, and cooperative with each
other when working and playing with their 3½-year-old. Furthermore, there is a
very strong concurrent association between parents' negatively toned behavior
toward each other (LV 5) and the quality of the relationships with their children
as observed during their separate visits to the playroom (LV 6). Fathers and
mothers in conflictful marital relationships tend to be less warm, and the fathers
are less likely to provide structure during the parent–child interaction sessions,
than parents who have found a way to work with each other more effectively.

*Individual Adaptation, Marital Quality, and Parenting Style.*    Life stressors
may be one of the mechanisms linking memories of men's and women's growing
up years with their parenting styles. Spouses who recall more conflict in the
families they grew up in (LV 1) tend to report more stressful life changes early in
their transition to parenthood, and the fathers tend to experience more stress in
their role as parents (LV 3). This finding is consistent with the view that life
changes, life events, and perceived stresses do not simply happen to people;
rather, they are reflections of individual and family coping skills available for
dealing with the challenges inherent in life transitions (cf. Patterson & Capaldi,
1991).

Families in which parents report more stress at the 6-month postpartum
follow-up appear to be at risk in two ways. First, there is a direct path from
parents' report of stressful life events (LV 3) to the quality of parenting (LV 6);
parents reporting higher stress when their child is 6 months old tend to show less
warmth and provide less structure with their child 3 years later. This direct path
may reflect the fact that there is some degree of continuity in life stress events

between 6 months and $3^{1}/_{2}$ years postpartum (men: $r = .37; p < .005$; women $r = .57; p < .001$). That is, the stressors parents experience early in the transition to parenthood continue to occur and to compromise the quality of parenting.

Life stress early in the transition to parenthood also functions as an indirect risk for parents. Couples experiencing high levels of stress at 6 months postpartum show a decline in marital quality from pregnancy to $1^{1}/_{2}$ years after their baby is born (LV 2 to LV 4), and this decline predicts marital conflict and ineffective parenting 2 years later.

*Marital Quality as an Independent Precursor of Parenting Quality.* We have seen that marital quality after the birth of a first child is implicated as one of the links in the chain connecting family of origin experiences and life stressors with parent–child relationship quality. Although we have drawn the arrows from marital quality to parenting style, we have noted previously that it is possible to interpret correlations across marital and parenting relationships as support for the bi-directional hypothesis that hard-to-manage children make it difficult for parents to be warm and structuring, and that the negative qualities of the parent–child relationship spill over into the marriage.

Because we have obtained reports of satisfaction with marriage and with the couple's role arrangements in pregnancy (LV 2), it is possible to be more precise about the direction of effects, at least in a statistical sense. Along the bottom of Fig. 4.1 we find a direct link between marital quality and parenting style. Low satisfaction with the couple relationship in pregnancy strongly predicts low marital cohesion as the parents describe it almost 2 years later (LV 4). The change in marital quality from pregnancy to $1^{1}/_{2}$ years postpartum (LV 2 to LV 4) predicts conflict and negative interaction between the partners (LV 5) 2 additional years later when the whole family works and plays together in our playroom. And, as we have seen, marital interaction quality correlates highly with how parents behave in the separate sessions with their $3^{1}/_{2}$-year-old child.

In summary, we have described three major "routes" to ineffective parenting. Conflict in the family of origin increases the probability of marital conflict between the parents, and increases the probability of life stress early in the transition to parenthood. Both these sources of difficulty are implicated in parenting that is low in warmth and structure. A third major route to ineffective parenting comes directly from the quality of the marriage as parents experience it several months before their first child is born.

Given this pattern of results it would be tempting to locate all of the power in our model in the family of origin, assuming that it shapes all of the other measures of adaptation in our model. However, memories of relationships in the family of origin are not correlated with couples' marital quality in pregnancy. How, then do we account for the path linking family of origin experiences with marital interaction 4 years later? It is possible that these findings are artifactual; family of origin experiences may not be as directly linked with self-report as with observational measures. It is also possible that the transition to parenthood establishes and amplifies the connection between the quality of past and present family relationships. Not until the baby arrives do the old (and continuing) patterns in the families that parents grew up in begin to color the quality of the interactions in the new families that they have created.

Path models can tell us how much of the variance in a given latent variable is accounted for by the preceding variables. Cumulatively, the latent variables assessing the couple's transition to parenthood (LV 1 to LV 4) account for 34% (Fig. 4.1) or 30% (Fig. 4.2) of the variance in partners' observed behavior toward one another when they are with their preschooler in our playroom (LV 5). Further, LVs 1 to 5 in total account for from 47% (Fig. 4.2) to 54% (Fig. 4.1) of the variance in mothers' and fathers' parenting style in the separate parent–child visits when the child is $3\frac{1}{2}$ years old (LV 6).[4] Consistent with our continuity hypothesis, when parents begin their transition to parenthood with negative feelings about their early family experiences and their marriage, and when their stress and marital dissatisfaction are sustained over the early family-making years, they tend to be less effective in their interactions with their preschoolers.

## Family Antecedents of the Child's Adaptation to School

Now we examine pathways to the outcome measures on the far right in Fig. 4.1 and 4.2. We begin by focusing on academic achievement in Fig. 4.1.

*Academic Achievement.* Both negative marital interaction (LV 5) and ineffective parenting style as observed in our laboratory playroom during the preschool period (LV 6) contribute to predictions of the child's low academic achievement scores on the Peabody Individual Achievement Test (LV 7; reading recognition, reading comprehension, spelling, mathematics, and general information). Overall, the family model using mothers' and fathers' data (LV 1 to LV 6) accounts for 52% of the variance in the child's achievement at the end of kindergarten. If we take into account parents' perceptions of their original families, their stress early in the transition to parenthood, their marital quality before and after the birth of their first child, and their level of warmth and structuring with their preschoolers, we can make very good predictions about their child's level of academic achievement at the end of kindergarten year.

*Peer Relationships.* When we enter exactly the same six latent variables described in Fig. 4.1 into a path model with aggressive and shy/withdrawn behavior with classmates as outcomes (Fig. 4.2), we find that the family variables account for a much smaller proportion of the variance than they did for

---

[4] Although LVs 1–6 contain identical measures in Fig. 4.1 and 4.2, they are mapped onto different outcomes, and so the path weights and percentage of variance accounted for differ slightly.

academic competence. LVs 1 to 6 predict 28% of the variation in shy/withdrawn behavior and 20% of the variation in children's aggressive behavior as rated by their kindergarten teachers in late spring. How we interpret the predictive strength of the social competence model, which is equivalent to correlations that range between .40 to .50, depends on our frame of reference. The same family variables that account for half the variance in children's academic competence, predict one fifth to one quarter of the variance in teacher-rated classroom peer relationships. In our view, the strength of the social competence predictions over a period of 2 to 6 years is still fairly impressive.

The direct links between parents' adaptation in pregnancy and the social competence outcomes differ in important ways from the path model describing academic achievement. In contrast with Fig. 4.1, in which family of origin memories (LV 1) and reports of marital quality in pregnancy (LV2) are uncorrelated with academic achievement at the end of kindergarten, here we find that conflict in the family of origin is moderately associated with both aggressive and shy/withdrawn behavior more than 6 years after the early memories were assessed. Our tentative hypothesis is that because the Family Environment Scale's measure of conflict and cohesion in the family of origin focuses on the quality of relationships in the early years, it is more likely to be correlated with children's peer relationships than with academic achievement.

One noteworthy feature of the family-to-school social competence model is the fact that marital conflict and competition during triadic family interactions with preschoolers predict very different kinds of peer relationship difficulties. Parents who are competitive and hostile in their marital interaction and do not work cooperatively in front of their preschooler tend to have children who show more aggressive interactions *or* who are shy and withdrawn with their classmates 2 years later.[5] Although we have known for some time that children whose parents divorce have more difficulties in school (see Hetherington et al., 1989; Wallerstein & Kelly, 1980), the findings in our study suggest that children whose married parents fail to regulate their conflicts are also at risk for social and academic problems as they set out on their school careers.

In Fig. 4.2 we also see that mothers' and fathers' style of parenting their preschoolers is a strong predictor of shy/withdrawn behavior, but not of aggressive behavior in the classroom. Why do children whose parents are low in warmth and structuring tend to be shy with their classmates? More research is needed to discover whether the relative lack of warmth and structuring behavior shown by parents somehow interferes directly with children's ability to relate comfortably with peers. Perhaps, however, the impact of less effective parenting is more complex and less direct—through the long-term effect of parenting style on the child's personality or through the parents' regulation of visits and super-

---

[5] There is a moderate negative correlation between LV 7 and LV 8 ($r = -24$). In general children who are described as Aggressive tend not to be described as Shy/withdrawn, but with the low negative correlation we can infer that a few children may be seen as having both types of problems.

vising the conditions under which their child can spend time with peers (see Parke, this volume).

We were surprised to see that there was no direct path from ineffective parenting style in the preschool period to aggressive behavior in kindergarten, as Baumrind (1967) found with young children and as research with older children implies (e.g., G. Patterson & Capaldi, 1991). In fact, structural models of our own concurrent data do show meaningful paths between parenting behavior and 3½-year-olds' externalizing behavior (anger, aggression, noncompliance), as described by parents and as rated by our observers in the laboratory (Miller et al., 1993). Miller et al.'s path analyses of these data created separate latent variables for warmth and structuring. The path models showed that only parents' warmth was associated with their 3½-year-olds' externalizing behavior. We reanalyzed the model presented in Fig. 4.2, eliminating the measure of structuring and using both warmth and responsiveness ratings of mothers and fathers in the separate parent–child interactions. This analysis yielded a path weight of −.25 linking low levels of warm, responsive parenting with high levels of classroom aggression 2 years later. We conclude, then, that both marital quality and parenting effectiveness during the preschool period predict academic and social competence at the end of kindergarten, but specific qualities of parenting are related to specific indices of social competence.

## IMPLICATIONS AND ISSUES

### The Five-Domain Family Model and Continuity Across Time

Our five-domain model of family adaptation receives additional support from the LVPLS models described in this chapter. Data concerning individual, marital, three-generational, parent–child, and outside the family variables (life stress events) combine to account for a substantial amount of the variation in children's adaptation to school. Furthermore, the continuity from parents' adaptation in pregnancy to children's adaptation to school occurs over a relatively long period in the life of a family. It may be that we have been able to identify this continuity because our measures were obtained during times of major family life transitions. Caspi and Moffitt (1991) suggest that because individuals tend to revert to tried and true coping mechanisms during periods of ambiguous, disequilibrating change, transitions heighten continuities of personality and character structure across time.

### The Importance of Cross-Generational Patterns

Parents' perceptions of growing up in conflictful families function as markers of future distress during the early years of family-making. In contrast with parents who report little or no family conflict in their growing up years, these parents report more life stress and parenting stress shortly after having a baby. Several years later, they show less warmth and more conflict as a couple in front of the child, and they are less warm and provide less structure for their children when they work and play together.

The fact that relationship quality in the family of origin, assessed before the birth of the child, is consistent with our observers' ratings of the couple and the parent–child relationship provides support for the conclusion that family patterns tend to be repeated across the generations (Caspi & Elder, 1988; Main & Gold-wyn, 1984). We do not have to assume here that the early memories are accurate in order to accord them some degree of importance as indicators of potential risk. Critical information for mental health professionals and educators with an interest in prevention can be gleaned from the fact that expectant parents' memories of their own early family relationships can predict their adjustment to parenthood *and* their children's adjustment to school. Further study of the processes that underlie the transmission of distress across the generations, and the conditions that help families break the negative generational cycles, will ultimately inform the design of preventive interventions for families at risk for distress and dysfunction (C. Cowan & P. Cowan, 1992).

## The Central Role of the Parents' Marriage in Children's Development

Stated in general terms, the finding that men's and women's difficulties in making the transition to parenthood predict negative marital interaction and less effective parenting during the preschool period is not surprising. It is consistent with the long-held assumption of family therapists (Bowen, 1978; Framo, 1981; Minuchin & Fishman, 1981; Satir, 1972) that the quality of the couple relationship is the key to understanding family dysfunction. Our results here suggest that the quality of the parents' marriage may be central to adaptation in nonclinic families as well.

The trends in Fig. 4.1 and 4.2 are similar to studies that show significant correlations between marital and parenting quality (e.g., Goldberg & Easterbrooks, 1984; Gottman & Fainsilber, 1989), especially links between prebirth marital quality and later parenting behavior (e.g., Belsky, Robins, et al., 1985; Cox, Owens, Lewis, & Henderson, 1989; Grossman et al., 1980; Heinicke & Guthrie, 1991). The findings reported here add support to the argument that parents' marital satisfaction and interaction in the child's early years are directly linked with the child's later ability to achieve academically and to establish positive relationships with other children at school.

## Gender

We must not forget that any analyses of the links between family processes and children's development, academic or social, must take into account both the gender of the parent and the gender of the child. Our approach in this chapter has been to combine parents' scores in single latent variables, but we know that path models based on data from mothers and fathers will rarely be identical (see Miller et al., 1993). And we know that fathers, even more than mothers, treat sons and daughters differently (Block, 1984; Fagot, 1985), especially when they are experiencing distress in their marriage (P. Cowan, C. Cowan, & Kerig, 1993). It is necessary, then, to examine the possibility that there may be different pathways from family relationships to school adaptation for boys and girls.

## Causality and the Direction of Effects

Although structural models have often been described as "causal models," the correlational data they yield cannot provide conclusive support for hypotheses about the impact of one variable on another. Nevertheless, in the analysis of longitudinal data sets, structural models can be used to explore the temporal *direction* of statistical relations. With only five latent variables, we have accounted for a substantial amount of the variance—approximately half—in the parents' style of interacting with their preschoolers (LV 6). Even so, despite the high predictability over time, we cannot conclude that parents' individual and marital distress during the transition to parenthood cause ineffective parenting 2 years later.

The structural models in Fig. 4.1 and 4.2 do tell us that not all of the parenting behavior we observe is a reaction to the child's behavior, development, and level of academic and social success. At least some of the correlates of parenting behavior can be traced back to the prebirth period before the child's temperament and behavior begin to influence the parents' reactions. Clearly, some of the ingredients of parenting style can be attributed to characteristics that the individual parents bring to their relationship and to the family-making enterprise.

To test the interpretation that marital quality functions as a prior ingredient of parent–child relationships, and not the reverse, we arranged the arrows so that the path would go from LVs 1 to 4, to LV 6, to LV 5. This order would be consistent with the hypothesis that family variables affect the quality of the parent-child relationship which, in turn, has a significant impact on marital quality. In this direction, the path weight connecting LVs 5 and 6 is reduced from .72 to .21 (for the model with academic achievement as outcome) and the cumulative predictive power of LVs 1 to 4 plus parenting quality (LV 6) accounts for only 28% of the variation in marital interaction (LV 5), in contrast with 47% of the variance in marital interaction explained in the original model. Thus, the statistical explanatory power of the model is stronger if we assume that marital quality contributes to the quality of the relationship between each parent and the child.

Although we cannot use correlations to prove hypotheses about causal mechanisms, we can speculate about the underlying processes that shape the trends represented in our structural models. The trends are certainly consistent with the notion that parents' adaptation to the birth of a first child colors the quality of the relationships they develop with that child. Furthermore, an argument can be made for the notion that the quality of parent–child relationships has a direct effect on the child's ability to succeed academically. A formulation consistent with Baumrind's (1979) work might be that when parents are able to provide a balance of warmth and structure, their authoritative style supports the child emotionally, which, in turn, facilitates the child's ability to pay attention, and to persist when faced with challenging intellectual tasks, thus promoting the acquisition of cognitive and instrumental skills.

Support for this formulation comes from Pratt et al. (1988) who have shown that authoritative parents tend to provide developmentally appropriate scaffolding for their children, moving in at the appropriate level when the child is having difficulty, and stepping back when the child is succeeding at the task alone. Similarly, parents' verbal responses to their children at 3½ predict their children's academic achievement 2 years later (Pratt, Kerig, P. Cowan, & C. Cowan, 1992) and their style of talking to their child is linked to the overall parenting styles they utilize. Mothers and fathers who feel good about themselves as individuals and as couples are more likely to select effective parenting styles encompassing teaching strategies that result in successful learning for children.

In our emphasis on the parents' influence on the parent–child relationship, we cannot ignore the child's contribution. By virtue of their temperaments, some children are easier to work and play with than others. And, given certain facilitating atmospheres, children are active in using adults to help them cope with challenging tasks and to regulate their emotions (e.g., Gottman & Fainsilber, 1989).

Given the limits of sample size, we have not been able to consider the important question of understanding the links between academic and social competence. Do social difficulties interfere with academic performance? Do the frustrations inherent in academic failure spill over onto the playground? Presumably the effects go both ways (Hinshaw, 1992). In our sample of kindergarten children, correlations between children's achievement test performance and teachers' ratings of aggressive and shy/withdrawn behavior are not statistically significant. But we expect that as the children proceed through their academic careers, the links between their academic and social adaptation at school will become stronger (Wetzel, 1991). Further research is necessary to explore whether the family pathways to these different outcomes will also change in strength over time and development.

## Risk, Resilience and the Limits of Structural Models

By documenting the amount of variance we can explain in children's developmental outcomes using a set of family-based measures, the structural models we have presented help us to define the magnitude of risk that can be attributed to family factors in children's adaptation to kindergarten. Interpretations of risk are always double-edged. On one hand, the combination of family variables we measured accounted for an impressive 52% of the variation in children's academic competence and 20%–28% of the variation in social competence, depending on the specific outcome. On the other hand, these figures caution us that the task of identifying sources of variation in children's competence inside and outside the family is far from completion.

The multiple regression or structural modeling approach to identifying combined risk has the advantage of specifying both the opportunities and the potential limits of specific interventions. In the present case, we can feel more optimistic about the potential of family-based interventions to enhance children's academic competence than to enhance their relationships with peers, at least at the kindergarten level. The fact that about half the variance in school achievement may be attributable to the family environment does not guarantee that any intervention will have an effect size approaching 50%. Included in the family variance are genetic risk factors that may be resistant to change, and entrenched family dynamics that also may be resistant to any specific intervention we put in place. Nevertheless, although interventions in other social systems may also have large payoffs, the prospects for family-based interventions seem promising in light of our results.

We have not given much attention to the possibility that at least some of the variance shared by parents' characteristics and children's development comes from a common genetic source. Structural models of the kind we have presented cannot untangle the genetic and psychological contributions of family functioning to children's coping with the academic and social demands of elementary school. Yet, we cannot assume that genetically influenced family behavior patterns are totally impervious to psychosocial interventions, just as we cannot assume that environmentally influenced marital or parenting behaviors will inevitably respond to these interventions. The critical question for intervention planing is not "how much of children's development is attributable to genetics and how much to family environment?", but "how much can children's development be affected by family-based interventions, regardless of how we conceptualize its origins?"

There is one final caveat concerning the use of multivariate techniques to define risk: The models we presented are likely to underestimate the sources of risk attributable to early family functioning. Because structural models almost invariably assume that risks and buffers are combined in linear ways, they do not test the possibility that some risks are multiplicative (e.g., that marital conflict and ineffective parenting are especially devastating when they occur together). Nor do they assess whether one protective factor (e.g., a good relationship with one parent) is sufficient to "cancel" the negative impact of many risks (cf. P. Cowan, C. Cowan, & Schulz, in press). Thus, structural models provide us with the "big picture" and with a good estimate of the main effects of each of the latent variables. More detailed analyses of the interactions among these variables will be necessary if we are to understand the family mechanisms linking risks to maladaptive and adaptive outcomes for children.

## AN EXPANDED FAMILY–SCHOOL MODEL

We have been focusing on the amount of variance in children's behavior that our path models explain. We turn briefly to other important sources of variation that are not accounted for in the models we have presented that might help to explain why some children do well and others do poorly at the beginning of their academic careers. Ultimately, we need an expanded conceptual model of school adaptation that encompasses all of the ecological contexts described by Bronfenbrenner (1986).

### The Impact of the Classroom Environment

When we left Teddy he was approaching the door of his kindergarten classroom. Our study followed Teddy's progress in school through his teacher's descriptions and an individually administered academic achievement test. Given the limits of our study design, we were not able to assess the qualities of his school, his classroom, and his particular teacher, key aspects of the school environment that may also be affecting how he copes with the academic and social challenges of elementary school.

Studies of the child's classroom environment show that a number of elements of the classroom environment can affect children's comfort levels, motivation, and competence. Among others, the way children are grouped by ability level for instruction (Rist, 1970), the cooperative versus competitive nature of the classroom climate (Aronson, Stephan, Sikes, Blaney, & Snapp, 1978), and the "openness" of the classroom structure (Minuchin & Shapiro, 1983), all affect children's learning. Teachers' instructional skills affect their students directly as do qualities of the teacher–student relationship. For example, just as we found with parents' styles, teachers who combine warmth and structuring in an authoritative classroom style tend to have students with higher achievement scores (Hansen, 1986).

Weinstein and her colleagues (Good & Weinstein, 1986; Weinstein, 1989; Weinstein, Marshall, Sharp, & Botkin, 1987) show how different aspects of school and classroom environments have interrelated effects on children's academic performance and well-being. Teachers' expectations of low achievement tend to have a negative impact on students primarily when they occur in classrooms in which children perceive that the teacher treats high and low ability students differently. In the elementary grades, the impact of teachers' expectations appears to increase over time (Weinstein et al., 1987). Most of these characteristics of schools and teachers have been explored in relation to children's achievement and personal adaptation (e.g., self-esteem). We have only beginning information about how teachers and classroom organization influence the structure and quality of children's peer relationships at school (cf. Bossert, 1984).

## The Similarity of Home and School

Epstein (1989) suggested that the families on the more adaptive end of the continuum in our study may be well organized and "schoollike." When parents regulate time and tasks, set standards, provide appropriate authority, establish a reward structure that recognizes children's accomplishments, and provide experiences that encourage positive social behavior, children do better at school. Epstein makes three important related points about family–school connections. First, the dimensions of family environments that she describes as facilitative of children's academic development are very similar to the dimensions of effective school environments. The study of parents' roles in their children's homework by Pratt and his colleagues (Pratt, Green, & MacVicar, & Bountrogianni, 1992), cited earlier, also supports this line of reasoning. Second, positive environments in both the home and the school have a dramatic impact on children's motivation to learn. This may be one of the intervening mechanisms that help to explain the links in our family–school model. Finally, Epstein implies that children tend to do best when there is something of a match between home and school environments. Hansen (1986), in an intriguing study of 11-year-old children in New Zealand, showed that students who experienced similar parenting styles and teaching styles achieved higher classroom grades; the home–school match had a more powerful effect than the specific styles in either environment. These results suggest that the impact of home and school environments on children's development might be interactive and synergistic rather than simply additive.

## Home–School Interaction

Epstein's work brings us out of what Bronfenbrenner described as the meso-system, in which separate family and school forces have a direct impact on children, and into the exosystem in which interactive processes occur between the systems in children's lives. Power and Bartholomew (1987) showed graphically that not only is there a combined or interactive effect of family and school environments on children's development, but there is also an important set of events at the interface of the two systems. How involved parents become in their children's school can affect the nature and quality of their adaptation (e.g., Stevenson & Baker, 1987). How involved schools are willing and able to be with families can have equally important effects.

## The Peer Group as an Independent Force

We have presented data suggesting that families influence the quality of children's relationships with their classmates, and hinted that school environments can also affect the quality of peer relationships (Bossert, 1984). We note here that the children's relationships with friends may have important effects of their own. First, early relationships with friends have an impact on the quality of later friendships. The research of Ladd and his colleagues (Ladd, 1989, 1990; Ladd & Price, 1987) demonstrates that children who develop more prosocial, cooperative play in preschool, who participate in many peer contexts, and who retain their friendships over the transition to school, are viewed more positively both by kindergarten teachers and classmates. In a full bi-directional model, we must also pay attention to the possibility that the children's peer relationships may affect their motivation and performance in the classroom, behavior at home, and, especially as they enter adolescence, their behavior in other societal settings (cf. G. Patterson & Dishion, 1985, 1988).

## The Societal Context

Finally, we are keenly aware that one important source of variance in children's adaptation to school lies in the ecology created by the socioeconomic circumstances affecting each member of the family. To examine whether there were gross effects of parents' income and education on the patterns in Fig. 4.1 and 4.2, we included them as covariates in the model and found no appreciable change in the results. Our sample is small, however, and there are no families at either of the economic extremes. In a larger study we would inevitably find that socioeconomic factors affect the links between family and school adaptation.

One probable pathway by which this influence occurs has been identified by McLoyd's (1990) research review and studies by Conger, Elder, Lorenz, Simmons, and Whitbek (1991) and G. Patterson and Capaldi (1991). Socioeconomic stressors affect children's social and emotional development because they have a disruptive impact on parenting effectiveness and marital relationships, which lead to more negative relationships between children and their peers. Another pathway will probably be found in the influence of socioeconomic factors on the nature, quality, and resources of the school system, on the social class and ethnicity of the school personnel, and on their attitudes, values, and behaviors with reference to the social class of their students.

## CONCLUDING REMARKS: TESTING THE FULL MODEL

In proposing that we work toward a more comprehensive ecological model of family system/school system interactions, we are not suggesting that every level of the family and the school must be assessed in each study. But if we are ever to draw a more complete map of the environments in which children develop, researchers must be cognizant of where their specialized and focused investigations fit in the overall territorial scheme of things.

We maintain a conviction that family studies can provide data for theory building and generate information that is vital for the planning of interventions. On the basis of the data presented in Fig. 4.1 and 4.2, we received funding for a new preventive intervention study with 150 families whose first children are in transition to elementary school. Given our findings that the quality of both couple relationship and parenting styles play a strong predictive role in children's adaptation to school, we are now examining the impact of two kinds of couples group intervention for parents in the year before their first child enters kindergarten. In small groups that meet weekly for 4 months, the leaders help one set of parents focus more on parent–child issues, and another explore normative and expectable marital issues facing couples at their stage of family life. We hope to show that improving the parenting effectiveness and marital quality of the couples in our study will enable their children to enter elementary school on a more positive academic and social trajectory. With family and child assessments in the preschool year, at the end of kindergarten, and at the end of first grade, we will have an opportunity to define through experiment the causal role of marital quality and marital interaction in children's adaptation to school. In future studies we hope to extend this kind of analysis to single-parent families, examining the role of parents' intimate relationships with family members and with lovers on their children's cognitive and social development.

The full model as we have outlined it suggests an even larger collaborative study in the future. From our perspective as family researchers, a family-based preventive intervention strategy makes sense, but we also appreciate the need for school-based interventions as well. We hope to encourage collaborative projects in which family-based and school-based interventions would be combined, coordinated, and evaluated. It will be too late to use this approach for Teddy as he faces the first of his thousands of days of formal schooling. But Teddy and his family have contributed to our vision of how family and school systems might work together to make his growing up years more satisfying and productive.

## APPENDIX: NOTES ON MANIFEST VARIABLES

*Role Arrangements (LV 2, LV 4).*    Satisfaction with role arrangements was inferred from the sum of the absolute discrepancies between "actual" and "ideal" descriptions of how the couple divided responsibility for household tasks, family decisions, and day-to-day child care on our Who Does What? questionnaire (C. Cowan & P. Cowan, 1988; P. Cowan & C. Cowan, 1990). The smaller the discrepancy between actual and ideal arrangements, the greater the inferred satisfaction.

*Marital Quality (LV 4).*    Self-reported family cohesion at 18 months postpartum (low conflict, high warmth, high expressiveness) as measured by the Family Environment Scale (Moos, 1974) showed a significant concurrent correlation with scores on the Locke–Wallace Short Marital Adjustment Test (husbands: $r =$ .47; $df = 42$; $p < .001$; wives: $r = .43$; $df = 42$; $p < .001$). This level of correlation indicates that the two measures are related, but far from identical measures of marital quality.

*Marital Interaction (LV 5).*    A male–female team rated the behavior of these mothers and fathers toward one another in the whole-family sessions on 12 items including warmth, anger, responsiveness, cooperation, and competition. A principal components factor analysis of the 12 items yielded two factors: conflict and negative interaction (anger, coldness, and competition) and positive interaction (warmth, responsiveness, and cooperation). Interrater reliabilities on the scales ranged from .76 to .92, and alpha coefficients assessing the internal reliabilities of the two factor scales were .88 and .83 respectively.

These observer ratings assess a quality of the couple's relationship different from that obtained in the partners' questionnaire responses. Neither negative nor positive couple interaction ratings of the parents' behavior toward each other were significantly correlated with husbands' self-reported marital satisfaction and conflict. Correlations between observed couple interaction and self-reported marital satisfaction for wives were statistically significant but low (negative interaction and marital satisfaction $r = -.34$; $p < .01$; positive interaction and marital satisfaction $r = .32$; $p < .02$).

*Parenting Style (LV 6).*    A male–female observer team rated the parent's behavior on 15 items, 14 of which were rated with adequate reliability: pleasure/displeasure, coldness/warmth, responsiveness, interactiveness, confidence in the parental role, anger, respect for the child's autonomy, limit setting, maturity demands, structure, creativity, activity level, respect for the child's autonomy, and clarity of communication. Each item was rated both for the highest level and the typical level of that behavior. Average interrater reliability (Pearson correlations) for mothers was .70 (range = 60 to .84) and for fathers .75 (range = .64 to .81).

Factor analyses of these items yielded five orthogonal parenting style factors for both mothers and fathers: (a) Negative affect (high ratings on anger, coldness, and displeasure); (b) Warmth/responsiveness (high ratings on warmth, responsiveness, and pleasure); (c) Limit setting (high ratings on setting limits and maturity demands, and low ratings on respect for the child's autonomy); (d) Engagement (interactive, and appears confident in the parental role; and (e) Structure (provides structure, and communicates clearly about the task). Alpha reliabilities of the five factor scores ranged from .73 to .93.

*Social Competence (LV 8 and LV 9).*    On the basis of content similarity we constructed 20 scales each containing three to seven items. Because we were interested specifically in the child's externalizing and internalizing aspects of relationships with peers, we selected three of the scales describing aggression (Antisocial, Negative, Hostile with alpha reliabilities of .86, .87, .86), and three describing shy and withdrawn behavior (Extraversion, Intraversion, and Interpersonal Tension with alpha reliabilities of .84, .87, and .80) for our latent variables. That is, the choices were rationally derived rather than based on a factor analysis. Although we are aware that children's relationships with peers are now most commonly assessed using sociometric or other information obtained from their peers beginning at age 8 and up (Coie, Dodge, & Kupersmidt, 1990), we assumed as Hartup did (1983) that teachers' ratings would provide reliable and valid measures of peer relationships as they occurred in the kindergarten classroom.

## ACKNOWLEDGMENTS

The longitudinal study has been supported throughout by NIMH grant MH 31109. Support for the analyses reported in this chapter came from a 1-year grant from the Spencer Foundation. We also want to acknowledge major contributions to the longitudinal study by members of the research team: Gertrude Heming served as data manager throughout the study, and Dena Cowan, Barbara Epperson, and Beth Schoenberger processed the immense data set. Ellen Garrett, William S. Coysh, Harriet Curtis-Boles, and Abner Boles III were the other two staff couples who along with the Cowans led intervention groups and followed couples over the first 4 years; Laura Mason Gordon and David Gordon interviewed couples in the final 3 years. Sacha Bunge, Michael Blum, Julia Levine, David Chavez, Marc Schulz, and Joanna Cowan worked with the children in the study; Linda Kastelowitz, Victor Lieberman, Marsha Kline, and Charles Soulé worked with the parents and children together. We thank Michael Pratt and Rhona Weinstein for their helpful comments on earlier drafts of this chapter.

## REFERENCES

Abidin, R. (1983). *Parenting stress index—Manual.* Charlottesville, VA; Pediatric Psychology Press.

Achenbach, T. M., & Edelbrock, C. S. (1981). Behavioral problems and competencies reported by parents of normal and disturbed children aged four through sixteen. *Monographs of the Society for Research in Child Development, 46* (Serial No. 188).

Ainsworth, M D. S., & Wittig, B. A. (1969). Attachment and exploratory behavior of one-year-olds in a strange situation. In B. M. Foss (Ed.), *Determinants of infant behavior* (Vol. 4, pp. 113–146). London: Methuen.

Alexander, K. L., & Entwisle, D. (1988). Achievement in the first 2 years of school: Patterns and processes. *Monographs of the Society for Research in Child Development, 53*(2, Serial No. 218).

Aronson, E., Stephan, C., Sikes, J., Blaney, N., & Snapp, M. (1978). *The jigsaw classroom.* Beverly Hills: Sage.

Asher, S. R., & Coie, J. D. (Eds.). (1990). *Peer rejection in childhood,* Cambridge: Cambridge University Press.

Baldwin, A. L., Cole, R. E., & Baldwin, C. P. (Eds.). (1982). Parental pathology, family interaction, and the competence of the child in school. *Monographs of the Society for Research in Child Development, 47* (5, Serial No. 197).

Barth, J. M., & Parke, R. D. (1993). Parent-child relationship influences on children's transition to school. *Merrill Palmer Quarterly, 39,* 173–195.

Baumrind, D. (1967). Child care practices anteceding three patterns of preschool behavior. *Genetic Psychology Monographs, 75,* 43–88.

Baumrind, D. (1979). The development of instrumental competence through socialization. In A. D. Pick (Ed.), *Minnesota symposia on child psychology* (Vol. 7, pp. 3–46), Minneapolis: University of Minnesota Press.

Baumrind, D. (1991). Effective parenting during the early adolescent transition. In P. A. Cowan & M. E. Hetherington (Eds.), *Advances in family research* (Vol. 2, pp. 111–163). Hillsdale, NJ: Lawrence Erlbaum Associates.

Belsky, J. (1984). The determinants of parenting: A process model. *Child Development, 55,* 83–96.

Belsky, J., Lang, M., & Rovine, M. (1985). Stability and change across the transition to parenthood: A second study. *Journal of Personality and Social Psychology, 50,* 517–522.

Belsky, J., Robins, E., & Gamble, W. (1985). The determinants of parental competence: Toward a contextual theory. In M. Lewis & L. Rosenblum (Eds.), *Beyond the dyad.* New York: Plenum.

Belsky, J., Rovine, M., & Fish, M. (1992). The developing family system. In M. Gunnar (Ed.), *Systems and development, Minnesota Symposium on Child Psychology* (Vol. 22). Hillsdale, NJ: Lawrence Erlbaum Associates.

Block, J. H. (1984). *Sex role identity and ego development.* San Francisco, CA: Jossey-Bass.

Block, J. H., & Block, J. (1980). The role of ego-control and ego-resiliency in the organization of behavior. In W. A. Collins (Ed.), *Minnesota Symposia on Child Psychology* (Vol. 13, pp. 39–101). Hillsdale, NJ: Lawrence Erlbaum Associates.

Block, J. H., Block, J., & Keyes, S. (1988). Longitudinally foretelling drug usage in adolescence: Early childhood personality and environmental precursors. *Child Development, 59,* 336–355.

Bossert, S. T. (1979). *Tasks and social relationships in classrooms.* Cambridge: Cambridge University Press.

Bowen, M. (1978). *Family therapy in clinical practice.* New York: Aronson.

Brody, G. H., Pellegrini, A. D., & Sigel, I. (1986). Marital quality and mother-child and father-child interactions with school-aged children. *Developmental Psychology, 22,* 291–296.

Bronfenbrenner, U. (1979). *The ecology of human development.* Cambridge, MA: Harvard University Press.

Bronfenbrenner, U. (1986). Ecology of the family as a context for human development: Research perspectives. *Developmental Psychology, 22,* 723–733.

Bronfenbrenner, U., & Crouter, A. C. (1983). The evolution of environmental models in developmental research. In P. H. Mussen (Series Ed.) & W. Kessen (Vol. Ed.), *Handbook of child psychology: Vol. 1. History, theory, and methods* (4th ed., pp. 357–414). New York: Wiley.

Brunquell, D., Crichton, L., & Egeland, B. (1981). Maternal personality and attitude in disturbances of childrearing. *American Journal of Orthopsychiatry, 51,* 680–691.

Campbell, S. B., March, C. L., Pierce, E. W., & Ewing, L. J. (1991). Hard to manage preschool boys: Family context and the stability of externalizing behavior. *Journal of Abnormal Child Psychology, 19,* 300–319.

Caspi, A., & Elder, G. H. Jr. (1988). Emergent family patterns: The intergenerational construction of problem behavior and relationships. In R. A. Hinde & J. Stevenson-Hinde (Eds.), *Relationships within families: Mutual influences* (pp. 218–240). Oxford: Clarendon Press.

Caspi, A., & Moffitt, T. E. (1991). Individual differences are accentuated during periods of social change. *Journal of Personality and Social Psychology, 61,* 157–168.

Chall, J. S., Jacobs, V. A., & Baldwin, L. E. (1990). *The reading crisis: Why poor children fall behind.* Cambridge, MA: Harvard University Press.

Clarke-Stewart, A. (1977). *Child care in the family.* New York: Academic Press.

Conger, R., Elder, G., Lorenz, F., Simmons, R. L., & Whitbeck, L. D. (1991, April). *A family process model of economic hardship influences on adjustment of early adolescent boys.* Paper presented at the Society for Research in Child Development, Seattle, WA.

Cowan, C. P., & Cowan, P. A. (1988). Who does what when partners become parents: Implications for men, women, and marriage. *Marriage & Family Review, 13,* 105–132.

Cowan, C. P., & Cowan, P. A. (1992). *When partners become parents: The big life change for couples.* New York: Basic Books.

Cowan, C. P., Cowan, P. A., Heming, G., Garrett, E., Coysh, W. S., Curtis-Boles, H., & Boles, A. J. (1985). Transitions to parenthood: His, hers, and theirs. *Journal of Family Issues, 6,* 451–481.

Cowan, C. P., Cowan, P. A., Heming, G., & Miller, N. B. (1991). Becoming a family: Marriage, parenting, and child development. In P. A. Cowan & E. M. Hetherington (Eds.), *Family transitions: Advances in family research* (Vol. 2, pp. 79–109). Hillsdale, NJ: Lawrence Erlbaum Associates.

Cowan, P. A. (1991). Individual and family life transitions: A proposal for a new definition. In P. A. Cowan & E. M. Hetherington (Eds)., Family transitions: *Advances in family research* (Vol. 2, pp. 3–30). Hillsdale, NJ: Lawrence Erlbaum Associates.

Cowan, P. A., & Cowan, C. P. (1990). Becoming a family: Research and intervention. In I. Sigel & G. Brody (Eds.), *Family research* (Vol. I, pp. 1–51). Hillsdale, NJ: Lawrence Erlbaum Associates.

Cowan, P. A., Cowan, C. P., & Kerig, P. (1993). Mothers, fathers, sons, and daughters: Gender differences in family formation and parenting style. In P. A. Cowan, D. Field, D. Hansen, A. Skolnick, & G. E. Swanson (Eds.) *Family, self, and society: Toward a new agenda for family research* (pp. 165–195). Hillsdale, NJ: Lawrence Erlbaum Associates.

Cowan, P. A., Cowan, C. P., & Schulz, M. (in press). *Risk and resilience in families.*

Cox, M. J., Owen, M. T., Lewis, J. M., & Henderson, V. K. (1989). Marriage, adult adjustment, and early parenting. *Child Development, 60,* 1015–1024.

Crockenberg, S. B., & Covey, S. L. (1991). Marital conflict and externalizing behavior in children. In D. Cicchetti & S. L. Toth (Eds.), *Rochester symposium on developmental psychopathology, Vol. 3.* Rochester, New York: Rochester University Press.

Dickie, J. (1987). Interrelationships within the mother–father–infant triad. In P. Berman & F. Pedersen (Eds.), *Men's transitions to parenthood: Longitudinal studies of early family experience.* Hillsdale, NJ: Lawrence Erlbaum Associates.

Dodge, K. A., Bates, J. E., & Petit, G. S. (1990). Mechanisms in the cycle of violence. *Science, 250,* 1678–1683.

Easterbrooks, M. A., & Goldberg, W. A. (1990). Security of toddler-parent attachment: Relation to children's socio-personality functioning during Kindergarten. In M. Greenberg, D. Cicchetti, & M. Cummings (Eds.), *Attachment in the preschool years: Theory, research and intervention.* Chicago: University of Chicago Press.

Epstein, J. L. (1989). Family structures and student motivation: A developmental perspective. In C. Ames & R. Ames (Eds.), *Research on motivation in education, Vol. 3: Goals and cognitions* (pp. 259–293). New York: Academic Press.

Fagot, B. I. (1985). Beyond the reinforcement principle; Another step toward understanding sex roles. *Developmental Psychology, 21,* 1097–1104.

Falk, R. F. (1987). *A primer for soft modeling*. Berkeley, CA: Institute of Human Development.

Falk, R. F., & Miller, N. B. (1991). A soft models approach to transitions. In P. A. Cowan & E. M. Hetherington (Eds.), *Family transitions: Advances in family research* (Vol. 2, pp. 273–301). Hillsdale, NJ: Lawrence Erlbaum Associates.

Falk, R. F., & Miller, N. B. (1992). *primer for soft modeling*. Akron, OH: The University of Akron Press.

Feldman, S. S., Wentzel, K. R., Weinberger, D. A., & Munson, J. A. (1990). Marital satisfaction of parents of preadolescent boys and its relationship to family and child functioning. *Journal of Family Psychology, 4*, 213–234.

Framo, J. L. (1981). The integration of marital therapy with sessions with family of origin. In A. S. Gurman & D. P. Kniskern (Eds.), *Handbook of family therapy*. New York: Bruner/Mazel.

Ginsburg, D., Gottman, J. M., & Parker, J. G. (1986). The importance of friendship. In J. M Gottman & J. G. Parker (Eds.), *Conversations of friends* (pp. 3–49). Cambridge, England: Cambridge University Press.

Guidubaldi, J., & Perry, J. D. (1984). Divorce, socioeconomic status, and children's cognitive-social competence at school entry. *American Journal of Orthopsychiatry, 54*, 459–468.

Goldberg, W. A., & Easterbrooks, M. A. (1984). The role of marital quality in toddler development. *Developmental Psychology, 20*, 504–514.

Good, T. L., & Weinstein, R. S. (1986). Schools make a difference: Evidence, criticisms, and new directions. *American Psychologist, 41*, 1090–1097.

Gottman, J., & Katz, L. (1989). The effects of marital discord on young children's peer interactions and health. *Child Development, 25*, 373–381.

Grossman, F., Eichler, L., & Winickoff, S. (1980). *Pregnancy, birth, and parenthood*. San Francisco: Jossey-Bass.

Hansen, D. A. (1986). Family-school articulations: The effects of interaction rule mismatch. *American Educational Research Journal, 23*, 643–659.

Hartup, W. W. (1983). Peer relations. In P. H. Mussen (Series Ed.) & E. M. Hetherington (Vol. Ed.) *Handbook of child psychology: Vol. 4. Socialization, personality and social development* (pp. 103–196). New York: Wiley.

Heinicke, C. (1984). Impact of prebirth parent personality and marital functioning on family development: A Framework and suggestions for further study. *Developmental Psychology, 20*, 1044–1053.

Heinicke, C. M., Diskin, S. D., Ramsay-Klee, D. M., & Oates, D. S. (1986). Pre- and postbirth antecedents of 2-year-old attention, capacity for relationships and verbal expressiveness. *Developmental Psychology, 22*, 777–787.

Heinicke, C. M., & Guthrie, D. (1991, April). *Pre-birth marital interaction and post-birth development*. Paper presented at the meetings of the Society for Research in Child Development, Seattle, WA.

Heming, G. (1987, April). *Predicting adaptation in the transition to parenthood*. Paper presented at the Society for Research in Child Development, Baltimore.

Hess, R. D., & Holloway, S. D. (1984). Family and school as educational institutions. In R. D. Parke, R. N. Emde, H. McAdoo, & G. Sackett (Eds.), *Review of child development research* (Vol. 7, pp. 179–221). Chicago: University of Chicago Press.

Hetherington, E. M., Cox, E. M., & Cox, R. (1982). Effects of divorce on parents and children. In M. E. Lamb (Ed.), *Nontraditional families*. Hillsdale, NJ: Lawrence Erlbaum Associates.

Hetherington, E. M., Stanley-Hagen, M., & Anderson, E. R. (1989). Marital transitions: A child's perspective. *American Psychologist, 44*, 303–312.

Hinshaw, S. P. (1992). Externalizing problems and academic underachievement in childhood and adolescence: Causal relationships and underlying mechanisms. *Psychological Bulletin, 111*, 127–155.

Holmes, T. H., & Rahe, R. H. (1967). The social adjustment rating scale. *Journal of Psychosomatic Research, 11*, 213–218.

Hochschild, A. (1989). *The second shift: Working parents and the revolution at home.* New York: Viking Penguin.

Horowitz, M., Schaefer, C., Hiroto, D., Wilner, N., Levin, B. (1977). Life event questionnaire for measuring presumptive stress. *Psychosomatic Medicine, 39,* 413–431.

Howes, P., & Markman, H. J. (1989). Marital quality and child functioning: A longitudinal investigation. *Child Development, 60,* 1044–1051.

Joreskog, K. G., & Sorbom, D. (1985). *LISREL-V Program manual.* Chicago: International Educational Services.

Kalinowski, A., & Sloane, K. (1981). The home environment and school achievement. *Studies in Educational Evaluation, 7,* 85–96.

Kaye, S. H. (1989). The impact of divorce on children's academic performance. *Journal of Divorce, 12,* 283–298.

Kellam, S. G., Simon, M. B., & Ensminger, M. E. (1982). Antecedents in first grade of teenage drug use and psychological well-being: A ten-year community-wide prospective study. In D. Ricks & B. Dohrenwend (Eds.), *Origins of psychopathology: Research and public policy.* New York: Cambridge University Press.

Kline, M., Cowan, P. A., & Cowan, P. A. (1991). The origins of parenting stress during the transition to parenthood: A new family model. *Early education and development, 2,* 287–305.

Kupersmidt, Coie, J. D., & Dodge, K. A. (1990). The role of poor peer relationships in the development of disorder. In S. R. Asher & J. D. Coie (Eds.), *Peer rejection in childhood* (pp. 274–305). Cambridge England: Cambridge University Press.

Ladd, G. W. (1989). Children's social competence and social supports: Precursors of early school adjustment? In B. H. Schneider, G. Attili, J. Nadel, & R. Weissberg (Eds.), *Social competence in developmental perspective* (pp. 277–291). Dordrecht: Kluwer Academic Publishers.

Ladd, G. W. (1990). Having friends, keeping friends, making friends, and being liked by peers in the classroom: Predictors of children's early school adjustment? *Child Development, 61,* 1081–1100.

Ladd, G. W., & Price, J. M. (1987). Predicting children's social and school adjustment following the transition from preschool to Kindergarten. *Child Development, 58,* 1168–1189.

Lambert, N. (1988). Adolescent outcomes for hyperactive children: Perspectives on general and specific patterns of childhood risk for adolescent educational, social, and mental health problems. *American Psychologist, 43,* 786–799.

Laosa, L. M. (1982). School, occupation, culture, and family: The impact of parental schooling on the parent-child relationship. *Journal of Educational Psychology, 74,* 791–827.

Lewis, J. M., Tresch-Owen, M. T., & Cox, M. J. (1988). The transition to parenthood: III. Incorporation of the child into the family. *Family Process, 27,* 411–421.

Locke, H., & Wallace, K. (1959). Short marital adjustment and prediction tests: Their reliability and validity. *Marriage and Family Living, 21,* 251–255.

Loeber, R., & Dishion, T. J. (1984). Boys who fight at home and school: Family conditions influencing cross-setting consistency. *Journal of Consulting and Clinical Psychology, 52,* 759–768.

Lohmoeller, J. B. (1989). *Latent variable path modeling with partial least squares.* New York: Springer-Verlag.

Long, N., Forehand, R., Fauber, R., & Brody, G. H. (1987). Self-perceived and independently observed competence of young adolescents as a function of parental marital conflict and recent divorce. *Journal of Abnormal Child Psychology, 15,* 15–27.

Lorenz, K. Z. (1952). *King Solomon's ring.* New York: Crowell.

Maccoby, E., & Martin, J. (1983). Socialization in the context of the family: Parent-child interaction. In P. H. Mussen (Series Ed.) & E. M. Hetherington (Vol. Ed.), *Handbook of child psychology: Vol. 4. Socialization, personality, and social development* (pp. 1–101). New York: Wiley.

Majoribanks, K. (1979). Family environments: Relations with children's cognitive performance and affective performance, In J. J. Walberg (Ed.), *Learning environments and effects.* Chicago: National Society for the Study of Education.

Masten, A. S., Garmezy, N., Tellegen, A., Pellegrini, D. S., Larkin, K., & Larsen. (1988). Competence and stress in school children: The moderating effects of individual and family qualities. *Journal of Child Psychology and Psychiatry, 29,* 745–764.

Main, M., & Goldwyn, R. (1984). Predicting rejection of her infant from mothers' representation of her own experience: Implications for the abused-abusing intergenerational cycle. *Child Abuse and Neglect, 8,* 203–217.

McCombs, A., & Forehand, R. (1989). Adolescent school performance following parental divorce: Are there family factors that can enhance success? *Adolescence, 24,* 871–880.

McDevitt, T. M., Hess, R. D., Kashiwagi, K., Dickson, W. P., Miyake, N., Azuma, H. (1987). Referential communication accuracy of mother-child pairs and children's later scholastic achievement: A follow-up study. *Merrill-Palmer Quarterly, 33,* 171–186.

McLoyd, V. (1990). The impact of economic hardship on black families and children: Psychological distress, parenting, and socioemotional development. *Child Development, 61,* 311–346.

Miller, N. B., Cowan, P. A., Cowan, C. P., Hetherington, E. M., & Clingempeel, G. (1993). *Externalizing in preschoolers and early adolescents: A cross-study replication of a family model. Developmental Psychology, 29,* 3–18.

Minuchin, S., & Fishman, H. C. (1981). *Family therapy techniques.* Cambridge: Harvard University Press.

Minuchin, P., & Shapiro, E. (1983). The school as a context for social development. In E. M. Hetherington (Ed.), *Handbook of child psychology. Vol. 4. Socialization and personality development* (pp. 573–672).

Moos, R. H. (1974). *Family Environment Scale.* Palo Alto: Consulting Psychologists Press.

O'Donnell, J. P., & VanTuinen, M. V. (1979). Behavior problems of preschool children: Dimensions and congenital correlates. *Journal of Abnormal Child Psychology, 7,* 61–75.

Parke, R. D., & Tinsley, B. (1982). The early environment of the at-risk infant: Expanding the social context. In D. D. Bricker (Ed.). *Intervention with at-risk and handicapped infants* (pp. 153–177). Baltimore: University Park Press.

Parke, R. D., & Tinsley, B. (1987). Family interaction in infancy. In J. Osofsky (Ed.), *Handbook of infancy* (2nd ed., pp. 579–641). New York: Wiley.

Patterson, C. J., Vaden, N. A., & Kupersmidt, J. B. (unpublished manuscript). *Family background, recent life events and peer rejection during childhood.*

Patterson, G. R. (1982). *Coercive family processes.* Eugene, OR: Castilia Press.

Patterson, G. R., & Capaldi, D. (1991). Antisocial parents: Unskilled and vulnerable. In P. A. Cowan & M. E. Hetherington (Eds.), *Family transitions. Advances in family research* (Vol. 2, pp. 195–218). Hillsdale, NJ: Lawrence Erlbaum Associates.

Patterson, G. R., & Dishion, T. J. (1985). Contributions of families and peers to delinquency. *Criminology, 23,* 63–77.

Patterson, G. R., & Dishion, T. J. (1988). Multilevel family process models: Traits, interactions, and relationships. In R. A. Hinde & J. Stevenson-Hinde (Eds.), *Relationships within families: Mutual influences* (pp. 283–310). Oxford: Clarendon Press.

Pettit, G. S., Harris, A. W., Bates, J. E., & Dodge, K. A. (1991). *Journal of social and personal relationships, 8,* 383–402.

Power, T. J., & Bartholomew, K. L. (1987). Family-school relationship patterns: An ecological assessment. *School Psychology Review, 16,* 498–512.

Pratt, M. W., Green, D., MacVicar, J., & Bountrogianni. (1992). The mathematical parent: Parental scaffolding, parenting style, and learning outcomes in long-division mathematics homework. *Journal of Applied Developmental Psychology, 13,* 17–34.

Pratt, M. W., Kerig, P. K., Cowan, P. A., & Cowan, C. P. (1988). Mothers and fathers teaching three year-olds: Authoritative parenting and adults' use of the zone of proximal development. *Developmental Psychology, 24,* 832–839.

Pratt, M. W., Kerig, P. K., Cowan, P. A., & Cowan, C. P. (1992). Family worlds: Couple satisfaction, parenting style, and mother' and fathers' speech to young children. *Merrill-Palmer Quarterly, 38,* 245–262.

Renken, B., Egeland, B., Marvinney, D., Mangelsdorf, S., & Sroufe, L. A. (1989). Early childhood antecedents of aggression and passive-withdrawal in early elementary school. *Journal of Personality, 57,* 257–281.

Rist, R. C. (1970). Student social class and teacher expectations: The self-fulfilling prophecy in ghetto education. *Harvard Educational Review, 40,* 411–451.

Rutter, M. (1987). Psychosocial resilience and protective mechanisms. *American Journal of Orthopsychiatry, 57,* 316–331.

Sameroff, A. J., Seifer, R., & Zax, M. (1982). Early development of children at risk for emotional disorder. *Monographs of the Society for Research in Child Development, 47*(7, Serial No. 199).

Satir, V. (1972). *Peoplemaking.* Palo Alto: Science and behavior books.

Schaefer, E. S., & Hunter, W. M. (1983, April). *Mother-infant interaction and maternal psychosocial predictors of kindergarten adaptation.* Paper presented at the meeting of the Society for Research in Child Development, Detroit.

Scott, J. P., Fredericson, E., & Fuller, J. L. (1951). Experimental exploration of the critical periods hypothesis. *Personality, 1,* 268–270.

Scott-Jones, D. (1984). Family influences on cognitive development and school achievement. In E. W. Gordon (Ed.), *Review of research in education* (Vol. 11, pp. 259–306). Washington, DC: American Educational Research Association.

Seginer, R. (1983). Parents' educational expectations and children's academic achievement: A literature review. *Merrill-Palmer Quarterly, 29,* 1–23.

Snow, C. E., Barnes, W. S., Chandler, H., Goodman, I. F., & Hemphill, L. (1991). *Unfulfilled expectations: Home and school influences on literacy.* Cambridge, MA: Harvard University Press.

Steinberg, L., Elmen, J. D., & Mounts, N. S. (1989). Authoritative parenting, psychosocial maturity, and academic success among adolescents. *Child Development, 60,* 1424–1436.

Stevenson, D. L., & Baker, D. P. (1987). The family-school relation and the child's school performance. *Child Development, 58,* 1348–1357.

Stevenson, H. W., Lee, S-y in collaboration with Chen, C. Stigler, J. W., Hsu, C., & Kitamura, S. (1990). *Monographs of the Society for Research in Child Development, 55,* Serial No. 221.

Tinbergen, N. (1951). *The study of instinct.* Oxford: Clarendon Press.

Wallerstein, J., & Kelly, J. (1980). *Surviving the breakup.* New York: Basic Books.

Weinstein, R. S. (1989). Perceptions of classroom processes and student motivation: Children's views of self-fulfilling prophecies. In R. E. Ames & C. Ames (Eds.), *Research on Motivation in education.* Vol. 3. Goals and cognitions (pp. 359–369). New York: Academic Press.

Weinstein, R. S., Marshall, H. H., Sharp, L., & Botkin, M. (1987). Pygmalion and the student: Age and classroom differences in children's awareness of teacher expectations. *Child Development, 58,* 1079–1093.

Wentzel, K. R. (1991). Relations between social competence and academic achievement in early adolescence. *Child Development, 62,* 1066–1078.

Werner, E. E., & Smith, R. S. (1982). *Vulnerable but invincible: A longitudinal study of resilient children and youth.* New York: McGraw-Hill.

Wold, H. (1982). Systems under indirect observation using pls. In C. Fornell (Ed.), *A second generation of multivariate analysis* (pp. 325–347). New York: Praeger.

# 5

# Family–Peer Relationships: A Tripartite Model

Ross D. Parke
*University of California, Riverside*

Virginia M. Burks
*Vanderbilt University*

James L. Carson
*University of California, Berkeley*

Brian Neville
*University of Washington*

Lisa A. Boyum
*National Jewish Hospital, Denver*

Families are linked with a variety of other socialization agents and settings. In this chapter, we explore the relationships between the family and the peer group—two social systems that are increasingly recognized as mutually interdependent and mutually influential (Parke & Ladd, 1992). Our goal is to explore the multiple ways in which these two systems are linked. Specifically, we present a three-part model that depicts alternative pathways that serve to connect families and peers and provide recent evidence in support of our three-tiered approach. The ways in which the model shifts across development are emphasized. Figure 5.1 outlines the model that guides our research and this chapter. This chapter discusses three modes by which parents may influence their children's peer relationships. First, parents are viewed as influencing their children's peer relationships indirectly through their childrearing practices and interactive styles. In this case, the impact of parent–child interaction on children's peer relationships is often indirect because the parent's goal is not explicitly to modify or enhance children's relationships with extra-familial social partners such as peers. Second, parents may influence their children's peer relationships directly in their role as a direct instructor or educator. In this role, parents may explicitly set out to educate their children concerning appropriate ways of negotiating the peer system. This mode of linkage may take one of a number of forms. Parents may serve as coaches as they provide advice, support, and directions about strategies for managing peer relationships. Parents may act as supervisors of peer interaction in which their child is participating or may directly assist their children to maintain play with other children (Lollis & Ross, 1987; Lollis, Ross, & Tate, 1992; Parke & Bhavnagri, 1989). In a third role, parents' function as managers of their

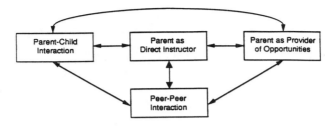

FIG. 5.1.  Family-peer relationships: Three modes of linkage.

children's social lives (Hartup, 1979; Parke, 1978) and serve as providers of opportunities for social contact with extra-familial social partners (Ladd, Profilet, & Hart, 1992; Parke & Bhavnagri, 1989).

## Parent—Child Play as a Context for the Development of Peer—Peer Competence

The goal of research in this area has been to provide a detailed description of the ways in which parent–child interaction patterns relate to children's peer group interaction. The foundation of this line of research has been the assumption that parent–child face-to-face interaction may provide opportunities to learn, rehearse, and refine social skills that in turn will be useful in children's interactions with peers. This research has employed a two-phase paradigm. In Phase 1, parent–child interaction is assessed in some manner. In our own lab, this phase has involved videotaping mothers and fathers on separate occasions interacting with their 3 to 5-year-old children. In our studies, a 10-minute period in which parents are specifically instructed to play physically with their children is included. Parents are given examples such as tickling, tumbling, or wrestling. In Phase 2, measures of peer-interactive competence are secured. These have varied across studies and include (a) teacher assessments, (b) sociometric ratings, and (c) observations of peer–peer interaction.

## Parent—Child Interactive Processes

In our initial study (MacDonald & Parke, 1984), 3- to 5-year-old boys and girls were observed interacting during free and physical play with their mothers and fathers in their homes. A variety of measures of verbal and physical behavior were derived from videotape of these play interactions, including the number of 10-second periods of parent–child physical play, verbal interchanges, directive statements, and ratings of children's positive affect. As a measure of peer status, teacher rankings of children's popularity were secured (see MacDonald & Parke, 1984, for details and other measures). Our results indicated that popular boys had mothers and fathers who were engaging and elicited positive affect during play, mothers who were verbally stimulating, and fathers who were low in directiveness but physically playful. Girls whose teachers rated them as popular had physically playful and affect-eliciting but nondirective fathers, and directive mothers.

Work by Burks, Carson, and Parke (1987) utilizing a molecular coding strategy and measures of sociometric status, confirmed our earlier work and extended our understanding of familial antecedents of peer-interactive competence. Popular and rejected 3- to 5-year-old boys and girls were observed interacting with their mothers and fathers on separate occasions for a 5-minute warm-up free-play period as well as a 10-minute physical play session in a lab playroom. Dyads of popular children and their parents had more sustained play bouts and played for a larger proportion of the time than dyads of rejected children and their parents. Initiation strategies varied by sociometric status. Popular parent–child dyads used noncoercive initiation tactics, such as questions, whereas dyads involving rejected children and their parents used more coercive tactics such as suggestions and directives. Similarly, responses to initiations differed across the status groups. Dyads involving rejected children were more likely to respond negatively than popular dyads.

The consistency of these findings with those from studies of parental disciplinary style increases our confidence in the ecological validity of the laboratory-based findings. For instance, children of mothers with power-assertive disciplinary styles have been found to be less accepted by peers than have children of mothers with inductive disciplinary styles (Hart, Ladd, & Burleson, 1990). Other data (Gottman & Fainsilber-Katz, 1989) provides further support for this parental profile. In an examination of the parent–child interaction, Gottman and Fainsilber-Katz found that a parenting style characterized as cold, unresponsive, angry, and low in limit setting and structuring leads to higher levels of anger and noncompliance as well as high levels of stress-related hormones. Children from such homes tend to play at a lower level with peers, display more negative peer interaction, and have poorer physical health. Maritally distressed couples were more likely to exhibit this parenting style—a finding consistent with other work (see Grych & Fincham, 1990, for a review of the impact of marital interaction on children's social adaptation).

One limitation of the studies reviewed in this section is their reliance on concurrent assessments of both parent–child interaction and peer competence. The nature of this cross-sectional approach limits the extent to which the direction of effects can be assessed as well as the long-term impact of familial effects on later adjustment to peers.

*Short-Term Longitudinal Evidence.*   Recent evidence suggests that both the ability of the parent–child dyad to maintain physical play and the style of parent–child interaction not only are concurrent correlates of children's peer behavior, but also are related to children's later adjustment after the transition to school

(Barth & Parke, 1993). In this study, the relation between parent–child interaction and children's social adjustment as they make the transition to elementary school was examined. Children who were entering kindergarten were observed in physical play sessions separately with their mothers and fathers 1 to 2 months prior to school entrance. Social adjustment in the school setting was assessed through parent ratings, teacher reports, and interviews with the children 2 weeks after school began and at the end of the first school semester.

Results from this study indicate that mother–child and father–child interaction both predicted subsequent school social adaptation. First, the amount of time that the parent and child spent in sustained play interaction was a significant predictor. For mothers, this "length of bout" measure was positively associated with teachers' ratings (Schaefer, Edgerton, & Aaronson, 1978; Classroom Behavior Inventory) of a child's consideration of others and negatively related with teachers' rating of dependence at both 2 weeks after school entry and again at the end of the semester. Similarly, there was a positive relation between the extent to which there was sustained parent–child interaction and children's attitudes toward school; children's attitudes were measured by the "One Child's Day" scale (Barth, 1988), which asks children to evaluate specific events that occur in a typical school day on a 3-point scale. For example, items asked children how much they liked getting ready for school, arriving at school, and playing with other children during free time. In addition, the children's positive attitudes toward school were associated with low ratings of loneliness (Barth, 1988) after the beginning of school and with low teacher hostility ratings at the end of the semester. Each parent independently completed the Home Behavior Questionnaire (HBQ), which assessed a child's interaction with adults and other children at home, school concerns, and physical signs of stress related to health, appetite, and sleep patterns. Parents completed the questionnaire for several days at the onset of school and at the end of the semester. Children who received higher parental ratings of their home behaviors in the 2-week period after school onset, spent more time in play bouts with their fathers, in addition, they engaged in more frequent positive social interaction and relatively infrequent nonsocial bystander behavior in the classroom as assessed by independent observations.

Style of interaction in addition to the quantity or amount of interaction was an important correlate of children's social adjustment. In contrast to earlier studies, in which independent measures of parent or child behaviors were examined, a dyadic measure of parent–child interaction style was used. Children who were highly directive and unwilling to accept maternal input during mother–child interaction were more likely to show poor social adjustment as indexed by high hostility and low consideration ratings from teachers, and higher levels of loneliness. Mother–child dyads characterized by a dominant mother and an uncooperative, resistant child were related to teacher ratings of dependency after the onset of school and higher ratings of hostility at the end of the semester. Similarly, father–child dyads characterized by a pattern of parent control and child resistance were also correlated with poor social adjustment in both home and school settings. Immediately after school entrance, this interaction style was associated with children's reports of loneliness and parents' reports of behavior problems at home. By the end of the semester, this style was negatively correlated with teachers' reports of consideration.

Many of the patterns that we have found in parent–child play are similar to patterns of peer interactions. Peer interactions with popular children generally involve more engaged activities that are of longer duration than interactions involving rejected children. Similarly, popular children tend to be less controlling and more willing to adapt to the activities of the group, whereas rejected children tend to be assertive and directive when they interact with peers (Dodge, 1983).

## Emotion: A Special Role in Parent–Child Interaction

Across these studies it is clear that the affective quality of the interactions of popular children and their parents differs from the interactions of rejected children and their parents. Consistently, higher levels of positive affect were found in the popular dyads than in the rejected dyads. This is evident not only for the children, but for the parents as well (Burks et al., 1987).

More recent work has revealed the nature of the specific emotional expressions displayed by parents and children during social interaction. Carson (1991) found differences in the types of emotions shown by popular or rejected preschool-age children and their parents during physical play. Popular children showed more happiness and laughter, whereas rejected children showed more neutral affect. In addition, the level of anger shown by fathers and their rejected children was positively correlated, which suggested that father and child may be engaged in reciprocal displays of anger. This pattern of positive correlations between paternal anger and either popular or rejected children's anger was not evident for mothers nor did fathers show this pattern with their popular offspring.

Similar evidence based on home observations of a relationship between peer acceptance and the type of affective expressions exhibited during the course of parent–child interaction comes from a study by Boyum (1991). Kindergarten children of varying levels of peer acceptance—as indexed by sociometric ratings by their classmates—and their parents were videotaped at home during a family dinner time. The affective expressions of mothers, fathers, and children were scored during 30-second intervals throughout the dinner time period. Boyum reported negative correlations between the level of a variety of father negative affects, including anger, disgust, and anxiety and their kindergarten children's sociometric status. There were no significant relationships found for mothers. Just as Carson (1991) found in his study of parent–child interaction in the laboratory, paternal negative affect is associated with lower levels of peer acceptance, in this home-based observational investigation.

These findings concerning the heightened degree of negative affects on the part of parents of less socially accepted children have several implications. First, children may transfer some of the negative affect from family to peer settings which may account for the heightened aggression among some rejected children. Second, others (Lindahl, 1991; Lindahl & Markman, 1990) suggest that high levels of maternal negative affect is associated with less ability to manage their negative emotions and higher levels of negative affect in their children.

Other evidence also implicates affect as an important factor in the links between family interaction and peer outcomes. Cassidy, Parke, Butovsky, and Braungart (1992), for example, recently found that parental emotional expressiveness in home contexts—as assessed by Halberstadt's family expressiveness index—is positively associated with children's greater competence with peers as assessed by sociometric and behavior measures. Learning to express emotions, especially in a socially appropriate fashion, may be an important ingredient of emerging social competence. Together these studies underscore the important role of affect in the family–peer relationship.

### In Search of Mediating Processes

A variety of processes have been hypothesized as mediators between parent–child interaction and peer outcomes. These include emotion encoding and decoding skills, emotional regulatory skills, cognitive representations, attributions and beliefs, and problem-solving skills (Ladd, 1992). It is assumed that these abilities or beliefs are acquired in the course of parent–child interchanges over the course of development and in turn, guide the nature of the child's behavior with their peers that, in turn, may determine their level of acceptance by their peers. In this chapter we focus on two sets of processes that seem particularly promising candidates for mediator status: emotional skills and cognitive representational processes.

## EMOTIONAL MEDIATING PROCESSES

### The Relationship Between Emotional Encoding and Decoding Abilities and Sociometric Status

One set of skills that are of relevance to successful peer interaction and may, in part, be acquired in the context of parent–child play, especially arousing physical play, is the ability to clearly encode emotional signals and to decode others' emotional states. Through physically playful interaction with their parents, especially fathers, children may be learning how to use emotional signals to regulate the social behavior of others. In addition, they may learn to accurately decode the social and emotional signals of other social partners.

To determine the role of the ability to decode affect cues in mediating peer relationships, we (Beitel & Parke, 1985) asked 3- and 4-year-old children to correctly identify facial expressions depicting the following emotional states: happy, sad, scared, angry, and neutral. Consistent with prior work (Field & Walden, 1982) there were significant positive relationships between emotional decoding ability and various measures of children's peer status. This evidence suggests that one component of peer acceptance may be a child's ability to correctly identify the emotional states of other children. It is assumed that this emotional identification skill would permit a child to more adequately regulate social interactions with other children; in turn, this could contribute to greater acceptance by peers.

Evidence suggests that emotional encoding is linked with children's social status as well. Others (Buck, 1975) have found positive relationships between children's ability to encode emotional expressions and children's popularity with peers. Carson, Burks, and Parke (1987) extended earlier work by examining how sociometric status is related to emotional production and recognition skills within the family. In our paradigm, parents and children were asked to identify each other's facial expressions (happy, sad, mad, scared, surprise, neutral, and disgust). There were no sociometric status group differences in parents' ability to recognize the faces of their children or in children's abilities to recognize their parents' faces. This suggests that within the family, children and parents, regardless of sociometric status, can recognize each other's facial expressions.

However, emotional expressions exchanged within the family might not be clear to individuals outside the family. Some families may utilize idiosyncratic affect cues that are not recognizable in interactions outside of the family. Their communications may reflect a "familycentric" bias. In support of this possibility, we found that there was a significant sociometric status difference in undergraduates' ability to accurately decode the children's facial expressions. The undergraduates were better able to recognize the facial expressions of the popular children than those of the rejected children. There were no status differences in the recognition of the facial expressions posed by parents. This suggests that the emotional production skills of popular children are greater than those of rejected children, because rejected children's facial expressions are not as well recognized outside the family. These studies provide support of the links between children's emotional encoding and decoding skills and children's sociometric status. Next we turn to the question of the role of parent–child play in the development of emotional encoding and decoding skills.

## Emotional Encoding and Decoding and Parent–Child Interaction

The aim of this phase of our project was to assess the relationship between affect decoding ability and parent–child interaction. Using the same facial production game described earlier, 4- and 5-year-old popular and rejected children were asked to identify facial expressions of different emotions produced by their mothers and fathers (Muth, Burks, Carson, & Parke, 1988). In support of the expected link between parent–child play and decoding ability, we found positive relationships between the length of the parent–child play bouts and the child's ability to correctly identify both maternal and paternal emotional expressions.

To evaluate the relationship between parent–child play and encoding ability, undergraduate recognition of children's emotional productions was correlated with the length of parent–child play bouts (see Burks et al., 1987). Children who had longer play bouts produced expressions that were more easily identified by undergraduate raters. These data support the link between parent–child play engagement (as assessed by the length of the play bouts) and children's ability to accurately produce emotional expressions.

## Beyond Encoding and Decoding: The Relationship of Emotional Understanding to Peer Competence

In order to develop a more comprehensive model of the role of affect in the emergence of peer competence, we recently examined other aspects of this issue. Successful peer interaction requires not only the ability to recognize and produce emotions, but also requires a social understanding of emotion-related experiences, of the meaning of emotions, of the cause of emotions, and of the responses appropriate to others' emotions. Cassidy et al. (1992) evaluated this hypothesized role of emotional understanding in a study of 5- and 6-year-old children. Based on interviews with the children about their understanding of emotions, they found that greater peer acceptance was associated with greater ability to identify emotions, greater acknowledgment of experiencing emotion, greater ability to describe appropriate causes of emotions, and greater expectations that they and their parents would respond appropriately to the display of emotions. Other evidence is consistent with this work. Denham, McKinley, Couchoud, and Holt (1990) found that children's understanding of the type of emotion that would be elicited by different situations was positively related to peer likability. These findings are consistent with other research that suggests connections between other components of social understanding and peer relations (Asher & Renshaw, 1981; Dodge, Pettit, McClaskey, & Brown, 1986; Hart et al., 1990). The next step, of course, is to determine how variations in family interaction may, in fact, contribute to individual differences in children's cognitive understanding of emotions (see Cassidy et al., 1992, for some relevant data).

Together, these studies suggest that various aspects of emotional development—encoding, decoding, and cognitive understanding—play an important role in accounting for variations in peer competence. Our argument is that these aspects of emotion may be learned in the context of family interaction and serve as mediators between the family and peer systems. Accumulating support for this view suggests that this is a plausible direction for future research.

## Cognitive Representational Models: Another Possible Mediator Between Family and Peer Systems

One of the major problems facing the area of family–peer relationships is how children transfer the strategies that they acquire in the family context to their peer relationships. A variety of theories assume that individuals process internal mental representations that guide their social behavior. Attachment theorists offer working model notions (Bowlby, 1969, 1973, 1980; Bretherton and Waters, 1985), whereas social and cognitive psychologists have provided an account involving scripts that could serve as a guide for social action (Nelson, 1986; Schank & Abelson, 1977).

The information-processing model proposed by Dodge (1986) provides a convenient framework for organizing some of these cognitive factors. According to this five-step model, the way in which children handle each decision point will determine how appropriately and competently the child will react to a social stimulus or event. These steps include the recognition of social cues, interpretation of these cues, the response search process, evaluation of the potential consequences of each response, and finally the enactment and monitoring of a chosen response. Support for most steps of this model have been generated mainly in work on aggressive children (Dodge, 1986) but also to some extent for children of differing sociometric status as well (Dodge et al., 1986). Briefly, there is evidence that aggressive children possess a bias toward perceiving hostile intent in their social partners. Negative and positive expectations concerning the behavior of social partners can alter the degree of social acceptance of rejected and popular children (Rabiner & Coie, 1989). Second, rejected as well as aggressive children generate fewer solutions to social problems but more antisocial solutions (Dodge, 1986; Renshaw & Asher, 1983). Third, aggressive children are more confident in their abilities to aggress, expect more positive payoffs and fewer negative outcomes for aggression (Perry, Perry, & Rasmussen, 1986). Other research suggests that children of various sociometric status have differing goals in social interaction contexts (Dodge, Asher, & Parkhurst, 1988; Renshaw & Asher, 1983) as well as different social values (Allen, Weissberg, & Hawkins, 1989). The work reviewed in the prior section concerning the role of emotional decoding and encoding could be viewed within the framework. Emotional decoding could be viewed as a necessary early step in recognizing social cues, whereas encoding abilities would be necessary skills for enactment of a chosen response. Only limited support for the role of the family in accounting for variations in some of these steps is available and is briefly reviewed.

## The Role of the Family in the Acquisition of Cognitive Representations Concerning Social Behavior

Some research supports the general underlying assumption that there is intergenerational continuity and/or influence concerning the cognitive representations about social behavior across parents and children. These studies show that there are relationships between maternal childrearing history and subsequent infant–caregiver attachment (Main, Kaplan, & Cassidy, 1985). Specifically, mothers' reports of the quality of their early relationships with their own caregivers were associated with secure or anxious patterns of attachment between these individuals and their subsequent offspring. The nature of the mechanisms by which this continuity is achieved is unclear; representational models of relationships that serve as guiding templates for social action have been suggested by Bowlby (1969) and others (Sroufe & Fleeson, 1986), but there is little direct evidence of the components of these models. Consistent with this evidence are other data that suggest continuity between the nature of early infant–mother attachment patterns and later social relationships with peers (Sroufe & Fleeson, 1986).

Next, we turn to an examination of the evidence in support of the general hypothesis that parents of children of different sociometric status vary in terms of their cognitive models of social relationships. Only a small amount of evidence exists in support of this proposition. In support of the assumption that parents of children of popular and rejected children provide different solutions to peer problems, Finnie and Russell (1988) found that mothers of low social status and high social status preschoolers differed in both number and adequacy in their solutions to hypothetical dilemmas involving peer-related problems. Closely related are the findings of Putallaz (1987) that suggest that the quality of a mother's advised solutions to a hypothetical situation involving her child being teased was predictive of the children's social status. At the same time, solutions to other hypothetical problems (e.g., entry into a new group) were not predictive, a result that is inconsistent with the Finnie and Russell findings. Clearly, more work is needed to reconcile these inconsistencies across studies. Finally, Pettit, Dodge, and Brown (1988) explored several aspects of this issue. Specifically, these investigators found that mothers' attributional biases concerning their children's behavior (e.g., the extent to which they view an ambiguous provocation as hostile or benign) and the endorsement of aggression as a solution to interpersonal problems were related to children's interpersonal problem-solving skill that, in turn, was related to their social competence. Moreover, Rubin, Mills, and Rose-Krasnor (1989) found a link between mothers' beliefs and their preschoolers' social problem-solving behavior in the classroom. Mothers who placed higher values on such skills as making friends, sharing with others, and leading or influencing other children had children who were more assertive, prosocial, and competent social problem solvers. Additionally, the degree to which mothers viewed social behavior as externally caused or controllable was associated with higher levels of social competence among their children. Finally, as others have found (Hart et al., 1990; Pettit et al., 1988) higher social competence was linked with low use of power-assertive disciplinary tactics. In related work, Spitzer, Estock, Cupp, Isley-Paradise, and Parke (1992) assessed perceptions of *parental influence* (e.g., how much influence that they feel they have regarding their children's social behavior) as well perceptions of *parental efficacy* (e.g., how easy or hard they found it to help their child's social behavior). Parents, especially mothers, who were high in both perceptions of influence and efficacy had children who were higher in their levels of social acceptance as rated by peers and teachers. Few effects were evident for father perceptions.

Other evidence suggests that parents hold different patterns of beliefs about problematic social behaviors such as aggression and withdrawal and that these patterns are associated with various sociometric status groups (Rubin & Mills, 1990). Parents were concerned about both types of problematic behavior, but expressed more negative emotions, such as anger and disappointment in the case of aggression. Few mothers or fathers made trait attributions to explain aggressive or withdrawn behavior, but instead attributed these behaviors to temporary or changeable conditions, much as "age or age-related factors." Strategies for dealing with these two types of behavior differed as well; the modal strategies were moderate power for dealing with aggression and low power for social withdrawal. This work is important because it suggests that parents do, in fact, have sets of beliefs concerning children's social behavior that may, in part, govern their behavior (Goodnow & Collins, 1991; Parke, 1978).

## Recent Evidence of the Links Between Parental and Child Cognitive Representations

Do parents and children have similar sets of beliefs about social behavior? A recent study by Burks and Parke (1991) explored this issue. The guiding framework is provided in Figure 5.2. Briefly, it is assumed that the child acquires a cognitive representation of social behavior in interaction with his or her parents that, in turn, serves as a guide in subsequent interactions with peers.

As a first step in this process we examined the degree of similarity in the cognitive representations of children and their mothers. Fourth and fifth graders were presented with a series of vignettes of common social problems, such as ambiguous provocation, mild rejection, and conflict resolution. The context of the vignette was also varied; children solved problems involving their peers as well as issues involving either their mother or father. Mothers solved a similar set of social problems that involved either their children in the family, their children in the peer group, or the parent in relation to his or her own adult peers. Participants were asked the following sets of questions in order to identify the specific components of their representational models: (a) *Attributions,* "Why do you think something like this might have happened to you?" (b) *Goals,* "What would you do in this situation and why would you do it? What would you be trying to accomplish?" (c) *Anticipation of Consequences:* "How do you think that other people are going to respond to you?" The results suggest that there were relationships between children and mothers in terms of their responses to the vignettes, although the links varied across components (attributions, goals, etc.) and the type of situation (ambiguous provocation, conflict resolution).

**PARENTS' PEER CONTEXT**        **FAMILY CONTEXT**        **CHILD'S PEER CONTEXT**

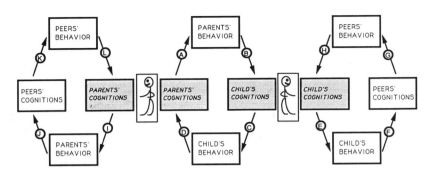

FIG. 5.2. A guiding model for assessing parent and child cognitive representations of social behavior in different contexts. From Burks and Parke (1991).

Children made similar attributions concerning ambiguous provocations when responding to a situation involving their father or a peer, which suggests that their cognitive representations about interactions in the family and in the peer group are similar. A similar pattern is evident when a child's responses to the conflict resolution vignette are examined. Specifically, the child's anticipation of consequences and their goals were similar when the vignette involved the child and either father or mother and when the child and his or her peer was involved. Again these data suggest that children's "cognitive representations," as indexed by their responses to these vignette-based social dilemmas, were similar across family and peer contexts. In turn, similar patterns of response to the vignettes are evident when the mother is asked to indicate how she would respond to situations in which she interacts with her child and how the child reacts to a situation involving the mother. This suggests that both mother and child view family situations in a similar fashion. Third, children respond in very similar ways to situations involving mothers and fathers; in other words, children's cognitive understanding of dilemmas involving family interactions do not differ as a function of the gender of the parent. This finding lends support to the view that children may develop a single representational model of family and that children's "cognitive representations" as indexed by their responses to these vignette-based social dilemmas were similar across family and peer contexts. Although the links between children and their peer group appear consistent, there were very weak connections between mothers' cognitive representations concerning family contexts (e.g., mother with child) and adult–peer contexts (e.g., mother with an adult peer) suggesting that mothers have rather distinct models for these two groups.

These data provide some evidence that the representations of parents and

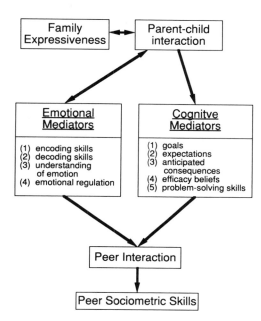

Fig. 5.3. Emotional and cognitive mediators: Links between parent-child interaction and peer sociometric status.

children are similar and also that representation concerning family and peer contexts are linked in expected ways. A next step would be to evaluate how these links vary as a function of children's sociometric status. In addition, the relationships between parent–child interaction and children's and parents' cognitive representations need to be examined in order to assess the hypothesis that these cognitive models are acquired, in part, in the context of parent–child interaction. This is a critical step in assessing the potential mediator role of cognitive models. It is important to examine other pathways by which cognitive models are acquired, such as modeling of parental solutions to common social dilemmas (Grych & Fincham, 1990), as well as the role of direct instruction and advice on the acquisition of these cognitive models (e.g., Finnie & Russell, 1988). Finally, the links between cognitive and emotional mediators needs to be explored more closely, because it is unlikely that these processes function independently of one another (Dodge, 1991; Grych & Fincham, 1990; Parke, Cassidy, Burks, Carson, & Boyum, 1992). Figure 5.3 summarizes the roles of emotion and cognitive representations as mediators between family and peer systems.

## PARENT AS MANAGER OF PEER RELATIONSHIPS

Parent–child play is only one avenue through which parents can influence their children's social relationships outside the family. A second way in which parents can influence their children's relationships is through their role as direct instructors who facilitate peer relationships by directly monitoring, supervising, and advising their children.

## Parent as Direct Instructor

In our laboratory we investigated one aspect of the parent role of direct instructor, namely as a supervisor of children's peer play (Bhavnagri & Parke, 1985, 1991). In a playroom, children's social competence with an unfamiliar peer was assessed under two conditions. In one condition, two children played without assistance from an adult. In this case, both mothers were present but were instructed not to assist or interfere with the children's play. In the contrasting condition, each mother, in turn, was asked to play an active supervisory role with the specific instruction "to help the children play together." Bhavnagri and Parke (1985) found that 24-month-old children's social competency was rated higher during periods of parental supervision. Children exhibited more cooperation, turn taking, and had longer play bouts when assisted by an adult than when playing without assistance. In a similar study, Bhavnagri and Parke (1991) found that both fathers and mothers were effective facilitators of their children's play with peers. However, supervision enhanced the quality of play for younger (2 to $3^{1}/_{2}$ years of age) more than older ($3^{1}/_{2}$ to 6 years of age) children. This suggests that parental facilitation may be more important for younger children, who are beginning to acquire social skills, than for older children.

Other studies have examined the conditions under which parents intervene during children's peer interactions. Lollis and Ross (1987), for example, found that mothers intervened more during peer conflicts than during other types of interactions and that their own child was more often the target of intervention than their child's play partner. As in other studies, parental intervention can yield positive outcomes, such as increased sharing of toys and materials. In addition to the specific interactional behaviors that may elicit parental involvement, the sociometric status of the child is related to the quality of parental interventions. Finnie and Russell (1988) examined the nature of maternal interventions among 4- and 5-year-old children of varying sociometric status. When mothers were observed assisting their child as he or she attempted to join two children playing, there were marked differences in the style of intervention of the mothers of well- versus low-accepted children. Mothers of well-accepted children used more skillful strategies (e.g., verbal coaching, positive discipline), whereas mothers of low-accepted children used less effective tactics (e.g., avoidance; talking exclusively to one child; power-assertive discipline). It is unclear whether these differences in maternal strategies may, in fact, have contributed to the emergence of these differences in children's sociometric status, or whether mothers are merely responding to previously established patterns of behavior.

## Parent as Advisor/Consultant

As children develop, the forms of management shift from direct involvement or supervision of the ongoing activities of children and their peers to a less public form of management, involving advice or consultation concerning appropriate ways of handling peer problems. This form of direct parental management has been termed *consultation* (Ladd, LeSieur, & Profilet, 1992) or *decontextualized discussion* (Lollis, Ross, & Tate, 1992). This role has received little attention, which is surprising in view of the extensive literature on coaching as a strategy to aid children with social skill deficits (Ladd, 1981). One important distinction between these two research traditions, however, is that the peer-coaching literature involves experimentally scripted training, whereas the more recent parental advisor/consultant work involves naturally occurring variations in the quality of parental advice as a function of children's social status or the type of situation or social problem. Consider this description of this type of parental management strategy:

> As consultants, parents may engage children in conversations about many aspects of their peer interactions and relationships, including how to initiate friendships, manage conflicts, maintain relationships, react to peer pressure and provocation, deflect teasing, repel bullies and so on. Parents may use these conversations to prepare children for social encounters or to resolve previously experienced interpersonal problems and difficulties. Other forms of "consulting" may be reactive in nature, as when children request help with interpersonal problems, or when parents recognize children's distress and become concerned about their performance in social situations. . . . Parents may offer expert advice or assistance with problem-solving. . . . Or parents may adopt less directive roles, perhaps by acting as a "sounding board" for children's self-generated assessments and solutions. (Kuczynski, 1984; Ladd, Profilet, & Hart, 1992, p. 28–29)

Cohen (1989), in a study of third graders and their mothers, found that some forms of consulting were associated with positive outcomes, whereas other forms were linked with poor social relationships. When mothers were supportive, but noninterfering, the outcomes were positive. On the other hand, mothers who were too highly involved (e.g., interfering) had children who were socially withdrawn. Direction of effects, of course, are difficult to determine and perhaps the overly involved mothers were simply being responsive to their children's poor social abilities. Alternatively, high levels of control may inhibit children's efforts to develop their own strategies for dealing with peer relations (Cohen, 1989).

In a later study, Russell and Finnie (1990) found that the quality of advice that mothers provided their children prior to entry into an ongoing play dyad varied as a function of children's sociometric status. Mothers of well-accepted children were more specific and helpful in the quality of advice that they provided. In contrast, mothers of poorly accepted children provided relatively ineffective kinds of verbal guidance, such as have fun, stay out of trouble. The advice was too general to be of value to the children in their subsequent instructions.

These studies suggest that parental management in the form of supervision can significantly increase the interactive competence of preschool children and illustrates the utility of examining parental management strategies as a way of increasing children's peer involvement.

## Parental Monitoring and Supervision

Another way in which parents can affect their children's social relationships is through monitoring of their children's social activities. Monitoring refers to a range of activities, including the supervision of children's choice of social settings, activities, and friends. A number of studies of adolescents have examined the use of parental monitoring. These studies indicate that parents of delinquent children engage in less monitoring and supervision of their children's activities, especially with regard to children's use of evening time, than parents of nondelinquent children (Belson, 1975; Pulkkinen, 1981). Others (Gold, 1963) found that parents of delinquents perceive themselves as less in control of their sons' choice of friends. Although earlier studies relied on a single self-report from either parents or children, a recent study by Patterson and Stouthamer-Loeber (1984), using multiple informants, found significant relationships between lack of parental monitoring (defined as awareness of the child's whereabouts) and court-reported delinquency, attacks against property, delinquent lifestyle, rule breaking outside the home, and an antisocial disposition (e.g., fighting with peers, talking back to teachers, being troublesome, breaking school rules) among Grade 7 and 10 boys. Monitoring is a composite measure that indexes how well the parents track their children's whereabouts, the kinds of companions they keep, or the types of activities they engage in. Adolescents who were monitored by their parents exhibited less antisocial behavior. Consistent with this study is the work of Steinberg (1986), who found that children in Grades 6 to 9, especially girls who are on their own after school, are more susceptible to peer pressure to engage in antisocial activity (e.g., vandalism, cheating, stealing) than are their adult-supervised peers. Any adolescent who indicated that at least one adult was present in the after-school setting (regardless of whether there was face-to-face contact with the adult) was categorized as supervised. It is important to note that not all forms of supervision are similar. As Steinberg (1986) suggested:

> Adolescents who are at home after school without an adult present may be supervised distally by their absent parents through telephone calls, an agreed-upon schedule followed by the adolescent, or the power of internalized parental controls which may be heightened by the adolescent's being in his or her own house. (p. 436)

In support of this distal monitoring, Steinberg found that adolescents who are on their own "hanging out" and not at home (e.g., unsupervised at a friend's house) are more susceptible to peer pressure than are adolescents who are on their own in their own homes. Further support for the distal monitoring notion is evident from the finding that adolescents whose parents know their whereabouts after school are less likely to be susceptible to peer pressure (Baumrind, 1978). Finally, Steinberg (1986) found that monitoring may be more important for some families than for others; specifically, children of parents who were high in their use of authoritative parenting practices (Baumrind, 1978) were less susceptible to peer pressure in the absence of monitoring. On the other hand, children of parents who were low in authoritative childrearing were more susceptible to peer pressure in nonsupervised contexts. The importance of monitoring varies with other aspects of the family environment, including childrearing practices. Nor are the effects of monitoring limited to a reduction in the negative aspects of peer relations. As Krappmann (1986) found in Germany, preadolescents of parents who were well informed about their children's peer relationships and activities had closer, more stable, and less problem-ridden peer relationships. Isolation of other conditions or variables that alter the impact of monitoring would be worthwhile. Developmental shifts may be important, because younger children are less likely to be left unsupervised than older children; moreover, it is likely that direct supervision is more common among younger children, whereas distal supervision is more evident among adolescents.

## PARENTS AS PROVIDERS OF OPPORTUNITIES FOR PEER CONTACTS

Young children, in particular, are dependent on their parents to provide opportunities for social contacts. In this section we look at a variety of ways in which this type of influence can occur, including the choice of neighborhood; the availability of child-centered activities, such as clubs and sports; and selection of day-care or preschool facilities (Rubin & Sloman, 1984). In addition, parents influence their child's opportunities directly by initiating and arranging social activities involving other children. Finally, we examine the impact of the role of adult social networks as a source of peer contacts for their children. We consider this third aspect of our model in this section.

### Neighborhoods as Determinants of Peer Contact

Neighborhoods vary in terms of their opportunities for peer–peer contact. Especially in the case of young children who have limited mobility, the neighborhood forms a significant proportion of their social world (Moore & Young, 1978). The most systematic evidence concerning the impact of variations in the quality of neighborhood environments comes from the work of Medrich (Berg & Medrich, 1980; Medrich, Roizen, Rubin, & Buckley, 1982). These investigators isolated a number of factors, such as safety, terrain, distance from commercial areas, and child population density, that affect the amount and type of peer social experience. Based on interviews with sixth-grade children, they found that children in neighborhoods in which houses are widely separated with few sidewalks tended to have fewer friends and travel longer distances in order to make contact. Their friendship patterns were more formal and rigid. In contrast, children in neighborhoods with little distance and few barriers between houses reported a higher number of friends and a more informal and spontaneous play pattern.

Safety was a further determinant of peer access. Children in neighborhoods with safety hazards such as major thoroughfares and unregulated traffic reported much less autonomy to visit playmates and gain access to play areas. Safety restraints limit the number of friends and amount of large-group play and are associated with rigidity of friendships. To compensate, children with these restraints report more play with siblings than did children in less-restrained neighborhoods (Medrich et al., 1982).

Other evidence (Cupp, Spitzer, Isley-Paradise, Bentley, & Parke, 1992) suggests that the parental perceptions of the quality of the neighborhood were related to children's sociometric status. As Fig. 5.4 shows, parents of well accepted children viewed their neighborhoods as less safe than parents of poorly accepted children, even though the actual features of the neighborhood were, in fact, similar for the two groups of children. This work underscores the importance of distinguishing between actual and perceived neighborhood qualities. Perhaps,

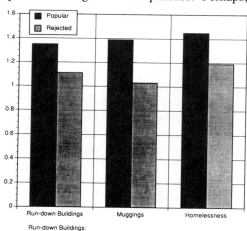

Fig. 5.4. Relationship between parental perceived neighborhood quality and children's sociometric status.

Run-down Buildings:
Univariate $F_{(1,66)} = 3.96$, p<.05

Muggings:
Univariate $F_{(1,66)} = 10.04$, p<.002

Homelessness:
Univariate $F_{(1,66)} = 4.07$, p<.05

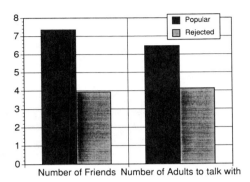

FIG. 5.5. Relationship between parental perceived social support and children's sociometric status.

Number of Friends in Neighborhood:
Univariate F (1, 50) = 5.23, p < .05

Number of Adults to talk with:
Univariate F(1, 50) = 5.57, p< .05

poorly accepted children receive less parental supervision and monitoring, which in turn leads to behavior patterns characteristic of rejected children.

Children's access to public facilities such as parks and schoolyards affects their play interaction. Children with less access report less large-group play and fewer friends than children with easy access to these facilities (Medrich et al., 1982). Moreover, a neighborhood with high social density was related to higher number of friends, more large-group play, and more spontaneity in play. Children in neighborhoods with fewer children reported having a smaller number of friends and more formal friendship patterns (Medrich et al., 1982). Finally, adult perceptions of the social support offered by their neighborhood is related to children's social acceptance (Cupp et al., 1992) (Fig. 5.5). Perhaps social support enhances parental child-rearing that promotes children's social competence and/or the availability of dense adult social networks may increse children's access to potential peers (see below).

Bhavnagri and Parke (1991) found that children's use of neighborhood varies with age, with younger children (2- to 3½-year-old) being permitted less unsupervised access to neighborhood facilities and playmates than older children (3½- to 6-year-old). Similarly older children played more outdoors with their friends in the neighborhood and had more playmates in the neighborhood than younger children.

What is the impact of neighborhood variations on peer competence? Bryant (1985) found that accessibility to neighborhood resources is a correlate of socioemotional functioning. Children who could easily access (by walking or bike) such community resources as structured and unstructured activities at formally sponsored organizations were higher in their acceptance of individual differences, as well as higher in perspective taking.

## Parental Participation in Children's Organized Activities

In addition to choosing a neighborhood as a way of increasing access to children, parents influence their children's social behavior by interfacing between children and institutional settings. More than 25 years ago, Coser (1964) recognized this function:

> Through her activities in the PTA, Brownies, Cub Scouts and the like, a mother helps both to maintain the communal social network and to integrate her children in it—hence the modern middle-class American mother performs a large share of the mediation between the community and the family; to use Parsons' phrase, she helps to adapt the family to the "external system." (p. 337, cited in O'Donnell & Stueve, 1983)

These mediational activities are important because they permit the child access to a wider range of social activities that may, in turn, contribute to their social and cognitive development.

As the early observations of Coser (1964) suggest, there are clear gender-of-parent differences in these activities. Mothers communicate more regularly with child-care staff than fathers (Joffe, 1977) and have more regular contact with teachers in elementary schools (Lightfoot, 1978) than fathers. In addition, Bhavnagri (1987) found that mothers and fathers differ in their views of the importance of preschool as an opportunity to learn social skills. Although both mothers and fathers indicated that the learning of social skills was an important factor in their choice of a preschool and an important goal of the preschool experience for their children, mothers' ratings of these factors were higher than fathers'. Together these findings suggest not only that mothers are more involved in the interface between the family and social institutions, but also that mothers view these settings as being more important for the development of social relationships than fathers.

Moreover, there are clear social-class variations in this activity. O'Donnell and Stueve (1983), in an interview study of 59 families with children between 5 and 14 years of age, found that 80% of the families were involved in community-based children's activities and only 22% of the mothers gave no evidence of volunteer activity, whereas 78% participated at least occasionally in one of the activities. Age determined to some extent the level of participation, with those families most involved in community-based activities having at least one child between the ages of 10 and 14 years of age. There were marked social-class differences both in children's utilization of community organizations and in the level of maternal participation. Working-class children were only half as likely to participate in activities as were their middle-class peers, and working-class children were more likely to use facilities on an occasional rather than a regular basis. Middle-class mothers were more likely to sign their children up for specific programs, whereas working-class mothers were less likely to involve their children in planned activities. The level of maternal participation varied by social class with better-educated and economically advantaged mothers participating more heavily than working-class mothers.

> By virtue of their purchasing power and their ability to manipulate the system, middle-class mothers were better prepared to act as social agents, and to introduce their children into the broader range of organized activities and resources beyond the boundaries of their homes and schools. (O'Donnell & Stueve, 1983, p. 123)

Unfortunately we know relatively little about how these opportunities for participation relate to children's social behavior with their peers. One exception is Bryant (1985), who found that participation in formally sponsored organizations with unstructured activities was associated with greater social perspective-taking skill among 10-year-old children, but had little effect on 7-year-olds. In light of the importance of this skill for successful peer interaction (Hartup, 1983), this finding assumes particular significance. Moreover, it suggests that activities that "allow the child to experience autonomy, control and mastery of the content of the activity are related to expressions of enhanced social-emotional functioning on the part of the child" (Bryant, 1985, p. 65).

Although we have limited understanding of how these activities vary as a function of children's age, it appears that there is an increase with age in participation in sponsored organizations with structured activities (e.g., clubs, Brownies, organized sports) with participation most prevalent among preadolescent children (Bryant, 1985; O'Donnell & Stueve, 1983). Finally, more attention to the ways in which fathers participate in these types of activities is needed, especially in light of their shifting roles (Parke & Tinsley, 1987).

## Parent as Social Initiator and Arranger

Parents play an important role in the facilitation of their children's peer relationships by initiating contact between their own children and potential play partners especially among younger children (Bhavnagri, 1987).

*Does Active Parental Initiation of Peer Contact Relate to Children's Social Competence?* A series of studies by Ladd and his colleagues suggests that parent's role as arranger may play a facilitory part in the development of their children's friendships. Ladd and Golter (1988) found that children of parents who tended to arrange peer contacts had a larger range of playmates and more frequent play companions outside of school than children of parents who were less active in initiating peer contacts. When children entered kindergarten, boys but not girls with parents who initiated peer contacts were better liked and less rejected by their classmates than were boys with noninitiating parents. Other evidence (Ladd, Hart, Wadsworth, & Golter, 1988) suggests that parents' peer management (initiating peer contacts; purchasing toys for social applications) of younger preschool children prior to enrollment in preschool was, in turn, linked to the time that children spent in peers' homes. In addition, work by Ladd and Hart (1991) provides further evidence of the importance of parental initiating and arranging activities. Parents who arranged a larger number of peer informal play contacts tended to have children with a larger range of playmates. In addition, these investigators found a positive relationship between the number of child initiations and the size of their playmate network. Moreover, these investigators confirmed earlier findings (Ladd & Golter, 1988) of a positive relationship between parents' initiations and higher levels of peer acceptance among boys, but not girls. In addition, parents who frequently initiated informal peer play opportunities tended to have children who were more prosocial toward peers and spent less time in onlooking and unoccupied behaviors.

Children's own initiation activity has been linked with measures of social competence. Children who initiated a larger number of peer contacts outside of school tended to be better liked by their peers in preschool settings. The work of Ladd and Hart (1991) serves as a corrective to the view that initiation activity is only a parental activity and reminds us that variations in how active a role children play in organizing their own social contacts is an important correlate of their social competence. Finally, Krappman (1986) reported that the quality of peer relationships of 10- to 12-year-old children in a German sample were related to parental management activity. Specifically, children of parents who played an active role in stimulating and arranging peer contacts on behalf of their children had more stable and closer peer relationships than children of less active parents.

Of interest for future research is to plot in more detail how parental and child initiating activities shift over the course of development. It is clear that parental initiating is important but over time it decreases and the factors that govern this decrease are important issues to explore. Moreover, it is critical to understand when parental initiation activity can, in fact, be detrimental to children's emerging social competence. By not providing a child with sufficient independence in organizing their social contacts, the child's social competence may, in fact, be negatively affected. At the least, a child may regard it as inappropriate for a parent to continue to initiate on their behalf beyond a certain age and parental micromanagement may be viewed as interfering rather than helpful and a potential source of embarrassment for the child.

Together these studies provide evidence of the possible facilitory role of parents in the development of social competence with peers. Little is known, however, about the possible determinants of parental utilization of neighborhood social resources, including other children as playmates. As noted earlier, one contributor may be the qualities of the neighborhood. If parents perceive the neighborhood as unsafe and unsupportive, it is less likely that they may utilize the neighborhood resources (Cupp et al., 1992). More work is needed on the determinants of parental initiating and arranging activities.

## Adult Social Networks as a Source of Potential Peer Contacts for Children

In addition to the role played by parents in arranging children's access to other children, parents' own social networks of other adults, as well as the child members of parental social networks, provide a source of possible play partners for children. Cochran and Brassard (1979) suggested several ways in which these two sets of relationships may be related. First, the child is exposed to a wider or narrower band of possible social interactive partners by exposure to the members of the parent's social network. Second, the extent to which the child has access to the social interactions of his or her parents and members of their social network may determine how well the child may acquire particular styles of social interaction. Third, in view of the social support function of social networks, parents in supportive social networks may be more likely to have positive relationships with their children which, in turn, may positively affect the child's social adjustment both within and outside the family.

Cochran and his co-workers (Cochran & Davila, 1992; Cochran, Larner, Riley, Gunnarsson, & Henderson, 1990) have provided support for the first issue, namely that there is overlap between parental and child social networks. Specifically, these investigators found that 30%–44% of 6-year-old children's social networks were also included in the mothers' networks. In other words, children often listed other children as play partners who were children of their mothers' friends. Finally, the overlap was higher in the case of relatives than nonrelatives but both kin and nonkin adult networks provided sources of peer play partners for young children.

Other evidence from Sweden (Tietjen, 1985) suggests that there is overlap in the social networks of parents and children. However, in this case, there was overlap only between mothers and their 8- to 9-year-old daughters; no relations were evident in the case of mothers and sons. In light of the failure to find gender differences in network overlap across generations in other studies (e.g., Cochran et al., 1990), this issue merits further examination, especially the potential role of culture in accounting for these findings.

Several other studies suggest that the quality of adult social networks do, in fact, relate to children's social behavior. In an Australian study, Hormel, Burns, and Goodnow (1987) found positive relationships between the number of "dependable" friends that parents report and 11-year-old children's self-rated happiness, the number of regular playmates, and maternal ratings of children's social skills. Second, parent's affiliation with various types of formal community organizations was related to children's happiness, school adjustment, and social skills. Unfortunately, the reliance on self-reports limits the value of these findings, but they do support the importance of parental, or at least maternal, social networks as a factor in potentially affecting children's social relationships.

Finally, Oliveri and Reiss (1987) suggested that it is important to consider both maternal and paternal social networks. These investigators found distinctive patterns between maternal and paternal networks and the networks of their adolescent children. The structural aspects (size, density) of networks were more closely related to maternal network qualities that is consistent with prior work that suggests that mothers function as social arrangers and "kin keepers" more than fathers (Ladd & Golter, 1988; Tinsley & Parke, 1984). In contrast, the relationship aspects of adolescent social networks (positive sentiment between individuals; help received from network members) more closely resembled these aspects of fathers' social network characteristics. This is consistent with the view that fathers may, in fact, play an important role in the regulation of emotion—a central ingredient in the maintenance of close personal relationships (Parke et al., 1992).

## CONCLUSIONS AND REMAINING ISSUES

As this review suggests, our multifaceted model of family–peer relationships has considerable support. At the same time there are a variety of issues that remain to be resolved.

First, although we have discussed different aspects of our model as separate influences, it is clear that these parental strategies often operate together in producing various peer outcomes.

As noted earlier,

> this array of socialization strategies that is available to parents can be viewed as analogous to a "cafeteria model" in which various combinations of items can be chosen or ignored in various sized portions. Are there family typologies in which different combinations are evident across families? If so, are these stable across time? Some parents may spend relatively little time in interaction but provide multiple opportunities for contact with peers. In contrast, other parents may be highly involved with their children in family settings but limit their children's peer contacts. Some parents may invest heavily in teaching their children social skills, whereas other parents may regard peer social skills as best acquired in interactions with other children. Do all combinations produce equally socially competent children or are some "ingredients" in this mix more important than others? Do different combinations produce different, but equally well-adjusted children—in recognition of the fact that developmental adaptations may be achieved through multiple pathways. Can heavy investment in one set of strategies compensate for limited utilization of another mode of influence? (Parke, 1992, p. 426)

Second, more work is needed to illuminate the nature of the intervening processes. Several candidates have been suggested in this chapter, namely emotional and cognitive processes. However, more work is needed to illuminate more specifically the nature of each of these processes. For example, a wider variety of emotional processes merit examination, especially the role of emotional regulation. Similarly on the cognitive side, more detailed specification of the dimensions (e.g., strategies, goals, expectations, anticipated consequences) that characterize cognitive models are needed. It is clear that cognition and emotion probably act interdependently rather than alone and greater attention to the ways in which these two classes of mediators function together is needed.

Third, the issue of the direction of effects needs more attention. Two forms of this issue merit distinction. In the first case, we need to assess the impact of the child on the parent as well as vice-versa in our studies of parent–child interaction. It is likely that both directions of influence are operative and the task is to delineate how the relative balance changes across age and setting. In the second case, it is important to assess the impact of experience in the peer group on family relationships in addition to the usual presumed direction of influence, namely family to peer influence. Some recent evidence will illustrate. Repetti (1993) found that daily fluctuations in a child's experience at school with peers and teachers can alter the nature of parent–child interactions on the same day. Children who had difficulties with peers (e.g., excluded from an activity) or teachers (e.g., received a bad grade or criticism) subsequently had more negative interchange with parents. This work is consistent with earlier reports concerning the carry-over effects of stressful adult work experiences on family life (Repetti, 1989).

Fourth, it is important to distinguish between short- and long-term models of family–peer linkage. The vast majority of research has focused on long-term models, in which the effects of stable family influences (e.g., intervention style, management style, disciplinary views, beliefs, and values concerning social behavior) are assessed and their relationship to some relatively enduring aspect of the child's relationship with other children is measured. In contrast, little attention has been devoted to short-term effects of fluctuations in either family functioning or peer experiences on the child's functioning in family or peer contexts. The Repetti work is a good illustration of the impact of short-term shifts in the quality of peer relationships on subsequent experiences with family members. On the family side, what is the impact of being involved in an argument with a sibling or parent prior to going to school on subsequent peer relationships? In both cases, events in which the target child is directly involved (e.g., argument with a friend, conflict with sibling) or events that are witnessed (e.g., watch a friend receive an injury or an insult at school, witness mother–father or parent–sibling conflict) are both worth examination.

In addition, a variety of temporary stressors of moderate duration merit exploration as well. The impact of divorce, parental job loss, or residential relocation may affect the quality of children's peer relationships. For example, Hetherington, Cox, and Cox (1979) found a significant deleterious impact of divorce on the peer relationships of preschool-age children, especially boys. Similarly, Ladd et al. (1988) found that families with two incomes and relatively stable residences (fewer moves) tended to have larger peer networks. More work on the impact of different types of family stress is needed and Patterson and her colleagues (Patterson, Griesler, Vaden, & Kupersmidt, 1992; Patterson, Vaden, & Kupersmidt, 1991) have made substantial progress along these lines, especially concerning the impact of family socioeconomic circumstances on children's peer relationships.

Fifth, a developmental analysis of these issues is clearly needed. As other research suggests (Grotevant & Cooper, 1986; Krappman, 1989) the direction of influence between parent and child is more balanced across development, as issues of autonomy become of more central importance to the child and adolescent. Even fundamental descriptive data concerning the ways in which different interactive strategies or managerial processes shift across development are lacking at this point. More importantly, the ways in which the family strategies relate to peer relational competence at different points in the child's development merit investigation.

Sixth, a major concern is our limited understanding of the generalizability of the processes that have been discussed. This issue takes a variety of forms. First, do variations in family structure impact on children's peer relationships. Although we have made significant progress in tracking single-parent versus two-parent families (Hetherington, 1989), the range of family forms and their impact is only beginning to be appreciated. In recent years, sociologists and epidemiologists have made us increasingly aware of the variety of family forms and household arrangements that exist in our own society (Cherlin, 1981). Even less is known about how variations in ethnicity, race, and class impact on how families orient their children for peer–peer interactions. Consider the pioneering work of Madsen (e.g., Madsen & Shapira, 1970) on how cooperative and competitive attitudes vary among Anglo and Mexican-American families. Mexican-American children were found to be more cooperative than their more competition-oriented Anglo peers. What implications do Asian-American family values of self-control in matters of emotional expression, aggression, and self-assertion (Suzuki, 1980) have for peer relationships?

These variations across ethnic lines represent important opportunities not only to explore the universality of processes and mechanisms of family–peer linkages, but they also provide naturally occurring variations in the relative salience of certain key determinants such as interactive style or emotional expressiveness. As we become aware of our own cultural diversity, it becomes important that we begin to make a serious commitment to an exploration of this diversity—both theoretically and through systematic empirical inquiry. The search for a balance between processes that are universal and processes that are unique to particular cultural, racial, or ethnic group represents one of our greatest challenges for the future.

## ACKNOWLEDGMENTS

Preparation of this chapter and the research reported were supported in part by NSF Grant BNS 89 19391 and a MacArthur Foundation Transition Network grant to Parke.

Thanks to Barbara J. Tinsley for her comments on the manuscript and to Donnalee Peccerilli, Jane-Ann Phillips, and Christine Strand for assistance in preparation of the manuscript.

## REFERENCES

Allen, J., Weissberg, R., & Hawkins, J. (1989). The relation between values and social competence in early adolescence. *Developmental Psychology, 25*, 458–464.

Asher, S. R., & Renshaw, P. D. (1981). Children without friends: Social knowledge and social skill training. In S. R. Asher & J. M. Gottman (Eds.), *The development of children's friendships* (pp. 273–296). New York: Cambridge University Press.

Barth, J. (1988). *Transition to school.* Unpublished doctoral dissertation, University of Illinois at Urbana-Champaign, IL.

Barth, J. M., & Parke, R. D. (1993). Parent–child relationship influences on children's transition to school. *Merrill-Palmer Quarterly, 39*, 173–195.

Baumrind, D. (1978). Parental disciplinary patterns and social competence in youth. *Youth & Society, 9*, 239–276.

Beitel, A., & Parke, R. (1985). *Relationships between preschoolers' sociometric factors and emotional decoding ability.* Unpublished manuscript, University of Illinois, Urbana, IL.

Belson, W. A. (1975). *Juvenile theft: The causal factors.* London: Harper & Row.

Berg, M., & Medrich, E. A. (1980). Children in four neighborhoods: Physical environment and its effects on play and play patterns. *Environment and Behavior, 12*, 320–348.

Bhavnagri, N. (1987). *Parents as facilitators of preschool children's peer relationships.* Unpublished doctoral dissertation, University of Illinois at Champaign-Urbana, IL.

Bhavnagri, N., & Parke, R. D. (1985, April). *Parents as facilitators of preschool peer–peer interaction.* Paper presented at the Biennial Meeting of the Society for Research in Child Development, Toronto.

Bhavnagri, N., & Parke, R. D. (1991). Parents as direct facilitators of children's peer relationships: Effects of age of child and sex of parent. *Journal of Personal and Social Relationships, 8*, 423–440.

Bowlby, J. (1969). *Attachment and loss* (Vol. 1). New York: Basic Books.

Bowlby, J. (1973). *Attachment and loss: Vol. 2. Separation.* New York: Basic Books.

Bowlby, J. (1980). *Attachment and loss: Vol. 3. Loss.* New York: Basic Books.

Boyum, L. (1991). *Family emotional expressiveness: A possible antecedents of children's social competence.* Poster presented at the Biennial Meeting of the Society for Research in Child Development, Seattle, WA.

Bretherton, I., & Waters, E. (Eds.). (1985). Growing points of attachment theory and research. *Monographs of the Society for Research in Child Development, 50*(1–2), Serial No. 209.

Bryant, B. (1985). The neighborhood walk: Sources of support in middle childhood. *Monographs of the Society for Research in Child Development, 50*(3, Serial No. 210).

Buck, R. (1975). Nonverbal communication of affect in children. *Journal of Personality and Social Psychology, 31*, 644–653.

Burks, V. M., Carson, J. L., & Parke, R. D. (1987). *Parent-child interactional styles of popular and rejected children.* Unpublished manuscript, University of Illinois, Urbana, IL.

Burks, V. M., & Parke, R. D. (1991, July). *Parent and child representations of social relationships: Mediators of children's social adjustment.* Paper presented at the International Society for the Study of Behavioral Development, Minneapolis, MN.

Carson, J. L. (1991, April). *In search of mediating processes: Emotional cues as links between family and peer systems.* Poster presented at the Biennial Meeting of the Society for Research in Child Development, Seattle, WA.

Carson, J. L., Burks, V. M., & Parke, R. D. (1987). *Emotional encoding and decoding skills of parents and children of varying sociometric status.* Unpublished manuscript, University of Illinois, Urbana, IL.

Cassidy, J., Parke, R. D., Butovsky, L., & Braungart, J. (1992). Family–peer connections: The roles of emotional expressiveness within the family and children's understanding of emotions. *Child Development, 63,* 603–618.

Cherlin, A. (1981). Trends in United States men and women's sex-role attitudes—1972 to 1978. *American Sociological Review, 46*(4), 453–460.

Cochran, M., & Brassard, J. A. (1979). Child Development and personal social networks. *Child Development, 50,* 601–616.

Cochran, M., & Davila, V. (1992). Societal influences on children's peer relationships. In R. D. Parke & G. W. Ladd (Eds.), *Family-peer relationships: Modes of linkage* (pp. 191–212). Hillsdale, NJ: Lawrence Erlbaum Associates.

Cochran, M., Larner, M., Riley, D., Gunnarsson, L., & Henderson, C., Jr. (1990). *Extending families: The social networks of parents and their children.* Cambridge, England, and New York: Cambridge University Press.

Cohen, J. S. (1989). *Maternal involvement in children's peer relationships during middle childhood.* Unpublished doctoral dissertation, University of Waterloo, Waterloo, Ontario, Canada.

Coser, R. L. (1964). Authority and structural ambivalence. In R. L. Coser (Ed.), *The family, its structure and functions* (pp. 325–340). New York: St. Martins.

Cupp, R., Spitzer, S., Isley-Paradise, S., Bently, B., & Parke, R. D. (1992, June). *Children's social acceptance: The role of parents' perceptions of the neighborhood.* Poster presented at the Annual Meeting of the American Psychological Society, San Diego, CA.

Denham, S., McKinley, M., Couchoud, E. A., & Holt, R. (1990). Emotional and behavioral predictors of preschool peer ratings. *Child Development, 61,* 1145–1152.

Dodge, K. A. (1983). Behavioral antecedents of peer social status. *Child Development, 54,* 1386–1399.

Dodge, K. A. (1986). A social information processing model of social competence in children. In M. Perlmutter (Ed.), *Minnesota symposia on child psychology* (Vol. *18,* pp. 77–126). Minneapolis: University of Minnesota Press.

Dodge, K. A. (1991). Emotion and social information processing. In J. Garber & K. Dodge (Eds.), *Emotion regulation* (pp. 159–181). New York: Cambridge University Press.

Dodge, K. A., Asher, S. R., & Parkhurst, J. T. (1988). Social life as a goal coordination task. In C. Ames & R. Ames (Eds.), *Research on motivation and education* (Vol. III, pp. 107–135). Orlando, FL: Academic Press.

Dodge, K. A., Pettit, G. S., McClaskey, C. L., & Brown, M. (1986). Social competence in children. Monographs of the Society for Research in *Child Development, 51*(2, Serial No. 213).

Field, T. M., & Walden, T. A. (1982). Production and discrimination of facial expressions by preschool children. *Child Development, 53,* 1299–1311.

Finnie, V., & Russell, A. (1988). Preschool children's social status and their mothers' behavior and knowledge in the supervisory role. *Developmental Psychology, 24,* 789–801.

Gold, M. (1963). *Status forces in delinquent boys.* Ann Arbor: University of Michigan Press.

Goodnow, J., & Collins, A. (1991). *Ideas according to parents.* Hillsdale, NJ: Lawrence Erlbaum Associates.

Gottman, J. M., & Fainsilber-Katz, L. F. (1989). Effects of marital discord on young children's peer interaction and health. *Developmental Psychology, 25,* 373–381.

Grotevant, H., & Cooper, C. (1986). Individuation in family relationships. *Human Development, 29,* 82–100.

Grych, J. H., & Fincham, F. D. (1990). Marital conflict and children's adjustment: A cognitive-contextual framework. *Psychological Bulletin, 108,* 267–290.

Hart, C. H., Ladd, G. W., & Burleson, B. R. (1990). Children's expectations of the outcomes of social strategies: Relations with sociometric status and maternal disciplinary styles. *Child Development, 61,* 127–137.

Hartup, W. W. (1979). The social worlds of childhood. *American Psychologist, 34,* 944–950.

Hartup, W. W. (1983). Peer relations. In P. Mussen & E. M. Hetherington (Eds.), *Manual of child psychology* (4th ed.). New York: Wiley.

Hetherington, E. M., Cox, M., & Cox, R. (1979). Play and social interaction in children following divorce. *Journal of Social Issues, 35,* 26–49.

Hetherington, E. M. (1989). Coping with family transitions: Winners, losers, and survivors. *Child Development, 60,* 1–14.

Hormel, R., Burns, A., & Goodnow, J. (1987). Parental social networks and child development. *Journal of Social and Personal Relationships, 4,* 159–177.

Joffe, C. E. (1977). *Friendly intruders.* Berkeley: University of California Press.

Krappman, L. (1986, December). *Family relationships and peer relationships in middle childhood: An explanatory study of the association between children's integration into the social network of peers and family development.* Paper presented at the Family Systems and Life-Span Development Conference at the Max Planck Institute, Berlin, FRG.

Krappman, L. (1989). Family relationships and peer relationships in middle childhood: An exploratory study of the associations between children's integration into the social network of peers and family development. In K. Kreppner & R. Lerner (Eds.), *Family systems and life-span development* (pp. 93–104). Hillsdale, NJ: Lawrence Erlbaum Associates.

Kuczynski, L. (1984). Socialization goals and mother-child interaction: Strategies for long-term and short-term compliance. *Developmental Psychology, 20,* 1061–1073.

Ladd, G. W. (1981). Effectiveness of a social learning method for enhancing children's social interaction and peer acceptance. *Child Development, 52,* 171–178.

Ladd, G. W. (1992). Themes and Theories: Perspective on processes in family-peer relationships. In R. Parke & G. Ladd (Eds.), *Family-peer relationships: Modes of linkage* (pp. 3–34). Hillsdale, NJ: Lawrence Erlbaum Associates.

Ladd, G. W., & Golter, B. S. (1988). Parents' management of preschoolers' peer relations: Is it related to children's social competence? *Developmental Psychology, 24,* 109–117.

Ladd, G. W., & Hart, C. H. (1991). *Parents' management of children's peer relations: Patterns associated with social competence.* Paper presented at the 11th Meeting of the International Society for Behavioral Development, Minneapolis, MN.

Ladd, G. W., Hart, C. H., Wadsworth, E. M., & Golter, B. S. (1988). Preschoolers' peer network in nonschool settings: Relationship to family characteristics and school adjustment. In S. Salzinger, J. Antrobus, & M. Hammer (Eds.), *Social networks of children, adolescents, and college students* (pp. 61–92). Hillsdale, NJ: Lawrence Erlbaum Associates.

Ladd, G. W., Le Sieur, K., & Profilet, S. M. (in press) Direct parental influences on young children's peer relations. In S. Duck (Ed.), *Learning about relationships* (Vol. 2). London: Sage.

Ladd, G. W., Profilet, S. M., & Hart, C. H. (1992). Parents' management of children's peer relations: Facilitating and supervising children's activities in the peer culture. In R. Parke & G. Ladd (Eds.), *Family-peer relationships: Modes of linkage* (pp. 215–253). Hillsdale, NJ: Lawrence Erlbaum Associates.

Lightfoot, S. L. (1978). *Worlds apart: Relationships between families and schools.* New York: Basic Books.

Lindahl, K. M. (1991, April). *Negative affect regulation in premarital, marital, and parent-child interactions: A longitudinal view.* Poster presented at the Biennial Meeting for the Society for Research in Child Development, Seattle, WA.

Lindahl, K. M., & Markman, H. J. (1990). Communication and negative affect regulation in the family. In E. Blechman (Ed.), *Emotions and the family* (pp. 99–116). Hillsdale, NJ: Lawrence Erlbaum Associates.

Lollis, S. P., & Ross, H. S. (1987, April). *Mothers' interventions in toddler-peer conflicts.* Poster presented at the Biennial Meeting of the Society for Research in Child Development, Baltimore, MD.

Lollis, S. P., Ross, H. S., & Tate, E. (1992). Parents regulation of children's peer interactions: Direct influences. In R. Parke & G. Ladd (Eds.), *Family-peer relationships: Modes of linkage* (pp. 255–281). Hillsdale, NJ: Lawrence Erlbaum Associates.

MacDonald, K., & Parke, R. D. (1984). Bridging the gap: Parent-child play interaction and peer interactive competence. *Child Development, 55,* 1265–1277.

Madsen, M. S., & Shapira, A. (1970). Cooperative and competitive behavior of urban Afro-American, Anglo-American, Mexican-American, and Mexican village children. *Developmental Psychology, 3,* 16–20.

Medrich, E. A., Roizen, J. A., Rubin, V., & Buckley, S. (1982). *The serious business of growing up: A study of children's lives outside school.* Berkeley: University of California Press.

Moore, R., & Young, D. (1978). Children outdoors: Toward a social ecology of the landscape. In I. Altman & J. F. Wohlwill (Eds.), *Children and the environment* (pp. 83–130). New York: Plenum.

Muth, S., Burks, V., Carson, J., & Parke, R. D. (1988). *Peer competence: Parent-child interaction and emotional communication skills.* Unpublished manuscript, University of Illinois at Champaign-Urbana, IL.

Nelson, K. (1986). Event knowledge and cognitive development. In K. Nelson (Ed.), *Event knowledge: Structure and function in development,* Hillsdale, NJ: Lawrence Erlbaum Associates.

O'Donnell, L., & Steuve, A. (1983). Mothers as social agents: Structuring the community activities of school aged children. In H. Lopata & J. H. Pleck (Eds.), *Research in the interweave of social roles: Jobs and families:* Vol. 3. *Families and Jobs* Greenwich, CT: JAI.

Oliveri, M. E., & Reiss, D. (1987). Social networks of family members: Distinctive roles of mothers and fathers. *Sex Roles, 17,* 719–736.

Parke, R. D. (1978). Children's home environments: Social and cognitive effects. In I. Altman & J. F. Wohlwill (Eds.), *Children and the environment* (pp. 33–81). New York: Plenum.

Parke, R. D. (1992). Epilogue: Remaining issues and future trends in the study of family-peer relationships. In R. Parke & G. Ladd (Eds.), *Family-Peer relationships: Modes of linkage.* (pp. 425–435), Hillsdale, NJ: Lawrence Erlbaum Associates.

Parke, R. D., & Bhavnagri, N. P. (1989). Parents as managers of children's peer relationships. In D. Belle (Ed.), *Children's social networks and social supports* (pp. 241–259). New York: Wiley.

Parke, R. D., Cassidy, J., Burks, V., Carson, J., & Boyum, L. (1992). Familial contribution to peer competence among young children: The role of interactive and affective processes. In R. Parke & G. Ladd (Eds.), *Family-peer relationships: Modes of linkage* (pp. 107–134). Hillsdale, NJ: Lawrence Erlbaum Associates.

Parke, R. D., & Ladd, G. W. (Eds.). (1992). *Family-peer relationships: Modes of linkage.* Hillsdale, NJ: Lawrence Erlbaum Associates.

Parke, R. D., & Tinsley, B. J. (1987). Family interaction in infancy. In J. D. Osofsky (Ed.), *Handbook of infant development* (2nd ed., pp. 579–641). New York: Wiley.

Patterson, C. J., Griesler, P. C., Vaden, N. A., & Kupersmidt, J. B. (1992). Family economic circumstances, life transitions, and children's peer relations. In R. D. Parke & G. Ladd (Eds.), *Family-peer relationships: Modes of linkage* (pp. 385–424). Hillsdale, NJ: Lawrence Erlbaum Associates.

Patterson, C. J., Vaden, N. A., & Kupersmidt, J. B. (1991). Family background, recent life events, and peer rejection during childhood. *Journal of social and personal relationships, 8,* 347–361.

Patterson, G. R., & Southammer-Loeber, M. (1984). The correlation of family management practices and delinquency. *Child Development, 55,* 1299–1306.

Perry, D., Perry, L., & Rasmussen, P. (1986). Cognitive social learning mediators of aggression. *Child Development, 57,* 700–711.

Pettit, G. S., Dodge, K. A., & Brown, M. M. (1988). Early family experience, social problem solving patterns, and children's social competence. *Child Development, 59,* 107–120.

Pulkkinen, L. (1981). Search for alternatives to aggression in Finland. In A. P. Medstein & M. Segall (Eds.), *Aggression in global perspective* (pp. 104–144). New York: Pergamon.

Putallaz, M. (1987). Maternal behavior and sociometric status. *Child Development, 58,* 324–340.

Rabiner, D., & Coie, J. (1989). Effect of expectancy inductions on rejected children's acceptance by unfamiliar peers. *Developmental Psychology, 25,* 450–475.

Renshaw, P. D., & Asher, S. R. (1983). Children's goals and strategies for social interaction. *Merrill-Palmer Quarterly, 29,* 353–374.

Repetti, R. L. (1989). Effects of daily workload on subsequent behavior during marital interaction: The roles of social withdrawal and spouse support. *Journal of Personality & Social Psychology, 57,* 651–659.

Repetti, R. L. (1993, April). *The effects of daily social and academic experiences on children's subsequent interactions with parents.* Poster presented at the Biennial Meeting of the Society for Research in Child Development, New Orleans, LA.

Rubin, K. H., & Mills, R.S.L. (1990). Maternal beliefs about adaptive and maladaptive social behaviors in normal, aggressive and withdrawn preschoolers. *Journal of Abnormal Child Psychology, 18,* 419–435.

Rubin, K. H., Mills, R.S.L., & Rose-Krasnor, L. (1989). Maternal beliefs and children's competence. In B. Schneider, G. Attili, J. Nadel, & R. Weissberg (Eds.), *Social competence in developmental perspective* (pp. 313–331). Amsterdam: Klewer Academic.

Rubin, Z., & Sloman, J. (1984). How parents influence their children's friendships. In M. Lewis (Ed.), *Beyond the dyad* (pp. 223–250). New York: Plenum.

Russell, A., & Finnie, V. (1990). Preschool children's social status and maternal instructions to assist group entry. *Developmental Psychology, 26*(4), 603–611.

Schaefer, E. S., Edgerton, M., & Aaronson, M. (1978). *Classroom behavior inventory.* Unpublished form, University of North Carolina at Chapel Hill, NC.

Schank, R. C., & Abelson, R. P. (1977). *Scripts, plans, goals and understanding.* Hillsdale, NJ: Lawrence Erlbaum Associates.

Spitzer, S., Estock, S., Cupp, R., Isley-Paradise, S., & Parke, R. D. (1992). *Parental influence and efficacy beliefs and children's social acceptance.* Unpublished manuscript, University of California, Riverside, CA.

Sroufe, L. A., & Fleeson, J. (1986). Attachment and the construction of relationships. In W. W. Hartup & Z. Rubin (Eds.), *Relationships and development* (pp. 51–72). Hillsdale, NJ: Lawrence Erlbaum Associates.

Steinberg, L. (1986). Latchkey children and susceptibility to peer pressure: An ecological analysis. *Developmental Psychology, 22,* 433–439.

Suzuki, H. H. (1980). The Asian-American family. In M. Fantine & R. Cardenas (Eds.), *Parenting in a multicultural society.* New York: Congman.

Tietjen, A. (1985). Relationships between the social networks of Swedish mothers and their children. *International Journal of Behavioral Development, 8,* 195–216.

Tinsley, B. R., & Parke, R. D. (1984). The person-environment relationship: Lessons from families with preterm infants. In D. Magnusson & V. Allen (Eds.), *Human development: An interactional perspective* (pp. 93–110). New York: Academic Press.

# 6

# The Social Adaptation of Children in Classrooms: A Measure of Family Childrearing Effectiveness

Sheppard G. Kellam
*The Johns Hopkins School of Hygiene and Public Health*

At any point in the life course, individuals in every society are involved in a set of social fields. A child in first grade might be a member of a family, a classroom, and the beginning of a peer group comprised mainly of classmates (Kellam, Branch, Agrawal, & Ensminger, 1975). The family has the primary role of preparing the child's transition and supporting the child's meeting the social task demands in each of these social fields. The effectiveness of childrearing family structure and processes can best be understood, therefore, by studies that include the child's successes and failures in other social fields along the life course.

Within each stage of life the family has a particular but varied relevance to the individual. In the first stages there is clearly a major responsibility in the family for obtaining and/or administering prenatal, perinatal, and preschool care and preparation for later transitions. But as the life course continues, different social fields become more important components in an individual's social adaptation. For instance, regulating the young child's peer relations is mostly under the family jurisdiction, whereas supporting the child's behavior and achievement in the classroom is more collaborative and supportive of the teacher's role, with jurisdiction regulated by law, school policy, and negotiation.

In this chapter we briefly summarize the *developmental epidemiological* orientation and a conceptual framework involving stages of life, social fields, and *social adaptation*. More extended discussions can be found in prior publications (Kellam, 1990; Kellam et al., 1975; Kellam & Ensminger, 1980; Kellam & Rebok, 1992). We then present data summarizing and extending earlier analyses of variation in the adult composition of the families raising elementary school children in Woodlawn, a very poor African American community on the south side of Chicago. We include similar new data for comparison

147

from five more varied urban areas in Baltimore, where prevention intervention trials have been carried out directed at early risk behaviors and characteristics of classroom and peer group. New family intervention trials are now being developed.

The role of family is then addressed in the children's behavioral responses to the specific tasks in the first-grade classrooms, and their course from first grade through middle adolescence. The evolving relationships among the child's maladaptive behavioral responses to each task is presented next. Finally, we describe studies of the malleability of the children's maladaptive behavioral responses, making use of two preventive trials aimed at specific early maladaptive behavioral responses. Gender differences are profoundly important in all of these steps involving the children and are addressed as they appear.

The central thesis of this chapter is that an important family role is to enhance the child's chances of success in responding to social task demands, including the child's capacity for correcting maladaptive responses. This does not mean that the child's failure or success is exclusively due to the family. Biological and prior social learning in the child, family resources, parental practices, characteristics of school, teacher, classmates, peers, and community all may contribute to the child's behavioral responses to social task demands. With so many influences, children will obviously vary greatly in their capacity for socially adaptive responses to social task demands in specific social fields. Such variation in children requires innovation sometimes beyond family capabilities, particularly in the case of children with limited capacity for adaptive innovation when faced with a specific social task demand.

Studies of variation in the success of children require developmental modeling within epidemiologically defined populations. Such modeling includes not only family characteristics, but also characteristics of the child and the adequacy of the child's responses to specific tasks in a specific social field such as classroom or peer group. The characteristics of the specific social field itself are also needed in the modeling. Three scientific perspectives are required by this view of research on family effectiveness. The first is a life course developmental perspective that assesses the child's career not only in the family but in other social fields over the life course. The second is an epidemiological perspective that assesses variation in families and children's courses in an ecologically defined population. The third is an intervention perspective that assesses malleability in the children's maladaptive responses when these occur (Kellam, 1990; Kellam & Rebok, 1992). Through these three perspectives this chapter is about understanding the child's behavioral responses to classroom social task demands as an outcome of family childrearing. The research we present for this purpose is developmental epidemiologically-based; the demand/response aspects are what we have termed *social adaptational*. The first step is a brief description of what we mean by *developmental epidemiology* and by *social adaptation* and *social adaptational status*.

# DEVELOPMENTAL EPIDEMIOLOGY, SOCIAL ADAPTATION, AND SOCIAL ADAPTATIONAL STATUS

Developmental epidemiology is derived from the integration of life course development with community epidemiology (Kellam, 1990; Kellam & Ensminger, 1980). Bringing these two core scientific perspectives together provides the conceptual framework and methods for mapping developmental paths within representative samples from an ecologically valid defined community population over significant portions of the life course. A core concept underlying this integrated perspective is the tracking of total populations or of representative samples of populations over time and defined stages of development.

In contrast to a more demographic epidemiological perspective concerned with larger population characteristics, community epidemiology is focused on fairly small populations in their environments such as the neighborhood or a factory and its work force. We hold constant general characteristics of the community such as poverty and ethnicity, and examine variation in processes within the community that explain variation in outcomes. In the earlier Woodlawn studies, for example, we asked why some children in this very poor, Black community achieved poorly or behaved aggressively, whereas others succeeded very well at both school achievement and prosocial behavior.

When coupled with the developmental perspective, community epidemiology allows study of the developmental paths within specific cohorts of children who develop toward health and social adaptation, compared to those in the same community and cohort who develop disorders and/or social maladaptation. This is accomplished by examining variation in the children and in characteristics of such social fields as family, classroom, or peer group within the community. From a developmental epidemiological perspective, our effort is to explain variation in developmental paths including antecedents, mediators, moderators, and outcomes within or across neighborhoods or other fairly small populations.

By starting with epidemiologically defined populations, we can control selection bias; calculate rates of the antecedents, mediators, moderators, and outcomes; and examine variation in the function of hypothesized mediators or moderators in their relationships to each other and to the outcome. This population-based strategy informs us about development and prevention in a particular community. It then requires direct and systematic replication in similar or different communities.

Social adaptation and social adaptational status (SAS) refer to the adequacy of performance of individuals within their immediate environments. Within the community and closely related to the developmental stages of its individuals are main social fields in which individuals face social task demands that require behavioral responses. SAS refers to the adequacy of behavioral responses of the individual to the social task demands in particular social fields at particular stages of life. We have termed this interactive process of demand/response *social adap-*

*tation,* and the judgments of adequacy of the individual's performance by powerful people such as parents, teachers, and supervisors SAS (Kellam et al., 1975).

A person or persons we have termed the *natural rater(s)* defines the specific social task demands that confront individuals and rates the adequacy of the individual's performance of the tasks. Parents function as natural raters in the family, teachers are natural raters of students in the classroom, and important peers are natural raters of the child's accommodation to peer demands. In addition to the actual performance of individuals, chance, idiosyncrasies of the natural rater, and the conformity of the individual with the others in the social field may all play roles in the natural rater's judgments of adequacy of performance (Kellam, 1990; Kellam et al., 1975; Kellam & Ensminger, 1980).

This framework distinguishes social task performance from *psychological well-being* (PWB). The latter concerns internal states such as symptoms, syndromes, or disorders involving anxiety, depression, bizarre feelings and thoughts, self-esteem, neuropsychological processes, and physiological status. On the other hand, social adaptational status is external to the individual.

The difference between SAS and PWB is subtle but distinct. The failing math grade is an example of SAS, whereas the depression the child may feel prior to taking the test or as a consequence of the grade is an example of PWB. The two domains may be highly interrelated, but they quite clearly represent two different conceptual domains; and problems in each have very different long-term outcomes. Gender differences in the developmental paths over the course of first grade through high school are strongly related to the distinction between SAS and PWB (Ensminger, Kellam, & Rubin, 1983; Kellam, Brown, Rubin, & Ensminger, 1983; Kellam et al., 1991).

It is important to family research concerned with child outcomes that SAS and PWB be measured separately to avoid confounding one with the other (Bank, Dishion, Skinner, & Patterson, 1990). Throughout our work in Woodlawn and now in Baltimore, the developmental relationships between these two domains have been central to the questions addressed in our developmental epidemiological and prevention research. What are the influences of SAS on PWB and vice versa? Are PWB and SAS reciprocal in their effects? How do characteristics of family and the other main social fields influence SAS and PWB and their interrelationships over time and life transitions?

*The Social Tasks of the Classroom.* In Woodlawn, we made assessments of the classroom performance of all first graders between 1964 and 1968 at first report card, mid-year, and at end of first grade, and again at end of third grade. There was a follow-up assessment of a sample of those children who were still in Woodlawn in third grade. These assessments were coupled with service and evaluation programs (Kellam et al., 1975) and were supported by a community board composed of leaders from the community's larger citizen organizations (Kellam & Branch, 1971; Kellam, Branch, Agrawal, & Grabill, 1972; Kellam & Rebok, 1992).

Our primary instrument, the Teacher's Observation of Classroom Adaptation (TOCA), was developed based on teacher reports of social tasks they expected children to perform in the classroom. To construct the TOCA scales, we asked the 57 Woodlawn first-grade teachers of 1964–1965 to submit lists delineating the ways children performed maladaptively in the classroom. Fifty-three teachers responded and 435 maladaptive behaviors were noted. Two research staff members then independently grouped these into five categories of social tasks: social contact, authority acceptance, maturation, cognitive achievement, and concentration (Kellam et al., 1975). An interview was constructed to be done in a private location in the school with a research staff member. The first phase was involved in defining the purpose and working through the trust issues such as whether we were rating the children or the teacher, ensuring confidentiality; the second part was the actual ratings of each child; and the third was devoted to termination, resolving concerns and discussing the next stages of the research. The interview was then tested for reliability and validity and employed as a core measure in the Woodlawn studies over the next decade.

A revised version of TOCA (TOCA-R) has been used as a major periodic assessment instrument for the Baltimore prevention trials. The TOCA-R further defines the basic social task demands of the teacher under the following groups: (a) social contact, (b) authority acceptance, (c) concentration, and (d) achievement. Psychometric properties of TOCA-R are reported by Werthamer-Larsson, Kellam, and Wheeler (1991).

## VARIATION IN CHILDREARING FAMILIES IN WOODLAWN AND BALTIMORE

In the late 1960s, individuals in U.S. society tended to perceive the family in a highly stereotyped fashion consisting of the two biological parents living with their two or three children in a single home or apartment (Schneider, 1968). Variation in the family has been an important interest of anthropologists, as illustrated by Minturn and Lambert's (1964) study of family structure in six cultures. However, it is still not a centrally prominent part of family research in our own society despite exceedingly high divorce rates in many strata and communities, important research on the consequences of marital discord and divorce, and the increasing number of families that are not stereotypical (Atkeson, Forehand, & Richkard, 1982; Emery, 1982; Fergusson, Horwood, & Lynskey, 1992; Hetherington, Cox, & Cox, 1985; Long & Forehand, 1987; Rutter, 1971, 1979; Wallerstein & Kelly, 1980).

Childbearing and childrearing by individuals or couples during marriage, divorce, and separation lead inexorably to variation in childrearing family types. This changing composition of family members taking part in the childrearing is highly likely to influence the rearing and the articulations of the family with the other main social fields to which the child must adapt. In addition, there are rising rates of young unprepared teen mothers and high poverty coupled with welfare systems that pay mothers only when they are without fathers. These combined factors should impel investigators to examine the resultant family types and how they operate in relation to childrearing and child outcomes.

Our developmental epidemiological orientation focuses on such variation within a community over a significant portion of the life course; and since 1977 we have published such studies of variation in family types in Woodlawn (Ensminger et al., 1983; Ensminger, & Slusarcick, 1992; Hunter, & Ensminger, 1992; Kellam, 1990; Kellam, Adams, Brown, & Ensminger, 1982; Kellam, Ensminger, & Turner, 1977; Kellam, Simon, & Ensminger, 1983; Pearson, Hunter, Ensminger, & Kellam, 1990).

In Woodlawn, there were 79 different combinations of adults in the homes of the total first-grade cohort in 1964 and 86 family types in 1966. This marked variation in the adult members of households of the children could be categorized at different levels of aggregation: the mother-alone family that included the mother as the only adult raising her children; mother/father families with and without other adults; mother/grandmother families in which the father was absent leaving the mother and grandmother raising the children; mother and aunt families in which father and grandmother were absent; mother/stepfather families with or without others present but the father being absent; and various other less frequent types of family membership (Kellam et al., 1977).

The frequencies of family combinations can be seen in the Woodlawn table (see Table 6.1), with mother alone being a prominent type. The Baltimore table (see Table 6.2) shows the frequencies of childrearing families in the five urban areas in which the prevention research described later is being done. These ares vary in socioeconomic status (SES) and other characteristics, and the frequencies of mother-alone families can be seen to reflect this variation.[1]

TABLE 6.1
Comparison of Family Type:
Chicago–Woodlawn Area ($N$ = 1,391)

| Relation | N | % |
|---|---|---|
| Mother-father | 563 | 40.5 |
| Mother-alone | 516 | 37.2 |
| Mother-grandmother | 76 | 5.4 |
| Mother-stepfather | 56 | 4.0 |
| Mother and others | 45 | 3.2 |
| Grandmother families | 41 | 2.9 |
| Mother-aunt | 29 | 2.0 |
| Other adult families | 24 | 1.7 |
| Father families | 20 | 1.4 |
| Aunt families | 12 | .8 |

[1] These data were analyzed by Drs. Jane Pearson and Andrea Hunter in the course of Annual follow up of two preventive intervention randomized field trials. It was a central activity of the Johns Hopkins Prevention Research Center.

TABLE 6.2
Comparisons of Family Type by Five Baltimore Urban Areas in Grade Four

| Relation | Area 1 | | Area 2 | | Area 3 | | Area 4 | | Area 5 | |
|---|---|---|---|---|---|---|---|---|---|---|
| | N | % | N | % | N | % | N | % | N | % |
| Mother-father | 57 | 51.4 | 21 | 9.4 | 42 | 20.1 | 49 | 35.5 | 76 | 65.0 |
| Mother Alone | 19 | 17.1 | 136 | 61.0 | 72 | 34.4 | 33 | 23.9 | 19 | 16.2 |
| Mother-grandmother | 9 | 8.1 | 13 | 5.8 | 33 | 15.8 | 13 | 9.4 | 5 | 4.3 |
| Mother-Stepfather | 8 | 7.2 | 7 | 3.1 | 7 | 3.3 | 4 | 2.9 | 5 | 4.3 |
| Mother and others | 7 | 6.3 | 21 | 9.4 | 19 | 9.1 | 16 | 11.9 | 5 | 4.3 |
| Grandmother Families | 3 | 2.7 | 10 | 4.5 | 13 | 6.2 | 13 | 9.4 | 1 | .9 |
| Mother-aunt | 2 | 1.8 | 4 | 1.8 | 12 | 5.7 | 3 | 2.2 | 2 | 1.7 |
| Other adult families | 0 | 0.0 | 4 | 1.8 | 3 | 1.0 | 3 | 2.2 | 0 | 0.0 |
| Father families | 5 | 4.5 | 4 | 1.8 | 5 | 2.4 | 4 | 2.9 | 2 | 1.7 |
| Aunt families | 1 | .9 | 3 | 1.3 | 4 | 1.9 | 0 | 0.0 | 2 | 1.7 |
| Missing | 58 | | 41 | | 57 | | 60 | | 70 | |
| Total* | 169 | 100.0 | 264 | 100.0 | 266 | 100.0 | 198 | 100.0 | 187 | 100.0 |

*Percentages equal 100.0 due to rounding.

The purpose in examining this variation is to call attention to the many combinations of adults and to variation in their frequencies across the communities in which they reside. Family processes of childrearing will vary as a function of both family and community variation.

In the Woodlawn studies, the stability of family types was assessed over the course of first grade through age 16 or 17. Seventy percent of mother-alone families were mother-alone 10 years after first-grade assessment. At some time during this decade, mother-alone families were at markedly increased risk of being on welfare, being at higher risk for depressive symptoms, having less membership in formal social organizations, and probably most important, having minimal or no help in childrearing (Brown, Adams, & Kellam, 1981; Kellam, Adams, Brown, & Ensminger, 1982). Although there may have been relatives or friends with whom they socialized, these mothers reported very consistently that seldom was anyone available to help in the daily affectional, rule-setting, behavior monitoring, and learning environment aspects of childrearing. The mothers who were alone raising their children were very likely to be teenagers, who if they had ever been married were highly likely to have had their marriages dissolved by the time the index children were in first grade.

Mother/grandmother families were particularly important and comprised 10% of the families of Woodlawn first graders in the 1966–1967 cohort. The parenting involvement of these grandmothers was considerable, second only to the mother in this cohort of families. It was characterized by roles involving punishment and support as well as control. The kinds of parenting by grandmothers differed by the type of family with greatest involvement in mother-absent homes. If the grandmother was employed, she was just as likely to be engaged in parenting activities (Pearson et al., 1990).

Children's family arrangements were not only varied, but over time they experienced great fluidity in the adults present in the home. By the time of third grade, the mother/grandmother families had decreased in number sharply, with the result most often being a mother-alone family (Kellam, Adams, Brown, & Ensminger, 1982). Changes in parents' martial status and entrances and exits of relatives were frequent causes of change in family composition (Hunter & Ensminger, 1992).

## SOCIAL ADAPTATIONAL STATUS AND VARIATION AMONG FAMILIES

The Woodlawn studies (Ensminger, 1990; Ensminger et al., 1983; Ensminger & Slusarcick, 1992; Kellam et al., 1975; Kellam, Brown, & Fleming, 1982; Kellam et al., 1983) demonstrate that as early as first grade, the period of transition into school, there are clearly identifiable antecedents leading to specific outcomes of psychopathology, delinquency, and heavy drug use in adolescence and beyond. Even though family processes that could explain the linkages were not included in the analyses, family variation played an important role in these studies. In the case of delinquency and violent behavior in adolescence, higher risk families such as mother alone produced more aggressive first grade children than did lower risk ones such as mother/father or mother/grandmother. However, the aggressive children raised in the lower risk families were at greater risk for later delinquency even though they were fewer in number (Ensminger et al., 1983).

We hypothesize that the lower risk families had more harmonious adults (Ferguson et al., 1992; Hetherington et al., 1985; Rutter, 1971, 1979); more effective behavior management (Patterson, 1982; Patterson, Reid, & Dishion, 1991); and/or parenting adults who combined warmth with consistent rules (Baumrind, 1971). Higher risk families not only are predicted to have less of the strengths, but also are poorer, live in worse neighborhoods, and send their children to schools with peers from similarly poor families (Kellam et al., 1977, 1982).

The role of the family in the social adaptational process is intricately woven together with that of the school, but in the context of the community with its social and physical environment. One example of how school environment influences the social adaptational process is the common policy of assigning children to ability-grouped classrooms where their aggressive or nonaggressive behavior is enhanced (Kellam, 1988; Werthamer-Larsson et al., 1991). Lower ability-grouped classrooms in Woodlawn had rates of aggression of 60% or higher, whereas higher ability-classrooms had rates often as low as 5%. In one class, being aggressive was deviant, whereas in another not being aggressive was deviant. Many of the findings from the Woodlawn developmental epidemiological studies suggest that families influence the early SAS of children in the classroom; and then the children's SAS in the classroom influences their school and later careers, with the family continuing to play a role as well.

The findings on early aggressive behavior as a predictor of later problems should be viewed as outcomes of this neighborhood/family/school/classroom social context. In Woodlawn, aggressive behavior by males in the first-grade classroom was a predictor of increased teenage delinquency and violence, and of drug, alcohol, and cigarette use. Similar findings have emerged in many other studies (Conger & Miller, 1966; Kaplan, 1980; Lefkowitz, Eron, Walden, & Huesman, 1977; Mitchell & Rosa, 1981; Robins, 1978; Spivak, Marcus, & Swift, 1986; Tremblay et al., 1992).

In Woodlawn and in other studies, the combination of early shy and aggressive behaviors in first-grade males was associated with higher levels of delinquency and substance use than aggressive behavior alone. This shy/aggressive combination takes the form of children who are loners but who break rules and fight as well. It is very much like the *DSM-III* undersocialized conduct disorder (Block, Block, & Keys, 1988; Ensminger et al., 1983; Farrington,

Gallagher, Morley, St. Ledger, & West, 1988; Farrington & Gunn, 1985; Hans, Marcus, Henson, Auerbach, & Mirsky, 1992; Kellam et al., 1983; McCord, 1988; Schwartzman, Ledingham, & Serbin, 1985). Learning problems have been found to predict psychiatric distress, particularly depressed mood (Kellam, 1990; Kellam et al., 1983; Kohlberg, Ricks, & Snarey, 1984; Shaffer et al., 1979). Poor achievement and early aggressive behavior together are important antecedents of school dropout as well (Ensminger & Slusarcick, 1992).

Another Woodlawn study linked poor family and classroom SAS in first grade to later maladaptive behaviors. Ensminger and Slusarcick (1992) examined the developmental paths toward high school graduation or dropout for the same cohort. Over half the cohort of first graders with school records did not graduate. Dropouts were compared with graduates in their family background, family environment, SAS during first grade, and their educational hopes and expectations. Low grades and aggressive behavior in first grade led to later dropout for males, with maternal education and poverty—both highly associated with family type—playing strong roles in this relationship to drop out.

Recent Woodlawn analyses have focused on the multiple problem children. One question is whether sexual activity is best considered in the same paradigm as adolescent substance use and assault or separately. Among Woodlawn adolescents ($N = 705$) followed longitudinally since first grade, three questions were examined: (a) How do these three behaviors co-occur? (b) What are their early and concurrent family and school precursors? (c) What are their relations with adolescent school behavior? The three most frequent patterns were compared: no problem behaviors; only sexual activity; and the combination of sexual activity, heavy substance use, and/or assault. In general, the multiproblem adolescents differed from the other adolescents in their behavior and in lower parental supervision. Sex-only females differed from the no-problem girls in their family origins, with maternal early sexual behavior an important antecedent in the context of family type (Ensminger, 1990).

These results suggest that by examining adolescent behaviors and their co-occurring combinations in epidemiologically defined populations, variations in pathways to deviance can be better understood. They also underline the importance of including family and school structure and processes in the context of community in the analytic modeling. Furthermore, the children's behavioral responses to the classroom social task demands are potentially both a consequence of family processes as well as antecedents of family processes and the child's life course in the school, the classroom, and beyond. The structure of the classrooms, the characteristics of the classmates and peer groups, and the characteristics of the schools can moderate the effects of family processes.

We turn now to the Baltimore studies for assessing the evolving patterns of maladaptation to first grade and their malleability in order to lay out what the SAS child outcomes should include for research on family structure and processes.

# EVOLVING RELATIONSHIPS AMONG SOCIAL
# MALADAPTATIONAL RESPONSES

The social adaptation to the classroom does not result in independent responses by the child, but rather a pattern of evolving interrelated behavioral responses. Family outcomes might be viewed in terms of the levels and relationships from fall to spring of first grade among teacher ratings of shy and aggressive behaviors, concentration problems, achievement test scores—all measures of social maladaptive responses to classroom social task demands and self-reports of depression, a PWB measure (Kellam et al., 1991). Such analyses were derived from the first of two cohorts of first-grade children in the Baltimore prevention trials, involving roughly 1,000 children who entered 19 public elementary schools in the eastern half of the city. Data were gathered at the time of the first report card, approximately 8 weeks into the school year, and again toward the end of the year.

Using multiple regression and log linear methods, we looked cross-sectionally and then longitudinally at aggressive and shy behaviors and concentration problems first, then added school achievement test scores to these three, and finally added child self-reports of depressive symptoms to the model. To assess the evolving relationships and directions, we used a cross-lagged regression model in which pairs of variables were isolated to study the longitudinal relationships among the five variables from fall to spring of first grade. The results summarized here are described in detail in Kellam et al. (1991).

Only data from the 473 control children were analyzed for the longitudinal studies because the data from the other children were confounded over the course of first grade by the two preventive intervention trials. Analyses were done separately by gender (234 males, 239 females).

The central role of concentration problems emerged in these analyses. From fall to spring in first grade, concentration problems led to shy and aggressive behavior and poor achievement in both genders and to depressive symptoms among females. Concentration problems almost never occurred by themselves; they were strongly associated with aggressive behavior, but equally strongly associated with shy behavior. A summary of the patterns of co-occurrence for each gender is contained in Fig. 6.1 and 6.2.

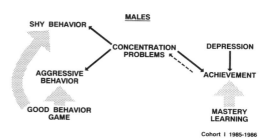

FIG. 6.1. Course of classroom social adaptational status and depression from fall to spring of first grade.

157

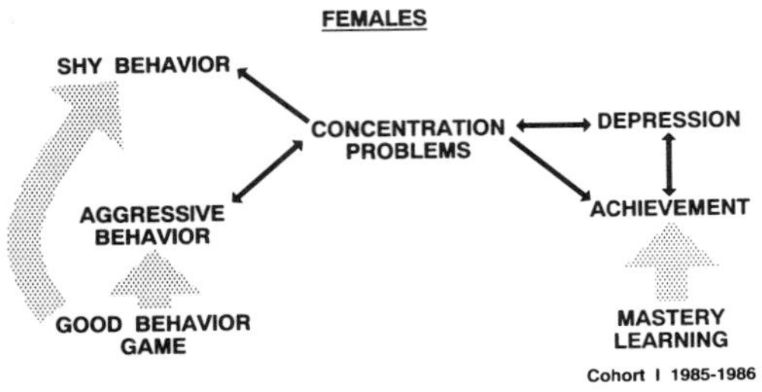

FEMALES

FIG. 6.2. Course of classroom social adaptational status and depression from fall to spring of first grade.

Based on these results, we hypothesize that concentration problems are a common latent condition underlying both social maladaptation and psychological well-being. Rather than a categorical attentional disorder, concentration problems may be evidence of general developmental psychopathology with potential for expression in many forms including shy and/or aggressive behavior, depressed affect, and poor learning.

Among females, but not males, there was evidence for reciprocal relationships between components of classroom SAS and between SAS and PWB (see Fig. 6.2). For example, depressive symptoms led to poor achievement in both males and females, whereas poor achievement led to depressive symptoms in females but not males, at least over the first-grade year. Similarly, for females, concentration problems in the fall preceded aggressive behavior in the spring, and aggressive behavior in the fall also predicted concentration problems later. The presence or absence of these reciprocal relationships may reflect an important aspect of gender differences that may be part of the explanation of later gender differences in prevalence of aggression and depression. The reciprocal relationships that characterize first-grade girls rather than boys suggests the hypothesis that girls in the first grade classroom, and possibly in other social fields, have greater concern with the judgments of natural raters than boys. These results support recent findings showing that first-grade girls are more responsive to parents' evaluation of their academic achievement, whereas first-grade boys rely more on self-evaluations (Entwisle, Alexander, Pallas, & Cadigan, 1987; Roberts, 1991).

These results on reciprocities provide important epidemiological data on the developmental paths leading to problem outcomes. A plausible reciprocal effects hypothesis is that depression leads to poor achievement, which in turn leads to more depression, and so on with increasing effects. The question facing family research is the role of family in these complex SAS responses to the classroom. The role of family in the development of the child's skills in attention, social participation, reducing aggression, enhancing achievement, and in psychological well-being are all specific aspects of family outcomes regarding child-rearing.

# THE USE OF PREVENTIVE TRIALS TO STUDY
## SOCIAL ADAPTATION

Preventive intervention trials represent an important strategy for examining influences on children's development. In our work at the Johns Hopkins Prevention Research Center in Baltimore, we have developed and implemented two experimental field trials directed at specific antecedents in the developmental models described here to help determine whether the risk of specific later problem outcomes can be reduced, and the role of family, classroom, and peer processes in the developmental outcomes (Kellam et al., 1991). Periodic longitudinal outcome evaluations of two Baltimore trials are being conducted for both these theoretical and utilitarian purposes. They provide data on the malleability of the early risk behavioral responses and their etiologic significance for outcomes, and these programs if effective may improve the risk of such outcomes in specific populations.

The behavioral responses targeted had been demonstrated to be predictors for later antisocial behavior, criminality, heavy substance use, and psychiatric distress. A team-based behavior management strategy called the Good Behavior Game (GBG; Barrish, Saunders, & Wolfe, 1969) targeted aggressive behavior in the classroom as measured by teacher and peer ratings (Dolan et al., in press). This preventive intervention promoted good behavior by rewarding teams that did not exceed maladaptive behavior standards. A second preventive intervention, Mastery Learning (ML), was aimed at improving cognitive skills involved in reading (Dolan et al., in press). The goal was to determine whether improved mastery of reading and other core skills would reduce the risk of later psychiatric symptoms, particularly depressive symptoms and possibly depressive disorder.

These ongoing population-based prevention trials are based on a strong collaborative relationship with the Baltimore City Public Schools and with the wider community of parents whose children are involved in the studies. Such close multiple community partnerships are essential for this type of population- and community-based research (Kellam et al., 1971; Kellam & Branch, 1972; Kellam, 1990; Rebok et al., 1991). In their collaborative role, leaders in the Baltimore City Public Schools designated a widely varied set of elementary schools in the eastern half of Baltimore City, where five quite different urban areas were selected. Some of the areas exhibited many of the characteristics of community decay and poverty that are associated with high risk of problem behavior. Some were more middle-class areas and had many characteristics of community organization and access to resources associated with lower risk. Each urban area was served by at least three public elementary schools with two or more first-grade classrooms.

One or two of the set of schools in each urban area was randomly assigned as a control school, another as a GBG school, and the third (or fourth) as an ML school. Within each intervention school, children were randomly assigned to an intervention classroom or a control classroom, with teachers also randomly designated. The interventions were implemented over 2 years for each cohort after intensive baseline assessments. Classrooms of children were kept together over the 2 years.

The design for this preventive trial was directed at control over (a) school differences; and (b) leakage or spillover effects that might happen if all or part of the intervention strategies were adopted in the comparison classrooms. These problems were addressed in the research design by having both internal comparison classrooms within the intervention schools and external comparison classrooms in schools not receiving any special intervention. This design also controlled for critical school level effects (Rutter, Maughan, Mortimore, Ouston, & Smith, 1979).

The results reported here focus on impact at the end of the first-grade year. To be included in the analyses, all students had to remain in the same design condition for the entire year. Students who transferred into the school system or who left the system during the first-grade year were not included in these analyses. Eight hundred sixty-four students met these criteria. The sample for the GBG condition was 182 students from eight classrooms; the sample for the GBG internal control condition was 107 from six classrooms; and the sample for the external control condition was 212 from 10 classrooms. The sample for the ML condition was 207 students from 9 classrooms; the sample for the ML internal control condition was 156 from 7 classrooms.

Teacher-rated aggressive behavior on the TOCA-R peer nominations of aggressive behavior, and standardized student achievement data from the California Achievement Test (CAT, Forms E and F) were assessed for the GBG, ML, internal control, and external control conditions. Assessments were conducted in the fall of first grade at first report card time and in the following spring near the end of first grade.

As hypothesized, short-term proximal or direct effects of both the GBG and ML interventions on their target antecedents were found in our initial analyses of impact (Dolan et al., in press). For both males and females, the GBG had a significant impact on aggressive behavior as rated by teachers. Peer nominations of aggressive behavior among males by their classmates also were significantly reduced. By examining scatterplots of aggressive behavior ratings in the fall and the spring along with the regression slopes, it appeared that the more severe end of aggressive behavior was affected by the GBG for both genders. We hypothesize that changes in aggressive behavior resulting from the GBG intervention were due to group pressure to respond to team contingencies and classroom rewards for altering behavior.

Cautions should be noted in the GBG reports. Although teacher ratings and peer nominations are considered important measures of SAS, they are contaminated by the fact that both the teacher and classmates were intervention agents and knowledgeable about specific outcome targets. Alternatively, they may have rated children more harshly because the consequences of maladaptation increased with the GBG. There was some evidence of this in the results from the earlier Woodlawn prevention trials (Kellam et al., 1975). Independent observers who were time-sampling classroom behavior were an important adjunct measure to gain control of this problem. These revealed an increase in on-task behavior in the GBG classrooms compared to the control classrooms (Brown, 1993).

For the ML intervention, we found significant short-term impact on reading achievement at the end of the spring of first grade for both males and females, in covariance analyses controlling for baseline achievement. Importantly, the nature of the intervention impact differed by gender. Female high achievers benefited more from the ML intervention than female low achievers, whereas male low achievers benefited more than male high achievers. From fall to spring of first grade neither intervention had impact on the proximal target of the other, either as a main effect or interaction that involved effects on their own proximal target as a condition for altering the proximal target of the other. Each intervention thus appears to be specific to its own proximal target (Dolan et al., 1993).

The choice of first grade as a context for experimental intervention is consistent with empirical evidence as well as with our developmental epidemiological and life-course perspective. Clearly, the transition to first grade entails adaptation to a new social field and a new and potentially difficult set of social, behavioral, and cognitive developmental tasks. It provides a specific time period during which family influences on the child's SAS and PWB are mediated in some way by school influences. Moreover, these early patterns of success or failure in social adaptation to the early elementary school environment have significant consequences across the life span in various social fields. The use of experimental interventions targeted at antecedent risk behaviors provides a powerful way of addressing questions about the mediating and moderating effects of contexts including but beyond the family on variations in behaviors.

In the prevention research approach we have described, the study populations and their environments are epidemiologically defined and deliberately varied. This enables us to examine the results as they apply to specific populations and to determine whether the impact of the trial differs for subpopulations or under varying ecological conditions. We examine whether the effects of intervention are greatest among the groups with highest risk or whether the effects are greater, equal, or less among the lower risk groups (Brown, 1993). Similarly, further analyses are under way on the influence of classroom, peer, and family environments on children's development.

Analyses of the results of the two Baltimore preventive interventions demonstrated impact particularly for children in high-risk groups. We were surprised to find that the GBG appeared to reduce the level of aggressive behavior for children who were highly aggressive in the fall of first grade. Finding malleability in this subpopulation suggested that the level of severity in the fall was not a reflection of immutability, even with what might be considered a fairly low intensity of intervention.

The ML intervention led to significant gains in reading achievement scores on the California Achievement Test, compared to internal or external control conditions. Importantly, the reading scores for a subgroup of children in the fall of first grade who reported symptoms of depression were significantly lower than those of the other children. It was those initially depressed, low-scoring children who gained most in reading through the ML intervention. Again, we found malleability where we might not have expected it.

We are continuing to follow annually the same children through the transition to middle school and beyond to assess the slopes of impact in the children as a whole and to model variation in the slopes of impact among subgroups of the children. This follow-up analysis will also allow us to examine lagged effects of interventions across time and to test for the possibility of so-called sleeper effects. The follow-up analyses of the Baltimore preventive trials contribute to theory building by providing data on the malleability of the models being tested (Kellam & Rebok, 1992).

## THEORETICAL AND EMPIRICAL IMPLICATIONS

The importance of these results to family research is that the children who respond well to the intervention can be compared to the children who respond poorly or not at all. This experimental intervention into classroom social adaptational processes offers a window into the family's role in not only the child's responses but the child's ability to correct maladaptive responses. Do families engender adaptive capacity in their children? This may be a critical element of childrearing success of families, one that extends the concept of childrearing to include capacities for coping with unforeseen social task demands in social fields later in the life course.

The classroom is one of three social fields in which children are faced with social task demands. Developmental modeling of the behavioral responses of children to the social task demands in the peer group, in the classroom, and in the family itself are equally important arenas. Peer rejection, classroom poor achievement, and parental rejection are each evidence of social maladaptation by the child to specific social task demands. The study of the child's responses to these demands is critical to assessing family effectiveness in preparing and supporting the child for the social adaptational process in each social field.

The geographic boundaries of these social fields overlap; and when the demands in one social field conflict with those of another, the child has the difficult responsibility of differentiating between very complex social task demands. The parental family overlaps in its jurisdiction with that of the teacher and the peer group. The structural arrangements regarding who has authority to set the social task demands and rate the child's performance are vital to the child's success. Teachers and parents vary in their understanding of the optimal arrangements, including how to transfer authority over the child from the parent to the teacher at the classroom threshold. The kinds of authority transferred and the conditions for its exercise by the teacher are largely unstudied from the family research and child developmental perspectives.

In the early elementary school years the classroom is the major location for the child, and classmates are the most important peers. Social adaptation in the peer group, the classroom, or the family may not be consistent; and bringing about consistency through regulation of peers and negotiation with the teacher is an important family role. Family effectiveness in this area of articulation with the other social fields is a centrally important aspect of family function. The articulation of these three social fields from a social structural point of view should include consistency of social task demands as we work toward preventive intervention programs that enhance each socialization structure.

Analyses of developmental epidemiological data from the Woodlawn and Baltimore projects suggest that the classroom environment is an important area for further study. Ability grouping cited in both our earlier chapter and this one should be a major subject of investigation (Kellam, 1990). In many school districts, school policy results in marked differences in achievement level and aggressive behavior in first-grade classrooms within the same school. With children assigned to classrooms based on their kindergarten records or readiness for school test scores, the result is the institutionalization of aggressive behavior in some classrooms and nonaggressive behavior in others. Mental health disciplines have not investigated the results of this policy or its implications for child development and family/classroom relationships and partnerships. Family studies concerned with the child's social adaptational success should take into account whether the child is in a predominantly aggressive and/or poor achieving classroom, or one that is well-behaved and/or high achieving.

Citations in our Woodlawn and Baltimore studies emphasize parallel variations in families and in classroom environment. Family processes related to aggression and achievement can be markedly influenced by classroom processes stemming from the teacher and classmates. Families that are less effective at behavior management may find their children assigned to classrooms where many children are aggressive; this would further undermine family efforts.

The community in which the child's family/classroom/peer group resides is probably of greater importance at this time when at other stages of life (Suttles, 1972). Dictated by school policy, families most often send their children to the public school in their residential area that typically has well-defined catchment boundaries. The population of families and the elementary school in a community influence each other in the child's choices of classmates and friends and the composition of school and classroom. The social task demands of the family, classroom, and peer group in the context of community are highly interrelated and provide a vitally important set of forces that enhance or inhibit the child's growth and development. Therefore, the next stage of family research should include the study of structures and processes that support or hinder the work among the three main social fields in the context of community.

The social adaptational processes involving natural raters in the classroom, family, and peer group in the context of community are the scene of the basic struggles of the child. As important as mapping variation in children's developmental courses is the possibility of influencing the child's development through preventive intervention efforts. A life course developmental orientation integrated with that of community epidemiology, in conjunction with preventive interventions aimed at particular specified targets represents a powerful strategy for the next stage of research. The evidence from the most recent set of preventive trials done by us and other population-based prevention researchers suggest that there is more malleability in the children's developmental paths than we supposed. This provides important opportunities for improving the life-course outcomes of children and adults that our society cannot afford to disregard.

## ACKNOWLEDGMENTS

The contributions of the City of Baltimore, its families and children, and the administration of the Baltimore City Public Schools have been and continue to be enormous. The same should be said of the City of Chicago and its families and children, particularly those who lived in Woodlawn. The Prevention Program is a collaboration between the Baltimore City Public Schools and the Prevention Research Center of the Department of Mental Hygiene, The Johns Hopkins University School of Hygiene and Public Health. This work of the Prevention Program would not have been possible without the participation and support of the leadership, faculty, and staff of the school district. Our work has been based on the search for mutual shared interests in the assessments and the interventions, and has been carried out under the aegis of the board of school commissioners and the superintendent.

Dr. Walter Amprey, superintendent of Baltimore City Public Schools, and Director Dr. Juanita Lewis have overseen and guided the current work on follow-up and the new work on the next stages of intervention development and evaluation. Originally, it was Ms. Alice Pinderhughes, former superintendent of the Baltimore City Schools who worked out with the Prevention Research Center the collaborative arrangements. The assistance and support of the following have been vital to our program: Dr. Leonard Wheeler, former assistant superintendent for elementary schools who was for many years our major coordinator and school district liaison. Dr. Carla Ford, former supervisor, Office of Early Childhood Education, made continuing contributions to the intervention design and implementation monitoring.

The original search for a behavioral intervention to address the social adaptational process between teacher and children was led by Dr. Alan Harris, and the first implementor and supervisor was Dr. Jaylin Turkkan. Dr. Larry Dolan was overall field supervisor the first 2 years, followed by Dr. Lisa Werthamer-Larsson, who is on the Department of Mental Hygiene faculty and continues to play a key leadership role in the Prevention Research Center. Dr. James C. Anthony is P.I. of the drug abuse aspects of the center's work and a leader in the original design of the two intervention trials. Dr. C. Hendricks Brown played a key biostatistical and methodological role in this work and continues to consult with us as well as to analyze the direct observation data.

The leadership of Ms. Elva Edwards and her staff in community base-building and crisis back-up are essential aspects of the Center's work and are gratefully acknowledged. Our editor, Ms. Fionnuala Regan and our manuscript producer Ms. Alice Brogden did their usual fine job in spite of the difficulties of scientific jargon and the complex styles of the authors.

Portions of this manuscript appeared in more elaborated form in earlier publications.

The studies on which this chapter is based have been supported by the following grants, with supplements from the National Institute on Drug Abuse: National Institute of Mental Health, NIMH Grant Number P50 MH38725, Epidemiologic Prevention Center for Early Risk Behavior; NIMH Grant Number 1R01 MH42968, Periodic Outcome of Two Preventive Trials; and NIMH Grant Number 1R01 MH40859, Statistical Methods for Mental Health Preventive Trials; and for the follow-up NIDA Grant DA-00787.

# REFERENCES

Atkeson, B. M., Forehand, R. L., & Rickard, K. M. (1982). The effects of divorce on children. In B. B. Lahey & A. E. Kazdin (Eds.). Advances in clinical child psychology (Vol. 5, pp. 255–281).

Bank, L., Dishion, T. O., Skinner, M., & Patterson, G. R. (1990). Method variance in structural equation modeling: Living with "GLOP". In G. R. Patterson (Ed.), *Depression and aggression in family interactions* (pp. 247–279). Hillsdale, NJ: Lawrence Erlbaum Associates.

Barrish, H. H., Saunders, M., & Wolfe, M. D. (1969). Good Behavior Game. Effects of individual contingencies for group consequences and disruptive behavior in a classroom. *Journal of Applied Behavioral Analysis, 2,* 119–124.

Baumrind, D. (1971). Current patterns of parental authority. *Developmental Psychology Monographs, 4*(1, part 2).

Block, J., Block, J. H., & Keyes, S. (1988). Longitudinally foretelling drug usage in adolescence: Early childhood personality and environmental precursors. *Child Development, 59,* 336–355.

Brown, C. H., Adams, R. G., & Kellam, S. G. (1981). A longitudinal study of teenage motherhood and symptoms of distress: The Woodlawn Community Epidemiological Project. *Research in Community and Mental Health, 2,* 183–213.

Brown, C. H. (1993). Statistical methods for preventive trials in mental health. *Statistics in Medicine, 12,* 289–300.

Conger, J. J., & Miller, W. C. (1966). *Personality, social class and delinquency.* New York: Wiley.

Dolan, L. J., Kellam, S. G., Brown, C. H., Werthamer-Larsson, L., Rebok, G. W., Mayer, L. S., Laudolff, J., Turkkan, J., Ford, C., & Wheeler, L. (1993). The short-term impact of two classroom-based preventive interventions on aggressive and shy behaviors and poor achievement. *Journal of Applied Developmental Psychology, 14,* 317–345.

Emery, R. E. (1982). Interparental conflict and the children of discord and divorce. *Psychological Bulletin, 92,* 310–330.

Ensminger, M. E. (1990). Sexual activity and problem behaviors among black urban adolescents. *Child Development, 61,* 2032–2046.

Ensminger, M. E., Kellam, S. G., & Rubin, B. R. (1983). School and family origins of delinquency: Comparisons by sex. In K. T. Van Dusen & S. A. Mednick (Eds.), *Prospective studies of crime and delinquency* (pp. 73–97). Boston: Kluwer-Nijhoff.

Ensminger, M. E., & Slusarcick, A. L. (1992). Paths to high school graduation or dropout: A longitudinal study of a first-grade cohort. *Sociology of Education, 65,* 95–113.

Entwisle, D. R., Alexander, K. L., Pallas, A. M., & Cadigan, D. (1987). The emergent academic self-image of first graders: Its response to social structure. *Child Development, 58,* 1190–1206.

Farrington, D. P., Gallagher, B., Morley, L., St. Ledger, R. J., & West, D. J. (1988). Are there successful men from criminogenic backgrounds? *Psychiatry, 51,* 116–130.

Farrington, D. P., & Gunn, J. (Eds.). (1985). *Aggression and dangerousness.* New York: Wiley.

Ferguson, D. M., Horwood, L. J., & Lynskey, M. T. (1992). Family change, parental discord and early offending. *Journal of Child Psychology and Psychiatry 33,* 1059–1075.

Hans, S. L., Marcus, J., Henson, L., Auerbach, J. G., & Mirsky, A. F. (1992). *Interpersonal behavior of children at risk for schizophrenia.* Manuscript submitted for publication.

Hetherington, E. M., Cox, M., & Cox, R. (1985). Long-term effects of divorce and remarriage on the adjustment of children. *Journal of American Academy of Psychiatry, 24,* 518–530.

Hunter, A. G., & Ensminger, M. E. (1992). Diversity and fluidity in children's living arrangement: Family transitions in an urban Afro-American community. *Journal of Marriage and the Family, 54,* 418–426.

Kaplan, H. G. (1980). *Deviant behavior in defense of self.* New York: Academic Press.

Kellam, S. G. (1990). Developmental epidemiologic framework for family research on depression and aggression. In G. R. Patterson (Ed.), *Depression and aggression in family interactions* (pp. 11–48). Hillsdale, NJ: Lawrence Erlbaum Associates.

Kellam, S. G., Adams, R. G., Brown, C. H., & Ensminger, M. E. (1982). The long-term evolution of the family structure of teenage and older mothers. *Journal of Marriage and the Family,* 539–554.

Kellam, S. G., & Branch, J. D. (1971). An approach to community mental health: Analysis of basic problems. *Seminars in Psychiatry, 3,* 207–225.

Kellam, S. G., Branch, J. D., Agrawal, K. C., & Ensminger, M. E. (1975). *Mental health and going to school: The Woodlawn program of assessment, early intervention, and evaluation.* Chicago: University of Chicago Press.

Kellam, S. G., Branch, J. D., Agrawal, K. C., & Grabill, M. E. (1972). Woodlawn Mental Health Center: An evolving strategy for planning in community mental health. In Golann, S. E. & Eisdorfer, C. (Eds.), *Handbook of community mental health* (pp. 711–727). New York: Appleton-Century-Crofts.

Kellam, S. G., Brown, C. H., & Fleming, J. P. (1982). Social adaptation to first grade and teenage drug, alcohol and cigarette use. *The Journal of School Health, 52,* 301–306.

Kellam, S. G., Brown, C. H., Rubin, B. R., & Ensminger, M. E. (1983). Paths leading to teenage psychiatric symptoms and substance use: Developmental epidemiological studies in Woodlawn. In S. B. Guze, F. J. Earls, & J. E. Barrett (Eds.), *Childhood psychopathology and development* (pp. 17–51). New York: Raven Press.

Kellam, S. G., & Ensminger, M. E. (1980). Theory and method in child psychiatric epidemiology. In F. Earls (Ed.), *Studies of children* (pp. 145–180). New York: Prodist.

Kellam, S. G., Ensminger, M. E., & Turner, R. J. (1977). Family structure and the mental health of children. *Archives of General Psychiatry, 34,* 1012–1022.

Kellam, S. G., & Rebok, G. W. (1992). Building developmental and etiological theory through epidemiologically based preventive intervention trials. In J. McCord & R. E. Tremblay (Eds.), *Preventing antisocial behavior: Interventions from birth through adolescence* (pp. 162–195). New York: Guilford Press.

Kellam, S. G., Simon, M. B., & Ensminger, M. E. (1983). Antecedents in first grade of teenage substance use and psychological well-being: A ten-year community-wide prospective study. In D. F. Ricks & B. S. Dohrenwend (Eds.), *Origins of psychopathology* (pp. 17–42). Cambridge: Cambridge University Press.

Kellam, S. G., Werthamer-Larsson, L., Dolan, L., Brown, C. H., Mayer, L., Rebok, G. W., Anthony, J. C., Laudolff, J., Edelsohn, G., Wheeler, L. (1991). Developmental epidemiologically based preventive trials: Baseline modeling of early target behaviors and depressive symptoms. *American Journal of Community Psychology, 19,* 563–584.

Kohlberg, L., Ricks, D., & Snarey, J. (1984). Childhood development as a predictor of adaptation in adulthood. *Genetic Psychology Monographs, 110,* 91–172.

Lefkowitz, M. M., Eron, L. D., Walden, L. O., & Huesman, L. R. (1977). *Growing up to be violent.* New York: Pergamon Press.

Long, N., & Forehand, R. (1987). The effects of parental divorce and parental conflict on children: An overview. *Developmental and Behavioural Pediatrics, 8,* 292–296.

McCord, J. (1988). Parental behavior in the cycle of aggression. *Psychiatry, 51,* 14–23.

Minturn, L., Lambert, W. W. (1964). *Mothers of six cultures.* New York: Wiley.

Mitchell, S., & Rosa, P. (1981). Boyhood behavior problems as precursors of criminality: A fifteen-year follow-up study. *Journal of Child Psychology, 22,* 19–33.

Patterson, G. R. (1982). *Coercive family processes.* Eugene, OR: Castalia.

Patterson, G. R., Reid, J., & Dishion, T. (1991). *Antisocial Boys.* Eugene, OR: Castalia.

Pearson, J. L., Hunter, A. G., Ensminger, M. E., & Kellam, S. G. (1990). Black grandmothers in multigenerational households: Diversity in family structure and parenting involvement in the Woodlawn community. *Child Development, 61,* 434–442.

Roberts, T. (1991). Gender and the influence of evaluations on self-assessments in achievement settings. *Psychological Bulletin, 109,* 297–308.

Rebok, G. W., Kellam, S. G., Dolan, L. J., Werthamer-Larsson, L., Edwards, E. J., Mayer, L. S., Brown, C. H. (1991). Early risk behaviors: Process issues and problem areas in prevention research. *The Community Psychologist, 24,* 18–21.

Robins, L. N. (1978). Sturdy childhood predictors of adult antisocial behavior: Replications from longitudinal studies. *Psychological Medicine, 50,* 611–622.

Rutter, M. (1971). Parent-child separation: Psychological effects on the children. *Journal of Abnormal Child Psychology, 12,* 223–260.

Rutter, M. (1979). Protective factors in children's responses to stress and disadvantage. In M. W. Kent & J. E. Rolf (Eds.) *Primary prevention of psychopathology* (Vol. 3, pp. 49–74). Hanover, NH: University Press of New England.

Rutter, M., Maughan, B., Mortimore, P., & Ouston, J. with Smith, A. (1979). *Fifteen thousand hours: Secondary schools and their effects on children.* Cambridge, MA: Harvard University Press.

Schneider, D. M. (1968). *American kinship: A cultural account.* Englewood Cliffs, NJ: Prentice-Hall.

Schwartzman, A. E., Ledingham, J. E., & Serbin, L. A. (1985). Identification of children at-risk for adult schizophrenia: A longitudinal study. *International Review of Applied Psychology, 34,* 363–380.

Shaffer, D., Stokman, C., O'Connor, P. A., Shafer, S., Barmack, J. E., Hess, S., & Spaulten, D. (1979). *Early soft neurological signs and later psychopathological development.* Paper presented at the meeting of the Society of Life History Research in Psychopathology and Society for the Study of Social Biology, New York.

Spivak, G., Marcus, J., & Swift, M. (1986). Early classroom behaviors and later misconduct. *Developmental Psychology, 22,* 124–131.

Suttles, G. D. (1972). *The social construction of communities.* Chicago: University of Chicago Press.

Tremblay, R. E., Masse, B., Perron, D., LeBlanc, M., Schwartzman, A. E., & Ledingham, J. E. (1992). Early disruptive behavior, poor school achievement, delinquent behavior, and delinquency personality: Longitudinal analyses. *Journal of Consulting and Clinical Psychology, 60,* 64–72.

Wallerstein, J. S., & Kelly, J. B. (1980). *Surviving the breakup.* New York: Basic Books.

Werthamer-Larsson, L., Kellam, S. G., & Wheeler, L. (1991). Effect of first-grade classroom environment on shy behavior, aggressive behavior, and concentration problems. *American Journal of Community Psychology, 19,* 585–602.

# 7
# The Contribution of Personal and Family Characteristics in Adolescence to the Subsequent Development of Young Adult Competence

William J. McCarthy
*University of California,*
*Los Angeles*

Peter M. Bentler
*University of California,*
*Los Angeles*

Michael D. Newcomb
*University of Southern California*

It is generally presumed that there exist two major sets of childhood determinants of competence in adult life: (a) the quality of striving that characterizes an individual's efforts to develop their talents, and (b) the quality of resources available to the individual during development, principally through the material, emotional, and appraisal support provided by the family. The first set of determinants includes traitlike characteristics such as motivation, intelligence, and values. The second set of determinants includes characteristics of the developmental environment, such as the cohesiveness of the family in which the individual was raised. Newcomb, McCarthy, and Bentler (1989) examined and confirmed the important role that teenagers' academic lifestyle orientation played in explaining young adult competence 8 years later, but they did not examine the concurrent impact of family-related influences on the development of competence. This chapter evaluates the impact of teenagers' academic lifestyle orientation, other indices of accomplishment and aspirations, and family-related qualities on subsequent young adult competence.

A child's psychological development is maximized when caretaker adults invest much time and attention in individualized tutoring and teaching of their child. The more children that caretaker adults have to teach and care for, the more that individualized attention available to each child is diminished. Not surprisingly, the literature suggests a pattern of diminished parenting effectiveness with increasing family size. A growing literature shows that there is a consistently negative relationship between family size and the quality of parent–child relations (Bell & Avery, 1985; Kidwell, 1981; Scheck & Emerick, 1976). Conger, McCarty, Yang, Lahey, and Kropp (1984) found that family size was correlated with self-reported maternal distress and to the percentage of negative parental interactions with children. The impact of family size on parent–child relations appears consistently small, however, explaining usually less than 5% of the variation. Related to the decreased quality of parenting in larger families is the much-replicated finding that the intellectual development of children is significantly lower in large families, even after controlling for the effects of parental socioeconomic status (SES; Mercy & Steelman, 1982; Velandia, Grandon, & Page, 1978; Zajonc, 1976, 1979).

Conversely, first borns and only children get more parental attention than do later borns (Falbo & Cooper, 1980; Gewirtz & Gewirtz, 1965; Hilton, 1967). Blake (1981) argued persuasively that the enhanced parental attention accorded to first-born and only-born children helps to explain their above average educational attainment and achievement motivation. Falbo (1984) theorized that internality is also greater in first borns and only children because of greater parental attention. In their recent meta-analysis of the literature on birth order and family size, Falbo and Polit (1986) found that only borns were not different from first borns of small families and were superior to later borns, especially from large families, on the dimensions of intelligence, achievement, and character (e.g., leadership, maturity).

In addition to the amount of attention that children need from adult monitors for optimal psychological growth, is the quality of attention received. Permanent guardians allow for a stability of standards and memory of baseline conditions that enable them to provide the kind of informed guidance required for optimal child growth. If children experience instability of guardians through divorce or by being moved repeatedly from one set of guardians to the next, they will be short-changed with respect to the quality of guidance that can best facilitate their social and psychological growth.

## Family Support (Closeness) and Child Development

There is little literature concerning the impact of family support per se on child development. What related literature exists suggests that family support facilitates child cognitive and social maturation. Relevant studies include the following measures of social support: (a) degree of closeness between parent(s) and child, (b) amount of satisfaction with social support, and (c) others' socially supportive behaviors. For instance, Baumrind (1985) reported from her longitudinal study of parental rearing practices that parents who did the most to encourage their children's autonomy and independent strivings and who negotiated with their children regarding what would be appropriate behaviors for their children, had children who were consistently rated as more competent than children from homes with parents who communicated less with their children because they were authoritarian or permissive. Authoritarian parents communicated less support to their children because they did not solicit input from their children with respect to appropriate child behavior. Permissive parents communicated less support to their children because they placed relatively few restrictions on their children's behavior. Specifically, the actively supportive parents had daughters who were more purposive, dominant, and achievement oriented than the average and sons who were more friendly and cooperative than the average.

In a recent review of adolescent coping with stress, Compas (1986) noted that there was a "strong" positive relation between social support and psychological and physical health. He cited the work of Barrera (1981), who found that better physical and psychological functioning was apparent among teenage mothers with family support than in those without. Cauce, Felner, and Primavera (1982) showed that family social support was positively related to academic performance in disadvantaged youth. Two additional studies showed that measures of adolescent social support were positively correlated with adaptive outcomes during academic transitions (Compas, Wagner, Slavin, & Vannatta, 1986; Felner, Ginter, & Primavera, 1982). Sandler (1980) and Sandler and Barrera (1984) also showed that social support helped poor adolescents cope with stress.

Insofar as family disruption contributes to strained relations between parents and children, there is considerable evidence that such strained relations are associated with decreased rates of cognitive and social maturation (Kinard & Reinherz, 1986) and increased deviance and emotional distress (Newcomb & Bentler, 1988b).

Finally, the effects of family characteristics on subsequent adult competence are expected to be mediated by the individual's perception of future opportunities for achievement. Bandura (1982) argued that parental characteristics probably influenced their children's perceived career options. He noted that Betz and Hackett (1981) had found that, although men judged themselves to be equally efficacious in performing either male-stereotyped or female-stereotyped jobs, women felt efficacious only in performing female-stereotyped jobs but not most male-stereotyped jobs. He further noted Hackett's (1981) report showing that how women were socialized influenced their perceived ability to acquire and use quantitative skills. These differences in the perceived career-related efficacy of Betz and Hackett's subjects were particularly striking because the subjects' scores on standardized tests indicated that the men and women did not differ in their verbal and quantitative abilities. Other observers have also noted that gender differences in career achievement are consistently associated with women's lower expectations for success, even though their measured ability did not differ from those of men (e.g., Basow, 1986).

The family conditions for optimal child growth presented here and the evidence that disrupted families are associated with antisocial and depressive behavior in children may explain why some children do poorly in school and perform poorly on tests of cognitive achievement. In summary, we expect the influence of such family factors as family size, family disruptedness, and family support to reduce the direct role of teenage academic lifestyle orientation in explaining subsequent adult competence.

In their investigation of the adolescent determinants of young adult psychological health and young adult cigarette smoking, Newcomb et al. (1989) found that teenagers' academic lifestyle orientation was a central organizing construct, with stronger within-time and across-time correlations with other constructs than such constructs as exposure to peer smoking models, social impact efficacy, and emotional well-being. The following investigation seeks to determine if teenagers' academic lifestyle orientation continues to play a central or explanatory role when such family factors as family size, family disruptedness, and family support are included. Subjects' perceived opportunities for future success are also assessed, because the effects of family factors on the development of subjects' perceived social abilities are expected to be mediated by their perceived future opportunities.

## METHOD

### Subjects

This study uses data from 654 individuals at two testings over a 4-year period from late adolescence to young adulthood (see Newcomb & Bentler, 1986a, 1988a). The study began in 1976 (Year 1) with a group of 1,634 students in the seventh, eighth, and ninth grades located at 11 Los Angeles County schools. These schools were roughly representative of all schools in that county regarding SES and ethnicity. Informed consent was obtained from both the teenager and his or her parents. Both parents and child were informed that responses to the questionnaire were protected legally by a grant of confidentiality from the U.S. Department of Justice, which has been maintained through all years of the study.

Data for this project were collected 4 years later when the subjects were late adolescents (Year 5) and again 4 years later when the participants were young adults (Year 9). These last data were collected in 1984. Data that were assessed in Year 1 were not included in the present analysis because adequate measures of family functioning were not gathered at that time. At the young adult follow-up, data were collected from 739 subjects from our original sample (654 participants provided data at both the Year 5 and Year 9 assessments). This represents a 45% retention rate over the entire 8-year period of the study. This rate of subject loss is not unusual among real-world studies of this type. An extensive series of attrition analyses, reported elsewhere (Newcomb, 1986; Newcomb & Bentler, 1986a, 1988a), revealed that patterns of dropping out of the study were only slightly systematic due to drug use, personality, or gender of the respondent. For example, in a comparison of 1976 data on subjects who either completed or did not complete the 1984 assessment, not one of 38 drug use and personality variables was able to significantly differentiate the lost from the continuing subjects. Thus, although the retention rate after 8 years was 45%, not surprising considering the nature and length of the research, results should not be gravely biased due to subject loss.

TABLE 7.1
Description of Sample

| Variable | Male | Female | Total |
|---|---|---|---|
| N | 192 | 462 | 654 |
| **Age** | | | |
| Mean | 21.86 | 21.90 | 21.90 |
| Range | 19-24 | 20-24 | 19-24 |
| **Ethnicity** | | | |
| Black | 12% | 16% | 15% |
| Hispanic | 8% | 11% | 10% |
| White | 70% | 64% | 66% |
| Asian | 10% | 9% | 9% |
| **High School Graduate** | | | |
| Yes | 94% | 93% | 93% |
| No | 6% | 7% | 7% |
| **Number of Children** | | | |
| None | 96% | 80% | 85% |
| One | 3% | 18% | 14% |
| Two | 1% | 1% | 1% |
| Three | 0% | 1% | 0% |
| **Income for Past Year** | | | |
| None | 3% | 4% | 4% |
| Under $5,000 | 31% | 34% | 34% |
| $5,001 to $15,000 | 51% | 44% | 45% |
| Over $15,000 | 15% | 10% | 12% |
| **Living Situation** | | | |
| Alone | 3% | 4% | 4% |
| Parents | 52% | 46% | 48% |
| Spouse | 7% | 21% | 17% |
| Cohabitation | 9% | 9% | 9% |
| Dormitory | 8% | 5% | 6% |
| Roomates | 16% | 11% | 12% |
| Other | 5% | 4% | 4% |
| **Current Life Activity** | | | |
| Military | 7% | 1% | 3% |
| Junior college | 9% | 13% | 12% |
| Four-year college | 24% | 20% | 21% |
| Part-time job | 14% | 14% | 14% |
| Full-time job | 46% | 47% | 47% |
| None or other | 0% | 5% | 3% |

Table 7.1 presents a description of the sample as young adults. Breakdowns are provided for gender, age, ethnicity, high school graduation, number of children produced, income level, living situation, and current life pursuit. In order to determine the representativeness of the remaining individuals, we compared our sample to other national samples and to individuals in studies similar to ours. When characteristics (e.g., income, living arrangements, etc.) of our participants were compared to U.S. national surveys of young adults (Glick & Lin, 1986; Johnston, O'Malley, & Bachman, 1987; Miller et al., 1983) and other samples of

young adults (Donovan, Jessor, & Jessor, 1983; Kandel, 1984) very similar patterns were noted. Our group of young adults did not appear to be markedly different from young adults in the United States. The main difference was that our sample had a greater percentage of women than men, which it has had since the beginning.

One would expect that more deviant subjects would drop out of a long-term study, leaving the resulting sample to be unrepresentative of the population. To evaluate such an effect, we compared reported drug use between this sample and a national representative sample of young adults (Miller et al., 1983). Lifetime prevalence levels were equal on hallucinogens, heroin, sedatives, analgesics, and cigarettes, whereas our sample reported significantly higher prevalence rates for use of cannabis, cocaine, stimulants, tranquilizers, and alcohol. Clearly, we have not lost substantial numbers of drug users as a result of attrition (see Newcomb & Bentler, 1988a, for further details).

## Measures of Late Adolescent Constructs

Twenty-two variables are used from the Year 5 assessment to reflect seven latent factors and three single-indicator constructs that are treated like latent factors even though they include measurement error. These measures are described in relation to the factor they represent. Table 7.2 presents the univariate statistics for all 42 variables assessed during late adolescence and young adulthood. The table is also organized into groups of variables related to each latent factor to facilitate description of the constructs.

*Family Support.* A latent construct of Family Support was reflected in two multi-item and two single-item variables assessed during adolescence. These scales included good relationship with parents, good relationship with family, happy with parents, and number of arguments with parents. The two multi-item scales (good relationship with parents and with family) are from a larger Social Support construct (see Newcomb & Bentler, 1986b). Each scale consists of four bipolar items rated on 5-point scales anchored at each end by opposing descriptions. For instance, an item on the good relationship with parents scale had endpoints of "parents don't think my ideas are worth much" and "parents usually respect my ideas." Similarly, endpoints of an item on the good relationship with family scale were "family is very close to each other" and "family is not very close to each other." The items typically assess the amount of respect, support, and inclusion experienced with parents and family. The single-item variable "happy with parents" asked the respondents to indicate how happy they felt about their relations with their parents. Responses were given on a 5-point rating scale that ranged from "very unhappy" (1) to "very happy" (5). The other single-item variable on this factor called "number of arguments with parents" asked the participants to indicate how many times during the past 6 months they had argued

TABLE 7.2
Summary of Variable Characteristics

| Variable | Mean | Range | Standard Deviation | Skew | Kurtosis | r Point Biserial Sex Differences |
|---|---|---|---|---|---|---|
| *Late Adolescence* | | | | | | |
| Good relationship with parents | 15.87 | 5-20 | 3.45 | -.76 | -.17 | .03 |
| Good relationship with family | 14.27 | 4-20 | 4.20 | -.47 | -.61 | -.01 |
| Happy with parents | 3.82 | 1-5 | 1.10 | -.91 | .07 | -.06 |
| Number of arguments with parents | 3.03 | 0-6 | 2.14 | .09 | -1.34 | .08* |
| Happy with future | 3.93 | 1-5 | .85 | -.52 | .05 | .05 |
| Happy with schooling up to now | 3.67 | 1-5 | 1.01 | -.71 | -.19 | .02 |
| Happy with chances to be what you want | 3.99 | 1-5 | .96 | -.66 | -.14 | .02 |
| Number of friends parents know | 3.32 | 1-5 | 1.05 | .02 | -1.13 | .12** |
| Number of friends parents like | 3.29 | 1-5 | 1.08 | .03 | -1.12 | .11** |
| Grade-point average | 2.62 | 0-4 | .92 | -.82 | 1.10 | .04 |
| Educational plans | 3.92 | 1-6 | 1.11 | -.18 | -.33 | .03 |
| Salary in July | 3.37 | 1-7 | 2.13 | 1.70 | .27 | -.14*** |
| Salary in October | 3.27 | 1-7 | 2.08 | 1.80 | .35 | -.10* |
| Salary in January | 3.46 | 1-7 | 2.14 | 1.66 | .29 | -.07* |
| Ambition | 14.67 | 4-20 | 3.62 | -.41 | -.46 | -.19*** |
| Leadership | 14.16 | 4-20 | 2.77 | -.12 | .35 | -.13*** |
| Law abidance | 13.15 | 4-20 | 4.03 | -.23 | -.75 | .16*** |
| Liberalism | 9.96 | 4-19 | 2.63 | .23 | -.05 | .02 |
| Religious commitment | 15.57 | 4-20 | 3.90 | -.75 | -.18 | .12** |
| Family size | 2.91 | 0-16 | 1.97 | 1.45 | 4.01 | .01 |
| Family disruption | .24 | 0-1 | .43 | 1.19 | -.60 | -.04 |
| Disruptive family events | .49 | 0-4 | .81 | 1.75 | 2.80 | .09* |
| *Young Adulthood* | | | | | | |
| Good relationship with parents | 16.54 | 4-20 | 3.21 | -1.24 | 1.41 | .07* |
| Good relationship with family | 14.87 | 4-20 | 3.78 | -.65 | -.11 | .07* |
| Happy with parents | 4.06 | 1-5 | 1.00 | -1.21 | 1.06 | .04 |
| Number of arguments with parents | 1.89 | 0-6 | 1.86 | .87 | -.23 | .07* |
| Happy with future | 3.91 | 1-5 | .86 | -.57 | -.06 | -.05 |
| Happy with schooling up to now | 3.53 | 1-5 | 1.06 | -.44 | -.77 | -.03 |
| Happy with chances to be what you want | 3.78 | 1-5 | .95 | -.57 | -.09 | -.07* |
| Educational plans | 3.53 | 1-6 | 1.44 | -.27 | -.57 | -.15*** |
| Educational expectations | 3.88 | 1-7 | 1.01 | .57 | 1.37 | -.10** |
| Salary in August | 3.49 | 1-8 | 1.66 | .31 | .06 | -.13*** |
| Salary in October | 3.39 | 1-8 | 1.69 | .42 | .05 | -.05 |
| Salary in December | 3.53 | 1-8 | 1.73 | .36 | -.04 | -.06 |
| Independence | 7.73 | 2-10 | 1.51 | -.78 | .49 | -.11** |
| Other's respect | 7.30 | 2-10 | 1.24 | -.39 | .66 | -.10** |
| Inner resources | 3.88 | 1-5 | .76 | -.56 | .62 | -.18*** |
| Ambition | 14.49 | 4-20 | 3.55 | -.43 | -.47 | -.20*** |
| Leadership | 14.27 | 5-20 | 2.86 | -.15 | -.30 | -.17*** |
| Law abidance | 14.19 | 4-20 | 3.42 | -.41 | -.42 | .14*** |
| Liberalism | 9.49 | 4-18 | 2.46 | .40 | .26 | .01 |
| Religious commitment | 15.62 | 4-20 | 3.99 | -.88 | .11 | .14*** |

*p < .05; **p < .01; ***p < .001.

[a]A positive correlation indicated that the women had the larger values.

or had a fight with either of their parents. Responses were given on a 7-point anchored rating scale that ranged from "none" (0) to "six or more times" (6).

*Perceived Opportunity.*    Three single-item variables were hypothesized to reflect a latent factor of Perceived Opportunity: happy with future, happy with schooling up to now, and happy with chances to be what you want. Each respondent indicated his or her degree of happiness with each of these three areas on 5-point anchored rating scales that ranged from "very unhappy" (1) to "very happy" (5).

*Peer–Parent Cohesion.*    Two single-item variables were assumed to reflect a latent construct of Peer-Parent Cohesion: number of friends parents know and number of friends parents like. Subjects indicated their responses to these items on 5-point anchored rating scales that ranged from "none" (1) to "all" (5).

*Academic Lifestyle.*    Two single-item variables were used as indicators of an Academic Lifestyle Orientation latent construct: grade point average (GPA) and educational plans. Grade point average for the past year was indicated in the standard manner (F = 0, D = 1, C = 2, B = 3, and A = 4). Educational plans were provided on a 6-point anchored rating scale that ranged from some "high school" (will drop out before completion) (1) to "doctor's degree" (6).

*Income.*    Three single-item measures were used as indicators of an Income latent construct: salary in July, salary in October, and salary in January. For these separate months during the previous year the respondents indicated their amount of earned income before taxes on 7-point anchored rating scales that ranged from "none" (1) to "more than $500" (7).

*Leadership Style.*    Two personality scales, ambition and leadership, were used to reflect the construct of Leadership Style. These traits were assessed using a self-rating test modified for this research program, but based on the Bentler Psychological Inventory (BPI; Bentler & Newcomb, 1978; Huba & Bentler, 1982). Although the BPI was developed with multivariate methods, the items have a high degree of face validity. Half of the items for each trait are reverse-scored to minimize response bias or acquiescence. Four items were used to assess each trait and each item was rated on a 5-point bipolar scale. Thus, each scale had a range of 4 to 20. The period-free test–retest reliability for ambition was .72 and the reliability for leadership was .71 (Stein, Newcomb, & Bentler, 1986). This construct of Leadership Style has been found to be one indicator of a higher order factor of Behavioral Coping Efficacy, and thus can be considered to overlap conceptually with self-efficacy (McCarthy & Newcomb, 1990) and be used as a prior measure of Social Impact Efficacy in the present analyses.

*Social Conformity.* This latent factor was identified by three measured variable scales: law abidance, liberalism, and religious commitment. These scales were taken from the BPI just described and each consists of four self-description items. This construct reflects a degree of adherence to traditional values and conformity to societal norms; it does not represent conformity to one's particular peer culture. It is a continuous latent construct, which at the low end reflects a rejection of traditional values and societal norms, and an embracing, or at least tolerance, of deviance, radical social change, and nonadherence to social control (e.g., laws). As such, low scores represent a tendency toward deviance, non-traditionalism, or problem behavior.

*Family Size.* This is a single-indicator factor that reflects the number of siblings (brothers and sisters) of the respondent. The actual number is used as the datum.

*Family Disruption.* This single-indicator factor was assessed with one measured variable that determined whether the adolescent's parents were still married to each other. An intact family was scored "0" and was defined as "mother married to father." Any other parental configurations were considered a disrupted or divorced family and were scored "1." As evident in Table 7.2, 24% of the sample reported having divorced parents. Although this question was first asked in Year 5 of the study, when subjects were in late adolescence, it is quite likely that an unknown percentage of the sample who reported living in a disrupted home at that time also lived in a disrupted home earlier in their life as well.

*Disruptive Family Events.* This is the third single-indicator factor from the late adolescent data. The variable represents the sum of five possible events that could occur to a family. If an event did not occur during the past year it was scored "0," whereas if it did happen it was scored "1." Events included family money problems, parent abusing alcohol, parents separated, parents argued or fought, and parent remarried (Newcomb, Huba, & Bentler, 1981).

## Measures of the Young Adult Constructs

Twenty variables were taken from the Year 9 young adult data to reflect seven latent constructs. Measures identical to those used in Year 5 were also used in Year 9 to form the factors of Family Support, Perceived Opportunity, Leadership Style, and Social Conformity. Descriptions of these measures were given earlier and are not repeated here. Those variables that were assessed differently or are newly introduced constructs are described here.

*Academic Lifestyle.* Two single-item scales are used to represent a latent construct of Academic Lifestyle Orientation in young adulthood: Educational plans and educational expectations. Educational plans were rated on a 6-point anchored scale that asked the respondents to indicate their long-range educational plans from "no more formal education" (1) to "doctor's degree" (6). The educational expectations item asked the young adult to indicate the highest level of education they expected to complete in the next few years. Responses were given on a 7-point anchored rating scale that ranged from "some high school" (will not finish) (1) to "doctor's degree" (7).

*Income.*    Three single-item measures were used as indicators of an Income latent construct: salary in August, salary in October, and salary in December. For these separate months during the previous year when the subjects were young adults, the respondent indicated their amount of earned income before taxes on 8-point anchored rating scales that ranged from "none" (0) to "more than $2,500" (7).

*Social Impact Efficacy.*    Three scales were used to reflect the Social Impact Efficacy construct. These scales were derived from the five-item scale of efficacy developed by Blatt, Quinlan, Chevron, McDonald, and Zuroff, (1982). Responses to these five items were given on 5-point anchored rating scales that ranged from "strongly disagree" (1) to "strongly agree" (5). The items were factor analyzed and found to reflect a unitary construct (only one eigenvalue greater than 1.00 and all factor loadings were greater than .4 on the first unrotated factor). As a result, these five items were combined into three scales based on content. Inner resources was assessed with a single item—"I have many inner resources." Independence was the average of two items—"I am a very independent person" and "I set my personal goals as high as possible." Others' respect was the average of two items—"Others have high expectations of me" and "What I do and say has a great impact on those around me."

## Controls for Demographic Differences

It is possible that differences between men and women or across ethnic groups may distort associations we find in the models. To reduce these potential confounds, gender (as one dichotomous variable) and ethnicity (as three dummy variables representing the four ethnic groups) were partialled from the data. As a result, our findings are not biased due to gender or ethnic differences among the variables.

## Analyses

Our first set of analyses use point-biserial correlations to test for mean differences between men and women on each of the 42 observed variables. Next, we use a confirmatory factor analysis with latent variables to evaluate the adequacy of our hypothesized factor structure as outlined earlier (e.g., Bentler, 1986, 1989; Bentler & Newcomb, 1986; Bollen, 1989; Newcomb, 1990). Table 7.2 presents the univariate statistics for all variables. An inspection of the skew and kurtosis estimates for the 42 observed measures indicates that most are normally distributed. As a result, we use the maximum likelihood structural model estimator, which, although historically has been assumed to require multivariately normal data, is often quite robust to normality violations (empirically, e.g., Harlow, 1985; theoretically, e.g., Mooijaart & Bentler, 1991; Satorra & Bentler, 1990). The demographic control variables of gender and ethnicity are statistically partialled from the data so that their influence is removed from the entire system of variables. If the initial hypothesized models do not adequately reflect the data (which is common in models with many variables and many subjects), additional correlated residuals are added until an acceptable fit is achieved. These modifications are made in a manner that does not disturb the critical features of the model. Once this is accomplished, we generate a structural model that predicts young adult constructs and variables from the adolescent factors and variables. This model will be over-fit by adding parameters and then nonsignificant paths will be deleted, as recommended by MacCallum (1986; see also Chou & Bentler, 1990). The resultant model summarizes the impact of teenage psychosocial factors and family conditions on aspects of young adult competence. All structural model analyses are performed with the EQS computer program (Bentler, 1989). In view of the large sample size, normed fit indexes (NFI) are used as adjuncts to model fit (Bentler, 1990a; Bentler & Bonett, 1980).

## RESULTS

### Gender Differences

Mean differences between men and women on the 42 variables were tested using point-biserial correlations. Males were coded 1 and females were coded 2, so that a positive correlation indicates that the women had the larger value and a negative correlation indicates that the men had the larger value. These mean difference correlations are presented in the right-hand column of Table 7.2.

Of the 22 variables assessed during late adolescence, significant mean differences were found on 11 of them. These differences indicated that the females, compared to the males, had more arguments with their parents, had more friends that their parents knew and liked, and earned less money in all three months that were sampled, reported less ambition and leadership, were more law abidant and religious, and reported more disruptive family events.

There were also 14 significant gender differences on the 20 variables assessed during young adulthood. These significant differences indicated that these young adult women had better relationships with their parents and family, more arguments with their parents, were less happy with their chances to be what they wanted, had fewer educational plans and aspirations, earned less money in August, felt less independent, had fewer inner resources, had less respect from others, had less ambition and leadership, and more law abidance and religious commitment, than did the men as young adults.

Although there were many mean differences between the males and the females, the magnitude of the differences was quite small. For instance, the largest difference accounted for only 4% of the variance between groups (on young adult ambition). Based on these rather small in magnitude mean differences between men and women, and previous results indicating that there were not different factor structures nor differential associations for men and women on similar or related variables (e.g., Newcomb & Bentler, 1986b, 1988b; Newcomb, Maddahian, & Bentler, 1986), we collapsed across gender for the remaining analyses. As a safeguard against any positive biases due to gender or ethnic variations, these were partialled from the data as described previously.

## Confirmatory Factor Analysis Models

In the initial confirmatory factor (CFA) model, the 14 latent constructs were hypothesized to "cause" or generate the variation in the 39 observed variables (three variables are used as single-indicator factors). In other words, we need to demonstrate that the variables we have chosen to reflect the latent factors with which we are concerned, in fact reflect these constructs in a statistically reliable manner. This is accomplished via a confirmatory factor analysis. The factor structure of this initial CFA model was simple in that each observed variable was allowed to load on only one latent construct. For instance, the variable "happy with the future" assessed during adolescence was allowed to load only on the Perceived Opportunity latent construct in adolescence.

An initial CFA model was run with the following specifications: (a) all factor variances were fixed at unity to identify the model; (b) all constructs (latent factors and single-indicator factors that are treated like factors) were allowed to correlate freely; and (c) across-time correlations between pairs of residuals on identical variables were included a priori. For instance, the residual of the late adolescent "good relationship with parents" scale was allowed to correlate with the young adult "good relationship with parents" variable residual.

This initial model did not adequately reflect the data ($p < .001$; see Table 7.3 for a summary of other-fit indices). This was not surprising considering the large number of subjects in the sample and variables in the model (Bentler & Bonett, 1980). However, the Normed Fit Index (NFI) was sufficiently large (.90) to suggest that minor modifications to the model should yield an acceptable fit. Factor intercorrelations for this initial CFA model are presented in the upper triangle of Table 7.4.

By examining selected multivariate Lagrangian Multiplier indices (Bentler &

TABLE 7.3
Summary and Model Fit Indices

| Model | $x^2$ | Degree of Freedom | P Value | Normed Fit Index |
|-------|-------|-------------------|---------|------------------|
| Initial CFA[a] | 1138.44 | 674 | <.001 | .90 |
| Final CFA[b] | 634.21 | 603 | .18 | .94 |
| Final Structural | 723.87 | 686 | .15 | .94 |

[a]CFA = Confirmatory Factor Analysis.

[b]Includes 70 correlated residuals and one variance constrained at zero to prevent it from being estimated as negative.

Chou, 1986; Chou & Bentler, 1990), correlations among 70 pairs of residuals were added to the model. No additional factor loadings were necessary. These modifications resulted in a model that adequately reflected the data ($p = .18$), or that could not be rejected as a plausible explanation for the data. Factor intercorrelations for this final CFA model are presented in the lower triangle of Table 7.5. All hypothesized factor loadings were significant. Standardized factor loadings for this final CFA model are given in Table 7.4.

In order to test whether adding the correlated residuals disturbed the fundamental associations among the latent constructs, the factor intercorrelation between the initial and final CFA models were correlated. This correlation was higher than .95, indicating that the model modifications did not alter the basic pattern of factor intercorrelations.

## Structural Model Analyses

The final stage in data analyses for this model was the creation of a structural or path model, which includes regression effects representing unidirectional or causal influences of one variable upon another from late adolescence to young adulthood. Regression paths were not included within time, because the causal interpretation of these may be ambiguous. Within-time associations were captured as correlations among constructs, factor loadings, or correlated residuals. The regression effects we are most interested in are those across time that may have a plausible causal inference.

Because some of the correlated residuals added in the model modifications to create the final CFA may be across-time regression effects, these empirically determined across-time correlated residuals were deleted in the initial structural model. This was done in hopes of capturing these associations as across-time causal paths. All constructs in adolescence were allowed to correlate freely, as were all factor residuals during young adulthood. All young adult constructs were initially predicted from all adolescent constructs.

This beginning model was modified by adding across-time regression paths

TABLE 7.4
Standardized Factor Loadings for the Final Confirmatory Factor Analysis Model

| Late Adolescence | | Young Adulthood | |
| --- | --- | --- | --- |
| Factor/Variable | Loading | Factor/Variable | Loading |
| Family Support | | Family Support | |
| Good relationship with parents | .82 | Good relationship with parents | .77 |
| Good relationship with family | .89 | Good relationship with family | .81 |
| Happy with parents | .81 | Happy with parents | .85 |
| Number of arguments with parents | -.45 | Number of arguments with parents | -.40 |
| Perceived Opportunity | | Perceived opportunity | |
| Happy with future | .82 | Happy with future | .88 |
| Happy with schooling up to now | .62 | Happy with schooling up to now | .55 |
| Happy with chances to be what you want | .66 | Happy with chances to be what you want | .68 |
| Peer-Parent Cohesion | | | |
| Number of friends parents know | .73 | | |
| Number of friends parents like | .88 | | |
| Academic Lifestyle | | Academic Lifestyle | |
| Grade-point average | .46 | Educational plans | .81 |
| Edicational plans | .70 | Educational expectations | .78 |
| Income | | Income | |
| Salary in July | .59 | Salary in August | .80 |
| Salary in October | 1.00[a] | Salary in October | .99 |
| Salary in January | .74 | Salary in December | .92 |
| Leadership Style | | Leadership Style | |
| Ambition | .72 | Ambition | .80 |
| Leadership | .49 | Leadership | .57 |
| Social Conformity | | Social Conformity | |
| Law abidance | .63 | Law abidance | .63 |
| Liberalism | -.46 | Liberalism | -.45 |
| Religious commitment | .40 | Religious commitment | .43 |
| Family Size | b | Social Impact Efficacy | |
| Family Disruption | b | Independence | .78 |
| Disruptive Family Events | b | Others' respect | .41 |
| | | Inner resources | .71 |

All factor loadinga are significant ($p < .001$).

[a]The residual of this variable was held at zero to prevent it from being estimated as negative.

[b]There is no factor loading for this variable since it is a single-indicator factor.

(based on selected modification indices) to over-fit the model and then nonsignificant parameters were deleted. The final model includes only significant paths and fit the data quite well ($p = .15$: see Table 7.3). Across-time effects between latent factors are graphically displayed in Fig. 7.1 and the across-time paths that include at least one observed variable are listed in Table 7.6 with their standardized regression weight. Within-time correlations between adolescent, independent factors are given in Table 7.7, whereas correlations among the young

TABLE 7.5
Factor Intercorrelations for the Initial (Above the Diagonal) and Final (Below the Diagonal) Confirmatory Factor Analyses

| Factors | | I | II | III | IV | V | VI | VII | VIII | IX |
|---|---|---|---|---|---|---|---|---|---|---|
| | | | | | *Late Adolescence* | | | | | |
| I | Family Support | 1.00 | .43*** | .41*** | .22*** | .04 | .18*** | .44*** | -.06 | -.17*** |
| II | Perceived Opportunity | .42*** | 1.00 | .19*** | .47*** | .05 | .24*** | .27*** | .00 | -.08* |
| III | Peer-Parent Cohesion | .39*** | .18*** | 1.00 | .09 | .12** | .16** | .27*** | -.17*** | -.06 |
| IV | Academic Lifestyle | .23*** | .42*** | .09 | 1.00 | -.08 | .47*** | .32*** | -.15** | -.09* |
| V | Income | .03 | .04 | .12** | .02 | 1.00 | .17* | -.01 | -.01 | -.04 |
| VI | Leadership Style | .13** | .24*** | .09* | .47*** | .13** | 1.00 | -.23*** | -.06 | .03 |
| VII | Social Conformity | .44*** | .28*** | .26*** | .37*** | -.01 | -.23*** | 1.00 | .07 | -.19*** |
| VIII | Family Size | -.06 | .00 | -.17*** | -.13** | -.02 | -.05 | .07 | 1.00 | .02 |
| IX | Family Disruption | -.17*** | -.08* | -.06 | -.10* | -.04 | .02 | -.19*** | .01 | 1.00 |
| X | Disruptive Family Events | -.32*** | -.06 | -.14*** | -.02 | -.02 | .02 | -.12* | .09** | .20*** |
| | | | | | *Young Adulthood* | | | | | |
| XI | Family Support | .59*** | .25*** | .22*** | -.01 | .09* | .06 | .23*** | .04 | -.17*** |
| XII | Perceived Opportunity | .34*** | .40*** | .16*** | .20*** | .08* | .09 | .22*** | .02 | -.13** |
| XIII | Academic Lifestyle | .11*** | .28*** | .03 | .78*** | -.07* | .27*** | .22*** | -.08* | -.09* |
| XIV | Income | -.01 | -.03 | .07 | -.08 | .22*** | .12*** | .03 | .03 | .04 |
| XV | Social Impact Efficiency | -.21*** | .32*** | .80*** | .36*** | .01 | .50*** | .11* | .03 | .05 |
| XVI | Leadership Style | .08 | .10* | .05 | .29*** | .00 | .82*** | -.19** | .03 | .06 |
| XVII | Social Conformity | .23*** | .11* | .16** | .10 | .05 | -.32*** | .80*** | .13** | -.20*** |

TABLE 7.5
(Continued)

## Late Adolescence

| Factors | | X | XI | XII | XIII | XIV | XV | XVI | VIII |
|---|---|---|---|---|---|---|---|---|---|
| I | Family Support | -.32*** | .59*** | .36*** | .14** | -.01 | .26*** | .09* | .25*** |
| II | Perceived Opportunity | -.05 | .26*** | .46*** | .28*** | -.03 | .40*** | .16** | .08 |
| III | Peer-Parent Cohesion | -.13** | .24*** | .18** | .03 | .07 | .15** | .10* | .16** |
| IV | Academic Lifestyle | .00 | .04 | .22** | .80*** | -.09* | .44*** | .28*** | .05 |
| V | Income | -.03 | .08* | .07 | -.08* | .23*** | .05 | .08* | .05 |
| VI | Leadership Style | .03 | .09 | .11* | .28*** | .15** | .62*** | .83*** | -.33*** |
| VII | Social Conformity | -.11** | .24*** | .25*** | .25*** | .03 | .13* | -.19** | .80*** |
| VIII | Family Size | .09* | .03 | .00 | -.08* | .04 | .04 | .04 | .13* |
| IX | Family Disruption | .20*** | -.16** | -.12** | -.09* | .03 | .05 | .06 | -.19*** |
| X | Disruptive Family Events | 1.00 | -.18*** | -.13** | .00 | .03 | .06 | .09* | -.10* |

## Young Adulthood

| Factors | | X | XI | XII | XIII | XIV | XV | XVI | VIII |
|---|---|---|---|---|---|---|---|---|---|
| XI | Family Support | -.19*** | 1.00 | .40*** | .03 | -.01 | .25*** | .05 | .20*** |
| XII | Perceived Opportunity | -.13** | .49*** | 1.00 | .27*** | -.01 | .52*** | .19*** | .25*** |
| XIII | Academic Lifestyle | .01 | .02 | .25*** | 1.00 | -.17*** | .40*** | .23*** | .05 |
| XIV | Income | .03 | -.01 | .00 | -.17*** | 1.00 | .12** | .15*** | .04 |
| XV | Social Impact Efficiency | .05 | .20*** | .44*** | .35*** | .09* | 1.00 | .77*** | .00 |
| XVI | Leadership Style | .08* | .01 | .13** | .20*** | .12** | .69*** | 1.00 | -.29*** |
| XVII | Social Conformity | -.10* | .21*** | .25*** | -.09 | .05 | -.03 | -.30*** | 1.00 |

*p < .05; **p < .01; ***p < .001.

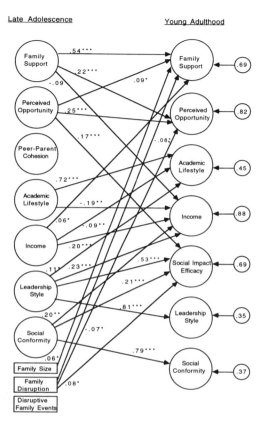

FIG. 7.1. Across-time effects between latent variables (large circles) and measured variables treated like constructs (rectangles) in the final structural model. Residual disturbances are variances and structural paths are standardized (*p < .05; **p < .01; ***p < .001). Nonstandard effects are given in Table 6, correlations among the late adolescent independent predictors are given in Table 7.7, and correlations among the young adult factor residuals are given in Table 7.8, and all are aspects of the same final structural model.

adult dependent-factor residuals are given in Table 7.7. The relationships presented in Fig. 7.1, and those listed in Tables 7.6, 7.7, and 7.8 are based on the same final model, and are presented separately only for reasons of clarity. It would require an extremely busy and overly complicated figure to depict graphically all of the significant relationships identified in the final structural model.

## Summary of Empirical Findings

The CFA models provide correlations among the 17 factors or constructs that are disattenuated for measurement error (except for those that are defined by only one indicator). As such, these correlations represent the "true" or error-free associations among the constructs and reveal important information about how the factors are related. Because the primary focus of this chapter is on the constructs related to family and academic interests, we direct our attention to the correlates of these factors.

TABLE 7.6
Direct Across-Time Causal Paths Not Depicted in Figure

| Adolescent Predictor Variable | | Young Adult Consequent Variable | | |
| Observed Variable | Latent Variable | Observed Variable | Latent Variable | Standardized Parameter Estimate[a] |
| --- | --- | --- | --- | --- |
| Good relationship with family (R) | | Good relationship with parents | | .10* |
| Number of friends parents like (R) | | Good relationship with parents | | .12* |
| Good relationship with parents (R) | | Good relationship with family | | .17*** |
| Happy with parents (R) | | Good relationship with family | | .11** |
| Educational plans (R) | | Happy with parents | | .11*** |
| | Family disruption | Number of arguments with parents | | -.12*** |
| | Perceived opportunity | Number of arguments with parents | | -.07* |
| Salary in January (R) | | Happy with schooling up to now | | -.06* |
| | Perceived opportunity | Happy with chances to be what you want | | .09** |
| Salary in July (R) | | Happy with chances to be what you want | | .06* |
| Ambition (R) | | Happy with chances to be what you want | | -.10** |
| Law abidance (R) | | Happy with chances to be what you want | | .08* |
| | Family disruption | Educational expectations | | -.05* |
| Good relationship with parents (R) | | Educational expectations | | .06* |
| Good relationship with parents (R) | | Other's respect | | .12** |
| Salary in July (R) | | Other's respect | | .09** |
| Leadership (R) | | Other's respect | | .09** |
| | Academic lifestyle | Inner resources | | .16*** |

186

| | | | |
|---|---|---|---|
| Number of arguments with parents (R) | | Law abidance | -.11** |
| Happy with chances to be what you want (R) | | Law abidance | .07* |
| | Academic lifestyle | Liberalism | .18*** |
| Happy with chances to be what you want (R) | | Perceived opportunity | .09* |
| Number of friends parents know (R) | | Academic lifestyle | .11** |
| Salary in July (R) | | Income | .11** |

[a]Significance level determined by a critical ratio of the unstandardized parameter estimate divided by its standard error.

[b](R) denotes variable residual.

*$p < .05$; **$p < .01$; ***$p < .001$.

In the final CFA model, the adolescent Family Support factor was significantly correlated with more Perceived Opportunity (at both time points), more Peer–Parent Cohesion, more adolescent Leadership Style, more Social Conformity and Academic Lifestyle (at both time periods), less Family Disruption, fewer Disruptive Family Events, more Family Support received as a young adult, and more Social Impact Efficacy (see Table 7.5). Large Family Size was significantly correlated with less Peer–Parent Cohesion, less interest in Academic Lifestyle (at both assessment times), more Disruptive Family Events, and more

TABLE 7.7
Correlations Among the Late Adolescent Independent Latent Factors in the
Final Structural Model (Figure 7.1)

| Factors | | I | II | III | IV | V | VI | VII | VIII | IX | X |
|---|---|---|---|---|---|---|---|---|---|---|---|
| *Late Adolescence* | | | | | | | | | | | |
| I | Family Support | 1.00 | | | | | | | | | |
| II | Perceived Opportunity | .39*** | 1.00 | | | | | | | | |
| III | Peer-Parent Cohesion | .35*** | .15*** | 1.00 | | | | | | | |
| IV | Academic Lifestyle | .15*** | .37*** | 0a | 1.00 | | | | | | |
| V | Income | 0a | 0a | .11** | 0a | 1.00 | | | | | |
| VI | Leadership Style | .12** | .10* | .09* | 0a | .09* | 1.00 | | | | |
| VII | Social Conformity | .38*** | .28*** | .20*** | .38*** | 0a | -.34*** | 1.00 | | | |
| VIII | Family Size | 0a | 0a | -.12** | -.13** | 0a | 0a | .10* | 1.00 | | |
| IX | Family Disruption | -.16*** | -.07* | 0a | .09* | 0a | 0a | -.17*** | 0a | 1.00 | |
| X | Disruptive Family Events | -.32*** | -.06* | -.13** | 0a | 0a | 0a | -.09* | .07* | .19*** | 1.00 |

*$p < .05$; **$p < .01$; ***$p < .001$.

[a]Fixed at zero in the final model.

TABLE 7.8
Correlations Among the Young Adult Latent Factor Residuals in the
Final Structural Model (Fig. 7.1)

| Factors | | XI | XII | XIII | XIV | XV | XVI | XVII |
|---|---|---|---|---|---|---|---|---|
| *Young Adulthood* | | | | | | | | |
| XI | Family Support | 1.00 | | | | | | |
| XII | Perceived Opportunity | .38*** | 1.00 | | | | | |
| XIII | Academic Lifestyle | 0ª | .20*** | 1.00 | | | | |
| XIV | Income | 0ª | 0ª | -.17** | 1.00 | | | |
| XV | Social Impact Efficacy | .16** | .42*** | .18** | 0ª | 1.00 | | |
| XVI | Leadership Style | 0ª | .20*** | 0ª | 0ª | .60*** | 1.00 | |
| XVII | Social Conformity | 0ª | .23*** | 0ª | 0ª | 0ª | 0ª | 1.00 |

*$p < .05$; **$p < .01$; ***$p < .001$.
ªFixed at zero in the final index.

Social Conformity as a young adult. Family Disruption was significantly corre-lated with less Family Support, reduced Perceived Opportunity, less Academic Lifestyle, and less Social Conformity (all at both time periods). Disruptive Fami-ly Events were significantly related to reduced Family Support, less Social Conformity (each at both time points), as well as less Peer–Parent Cohesion, larger Family Size, and more Family Disruption in adolescence and reduced Perceived Opportunity and more Leadership Style as young adults. Finally, in addition to the associations just noted, adolescent Academic Lifestyle was signif-icantly related to more Perceived Opportunity, more Leadership Style (each at both time periods), more adolescent Social Conformity, more young adult Aca-demic Lifestyle orientation, and more young adult Social Impact Efficacy.

In the final structural model, several interesting significant relationships emerged. These are summarized in Table 7.6 and Fig. 7.1.

The figure shows the major effects as directional arrows connecting the vari-ables involved. As shown in the figure, there were significant stability effects for all repeatedly measured constructs, as would be expected from attitude and behavior consistency theories. For example, Family Support during late adoles-cence significantly predicted Family Support in young adulthood. These stability effects were quite large, given the long interval between measurement points (4 years apart), for Family Support (.54; all parameter estimates are standardized), Academic Lifestyle (.72), Leadership Style (.81), and Social Conformity (.79). The development of these constructs appears to be quite well established by late adolescence. Although significant, the stability effects for Perceived Opportunity (.25) and Income (.20) were substantially lower, indicating that these behaviors and perceptions were not firmly established by late adolescence and continued to develop into young adulthood. Even the more stable factors were not perfectly predicted across time, revealing that other forces could influence their development into young adulthood.

The figure also shows a number of cross-time, cross-variable effects. Young adult Family Support was significantly predicted by more adolescent Perceived Opportunity, adolescent Income, and Family Size, and less adolescent Family Disruption. These effects are shown as arrows ending on young adult Family Support and originating at the named adolescent factors and variables. Similarly, young adult Perceived Opportunity was generated by earlier Family Support and less Family Disruption. Young adult Academic Lifestyle orientation was significantly predicted from less earlier Income and greater earlier Leadership Style. Increased young adult Income was a function of less earlier Family Support, less Academic Lifestyle orientation, greater Leadership Style, and more social Conformity. Young adult Social Impact Efficacy was significantly predicted from late adolescent Perceived Opportunity, Leadership Style (its proxy stability effect), Social Conformity, and Family Disruption.

Other significant regression effects across time that were not strictly between latent constructs are summarized in Table 7.6. There were 24 such nonstandard effects. See Bentler (1989, chapter 5, 1990b) and Newcomb (1990) for a discussion of nonstandard effects. In several instances, they corroborate the latent factor results, but with more specificity of content. For instance, adolescent Perceived Opportunity significantly reduced the number of arguments with parents as a young adult. On the other hand, many of these nonstandard effects capture small relationships not detected by the latent factors. For example, adolescent Academic Lifestyle orientation significantly increased inner resources and liberalism as a young adult. Similarly, Family Disruption significantly reduced the number of arguments with parents and educational expectations as young adults. In general, these effects are rather small, substantially data-driven, and require validation in future research on other samples.

All of the nonstandardized effects are not summarized in the text, but are given in Table 7.6. Examples from these nonstandard paths are included in our theoretical integration and implications of our findings discussed here.

## DISCUSSION

The relations between leadership style, family disruption, family support, and perceived opportunity can be understood in light of Stewart's theory of adaptation to life changes. Stewart and her colleagues (Healy & Stewart, 1984; Stewart, 1982; Stewart, Sokol, Healy, & Chester, 1986) have repeatedly shown for both children and adults that life changes precipitate a receptive, dependent stance toward the environment and that a subsequent period of stability is associated with a return to a more assertive stance toward the environment. Stewart theorized that it is adaptive for individuals to cope with marked environmental changes by giving up, temporarily, the sense of autonomy and competence that they normally enjoy, in order to observe and learn about the new environment they are in. As the new environment becomes more familiar, a more assertive stance is adopted with a concomitant decrease in attention to the environment, which then frees the individual from investing energy in being vigilant and enables personal action.

The importance of Stewart's perspective for explaining the consequences of life change on self-concept is the value that it places on periods of stability for enabling more assertive behavior. The instability associated with disrupted families, according to Stewart's perspective, is likely to retard children's developmental striving for a sense of autonomy. Corroborative of this perspective is the earlier work of Turner (1962) showing that high school students' levels of ambitiousness were positively related to family stability.

If one views young adult Leadership Style, Social Impact Efficacy, Academic Lifestyle, and Income as constructs reflecting young adult competence, it is clear that such adolescent family-related characteristics as family size and disruptive family events had no direct effects on young adult competence. Nevertheless, family size was inversely related to aspects of young adult competence through its correlation with adolescent Academic Lifestyle. These modest effects conform with the general finding that increased family size adversely influences achievement (e.g., Falbo & Polit, 1986; Zajonc, 1976). The net effect of family size on later adult competence is negligible, because the weak negative influence inferred via association with adolescent Academic Lifestyle was offset by a direct small effect that increased later Family Support.

Family disruption, as the literature would suggest, had significant negative effects on young adult Family Support and on young adult Perceived Opportunity, and reduced educational expectations, but, contrary to hypothesis, had a small, positive effect on young adult Social Impact Efficacy. Such a result is difficult to interpret in the absence of mediational data (e.g., whether disruption led to earlier independence from the family). Adolescent Family Support was also relatively unimpressive in regard to its range and magnitude of direct effects, having a small negative effect on young adult Income, a moderate effect on increasing Perceived Opportunity and a small influence on reducing arguments with parents. These effects are quite interpretable.

The relatively small and few direct effects of such adolescent family-related characteristics as family size, disruptive family events, family disruption, and family social support stand in contrast to the considerably stronger effects of adolescent Academic Lifestyle, Leadership Style, Social Conformity, and Perceived Opportunity on young adult constructs of competence.

Academic Lifestyle, Leadership Style, and Social Conformity measured in adolescence had strong stability effects and strong cross-time effects with young adult constructs of competence over a 4-year period. Adolescent Income and Perceived Opportunity had relatively smaller cross-time effects, probably reflecting their lack of stability during a developmental period when neither is usually well established. The negative relations across time between income and academic lifestyle reflect the fact that college students defer income as young adults even as their noncollege age-mates involve themselves in full employment. This finding also accords with the literature showing that early job involvement in adolescence is associated with lower academic achievement (Steinberg, Greenberger, Garduque, Ruggiero, & Vaux, 1982) and may reflect a general tendency toward deviance or precocious development (Newcomb, 1987; Newcomb & Bentler, 1988a).

Despite its weak stability, Perceived Opportunity had a significant cross-time effect on Social Impact Efficacy. Assuming that Perceived Opportunity partially reflects experience with success and failure in one's environment, this across-time effect suggests that environmental transactions as adolescents can contribute significantly to internal percepts of efficacy later in life. For instance, Scheier and Carver (1985) explicitly presumed that optimists derive their sense of optimism from a history of successes in which personal mastery over difficult situations was the outcome.

Across a longer follow-up period, Newcomb et al. (1989) found that adolescent Academic Lifestyle was a central organizing construct, with the strongest within-time and across-time correlations with other constructs. Family-related characteristics were not included as predictors or outcomes, however. As expected, the introduction of family-related factors in this study appears to reduce the cross-time effects of adolescent Academic Lifestyle on adult Social Impact Efficacy. Some of the strongest cross-time regression effects on adult Social Impact Efficacy, however, were with constructs measuring individual characteristics that were highly correlated with both family characteristics and with adolescent Academic Lifestyle. For instance, as shown in Table 7.7, Perceived Opportunity correlated highly with Family Support ($r = .39$) and with Academic Lifestyle ($r = .37$); Social Conformity correlated highly with Family Support ($r = .38$); with Family Disruption ($r = -.17$), and with Academic Lifestyle ($r = .38$). It is worth noting, however, that adolescent Academic Lifestyle did have a direct cross-time effect on the inner resources indicator of adult Social Impact Efficacy ($r = .16$; Table 7.6).

In the present analyses, Perceived Opportunities rather than Academic Lifestyle served as a central organizing construct. Perceived Opportunities had the strongest within-time correlations with most other constructs, particularly for the young adult constructs (see Table 7.5), and had a significant cross-time effect on Social Impact Efficacy. The lesser importance of Academic Lifestyle, as compared to the findings of Newcomb et al. (1989), may be attributed either to the inclusion of subjects 4 years younger than the teenagers examined in this study or to the inclusion of Perceived Opportunities and various family factors in this study. As mentioned earlier, Newcomb et al. did not have Perceived Opportunities and family factors measures available for the younger cohort in their study.

The cross-time effect of family disruption to increase slightly Social Impact Efficacy was not expected (i.e., in an unexpected direction), but its impact on Perceived Opportunities and Family Support was negative as expected. There were strong within-time correlations between Perceived Opportunities and several of the other young adult constructs, notably with Family Support and Social Impact Efficacy. If Family Disruption had stronger cross-time effects, the relatively high correlations among these young adult indicators of competence would, no doubt, have been substantially reduced because then they would have shared a common cause. However, Family Disruption and the other family factors were relatively weak in their causal impact.

The conceptual importance of Perceived Opportunities for explaining the development of teenagers' social competence is affirmed, indirectly, by the recent literature on dispositional optimism (Scheier & Carver, 1985, 1989; Scheier, Weintraub, & Carver, 1986). Scheier and Carver (1985) defined *dispositional optimism* as a generalized expectancy for favorable outcomes for oneself. The items that comprise their scale (e.g., "I'm always optimistic about my future") have substantial conceptual overlap with the items defined by Perceived Opportunities. Across multiple studies, Scheier, Carver and their associates found that individuals scoring high on dispositional optimism tended to use more adaptive coping methods in controllable and uncontrollable situations (Scheier et al., 1986), reported fewer physical complaints when subjected to significant stress (Scheier & Carver, 1985), and suffered less postpartum depression after giving birth (Carver & Gaines, 1987). They also reported strong positive correlations between optimism and particular coping styles that they viewed as empirically adaptive, such as a tendency to seek out social support when confronted by a stressful challenge and a tendency to engage in problem-focused coping (Scheier et al., 1986). The strong cross-time correlation in the study reported here between Perceived Opportunities and Social Impact Efficacy (.32; Table 7.5) is consistent with the correlations between optimism and coping efficacy obtained by Scheier and Carver. The causal impact of this variable, however, as shown in Fig. 7.1, is not as strong as the correlation would imply.

The overall picture that emerges from these analyses suggests that an individual's personal beliefs, values, and lifestyle in late adolescence are more important direct determinants of young adult competence than are the characteristics of the individual's family. Family characteristics of the late adolescent are, nevertheless, statistically significant predictors of young adult perceived social competence. As expected, inclusion of family-related characteristics did attenuate the observed relation between adolescent Academic Lifestyle and adult perceived competence measures. Family characteristics of the late adolescent are, of course, important influences on personal beliefs, values, and lifestyle that have been shown to contribute more directly to predicting adult competence, and thus are important mediators. It is also possible that family influences may have had an earlier impact (during childhood and early adolescence) on generating the personal values, beliefs, and lifestyle that are conducive to the subsequent development of an adolescent's individual characteristics and thus to young adult sense of competency and efficacy. The present analyses suggest that these family influences may not contribute directly to the development of adult competence once their impact has been originally registered earlier in life. This would account for the high within-time correlations between family-related variables and competency measures in the present study, while also explaining the lack of substantial direct, cross-time effects between these sets of factors.

The empirically determined important role of Perceived Opportunities in this study obviously needs replication. The weak stability effect of Perceived Opportunities, the stronger within-time correlations of Perceived Opportunities with other constructs at the young adult measurement period than during the late adolescent period, and the relatively strong cross-time effect of Family Support on Perceived Opportunities suggest that Perceived Opportunities (and, perhaps, dispositional optimism) only becomes a stable characteristic of the individual at young adulthood. Future research should confirm whether or not adult Perceived Opportunities is more stable over time than teenage Perceived Opportunities.

In conclusion, it must be noted that the measures in this study included self-reported perceptions of ability, not observed behavior. Future research needs to examine if similar results obtain over a similar period in life for the effects of family factors, academic lifestyle orientation, and perceived opportunities on observed young adult social competence.

## ACKNOWLEDGMENTS

This research was supported by grant DA01070 from the National Institute on Drug Abuse. This chapter was prepared subsequent to Bentler's invited presentation "Methodological Reflections on Analyzing Cross-Context Relationships" at the fourth annual Summer Institute, Family Research Consortium, Cape Cod, MA, May 1989, and is based on a paper presented by Newcomb at the Life History Research Society meeting, Montreal, June 1989. The assistance of Tove Davison is gratefully acknowledged.

## REFERENCES

Bandura, A. (1982). Self-efficacy mechanism in human agency. *American Psychologist, 37,* 122–147.

Barrera, M. (1981). Self-referent thought: A developmental analysis of self-efficacy. In J. M. Flavell & L. Ross (Eds.), *Social cognitive development: Frontiers and possible futures* (pp. 200–239). Cambridge, England: Cambridge University Press.

Basow, S. A. (1986). *Gender stereotypes: Traditions and alternatives* (2nd ed.). Monterey, CA: Brooks/Cole.

Baumrind, D. (1985). Familial antecedents of adolescent drug use: A developmental perspective. In

194    McCARTHY ET AL.

C. L. Jones & R. J. Battjes (Eds.), *Etiology of drug abuse: Implications for prevention* (pp. 13–44). Rockville, MD: National Institute on Drug Abuse.

Bell, N. J., & Avery, A. W. (1985). Family structure and parent-adolescent relationships: Does family structure really make a difference? *Journal of Marriage and the Family, 47*, 503–508.

Bentler, P. M. (1986). Structural modeling and *Psychometrika:* An historical perspective on growth and achievements. *Psychometrika, 51*, 35–51.

Bentler, P. M. (1989). *EQS structural equations program manual.* Los Angeles: BMDP Statistical Software.

Bentler, P. M. (1990a). Comparative fit indexes in structural models. *Psychological Bulletin, 107*, 238–246.

Bentler, P. M. (1990b). Latent variable structural models for separating specific from general effects. In L. Sechrest, E. Perrin, & J. Bunker (Eds.), *Research methodology: Strengthening causal interpretations of nonexperimental data* (pp. 61–83). Rockville, MD: Department of Health and Human Services.

Bentler, P. M., & Bonett, D. G. (1980). Significance tests and goodness of fit in the analysis of covariance structures. *Psychological Bulletin, 88*, 588–606.

Bentler, P. M., & Chou, C. P. (1986, April). *Statistics for parameter expansion and construction in structural models.* Paper presented at the American Educational Research Association meeting, San Francisco.

Bentler, P. M., & Newcomb, M. D. (1978). Longitudinal study of marital success and failure. *Journal of Consulting and Clinical Psychology, 46*, 1053–1070.

Bentler, P. M., & Newcomb, M. D. (1986). Personality, sexual behavior, and drug use revealed through latent variable methods. *Clinical Psychology Review, 6*, 363–385.

Betz, N. E., & Hackett, G. (1981). The relationships of career-related self-efficacy expectations to perceived career options in college women and men. *Journal of Counseling Psychology, 28*, 399–410.

Blake, J. (1981). The only child in America: Prejudice versus performance. *Population and Development in Review, 1*, 43–54.

Blatt, S. J., Quinlan, D. M., Chevron, E. S., McDonald, C., & Zuroff, D. (1982). Dependency and self-criticism: Psychological dimensions of depression. *Journal of Consulting and Clinical Psychology, 50*, 113–124.

Bollen, K. (1989). *Structural equations with latent variables.* New York: Wiley.

Carver, C. S., & Gaines, J. G. (1987). Optimism, pessimism, and post partum depression. *Cognitive Therapy and Research, 11*, 449–462.

Cauce, A. M., Felner, R. D., & Primavera, J. (1982). Social support in high-risk adolescents: Structural components and adaptive impact. *American Journal of Community Psychology, 10*, 417–428.

Chou, C.-P., & Bentler, P. M. (1990). Model modification in covariance structure modeling: A comparison among likelihood ratio, Lagrange Multiplier, and Wald tests. *Multivariate Behavioral Research, 25*, 115–136.

Compas, B. E. (1986). Coping with stress during childhood and adolescence. *Psychological Bulletin, 101*, 393–403.

Compas, B. E., Wagner, B. M., Slavin, L. A., & Vannatta, K. (1986). A prospective study of life events, social support, and psychological symptomatology during the transition from high school to college. *American Journal of Community Psychology, 14*, 241–257.

Conger, R. D., McCarty, J. A., Yang, R. K., Lahey, B. B., & Kropp, J. P. (1984). Perception of child, child-rearing values, and emotional distress as mediating links between environmental stressors and observed maternal behavior. *Child Development, 55*, 2234–2247.

Donovan, J. E., Jessor, R., & Jessor, L. (1983). Problem drinking in adolescence and young adulthood: A follow-up study. *Journal of Studies on Alcohol, 44*, 109–137.

Falbo, T. (1984). Only children. A review. In T. Falbo (Ed.), *The single child family* (pp. 1–24). New York: Guilford Press.

Falbo, T., & Cooper, C. R. (1980). Young children's time and intellectual ability. *Journal of Genetic Psychology, 173,* 299–300.

Falbo, T., & Polit, D. F. (1986). Quantitative review of the only child literature: Research evidence and theory development. *Psychological Bulletin, 100,* 176–198.

Felner, R. D., Ginter, M., & Primavera, J. (1982). Primary prevention during school transitions: Social support and environmental structure. *American Journal of Community Psychology, 10,* 277–290.

Gewirtz, J. L., & Gewirtz, H. B. (1965). Stimulus conditions, infant behaviors, and social learning in four Israeli childrearing environments: A preliminary report illustrating differences in environment and behavior between "only" and "youngest" child. In B. M. Foss (Ed.), *Determinants of infant behavior* (pp. 192–220). New York: Wiley.

Glick, P. C., & Lin, S. (1986). More young adults are living with their parents: Who are they? *Journal of Marriage and the Family, 48,* 107–112.

Hackett, G. (1981, August). *Mathematics self-efficacy and the consideration of math-related majors: A preliminary path model.* Paper presented at the meeting of the American Psychological Association, Los Angeles.

Harlow, L. L. (1985). *Behavior of some elliptical theory estimators with nonnormal data in a covariance structures framework: A Monte Carlo study.* Unpublished doctoral dissertation, UCLA, Los Angeles.

Healy, J. M., Jr., & Stewart, A. J. (1984). Adaptation to life changes in adolescence. In P. Karoly & J. J. Steffen (Eds.), *Adolescent behavior disorders: Foundations and applications.* Lexington, MA: Health Books.

Hilton, I. (1967). Differences in the behavior of mothers toward first-born and later-born children. *Journal of Personality and Social Psychology, 7,* 282–290.

Huba, C. G., & Bentler, P. M. (1982). A developmental theory of drug use: Derivation and assessment of a causal modeling approach. In B. P. Baltes & O. G. Brim, Jr. (Eds.), *Life-span development and behavior* (Vol. 4, pp. 147–203). New York: Academic Press.

Johnston, L. D., O'Malley, P. M., & Bachman, J. G. (1987). *National trends in drug use and related factors among American high school students and young adults: 1975–1985.* Rockville, MD: National Institute on Drug Abuse.

Kandel, D. B. (1984). Marijuana users in young adulthood. *Archives of General Psychiatry, 41,* 200–209.

Kidwell, J. S. (1981). Number of siblings, sibling spacing, sex, and birth order: Their effects on perceived parent-adolescent relationships. *Journal of Marriage and the Family, 43,* 315–332.

Kinard, E. M., & Reinherz, H. (1986). Effects of marital disruption on children's school aptitude and achievement. *Journal of Marriage and the Family, 48,* 285–293.

MacCallum, R. (1986). Specification searches in covariance structure analyses. *Psychological Bulletin, 100,* 107–120.

McCarthy, W. J., & Newcomb, M. D. (1990). Two dimensions of perceived self-efficacy: Cognitive control and behavioral coping ability. In R. Schwarzer (Ed.), *Self-efficacy: Thought control of action* (pp. 39–64). Washington, DC: Hemisphere.

Mercy, J. A., & Steelman, L. C. (1982). Familial influence on the intellectual attainment of children. *American Sociological Review,* 532–542.

Miller, J. D., Cisin, I. H., Gardner-Keaton, H., Harrell, A. V., Wirtz, P. W., Abelson, H. I., & Fishburne, P. M. (1983). *National survey on drug abuse: Main findings 1982.* Rockville, MD: National Institute on Drug Abuse.

Mooijaart, A., & Bentler, P. M. (1991). Robustness of normal theory statistics in structural equation models. *Statistica Neerlandica.*

Newcomb, M. D. (1986). Nuclear attitudes and reactions: Associations with depression, drug use, and quality of life. *Journal of Personality and Social Psychology, 50*, 906–920.

Newcomb, M. D. (1987). Consequences of teenage drug use: The transition from adolescence to young adulthood. *Drugs and Society, 1*, 25–60.

Newcomb, M. D. (1990). What structural modeling techniques can tell us about social support. In I. G. Sarason, B. R. Sarason, & G. R. Pierce (Eds.), *Social support: An interactional view* (pp. 26–63). New York: Wiley.

Newcomb, M. D., & Bentler, P. M. (1986a). Drug use, educational aspirations, and work force involvement: The transition from adolescence to young adulthood. *American Journal of Community Psychology, 14,* 303–321.

Newcomb, M. D., & Bentler, P. M. (1986b). Loneliness and social support: A confirmatory hierarchical analysis. *Personality and Social Psychology Bulletin, 12*, 520–535.

Newcomb, M. D., & Bentler, P. M. (1988a). *Consequences of adolescent drug use: Impact on psychosocial development and young adult role responsibility.* Beverly Hills, CA: Sage.

Newcomb, M. D., & Bentler, P. M. (1988b). The impact of family context, deviant attitudes, and emotional distress on adolescent drug use: Longitudinal latent variable analyses of mothers and their children. *Journal of Research in Personality, 22*, 154–176.

Newcomb, M. D., Huba, G. J., & Bentler, P. M. (1981). A multidimensional assessment of stressful life events among adolescents: Derivation and correlates. *Journal of Health and Social Behavior, 22*, 400–415.

Newcomb, M. D., Maddahian, E., & Bentler, P. M. (1986). Risk factors for drug use among adolescents: Concurrent and longitudinal analyses. *American Journal of Public Health, 76*, 525–531.

Newcomb, M. D., McCarthy, W. J., & Bentler, P. M. (1989). Cigarette smoking, academic lifestyle, and self-efficacy: An eight-year study from early adolescence to young adulthood. *Journal of Applied Social Psychology, 19*, 251–281.

Sandler, I. N. (1980). Social support resources, stress and maladjustment of poor children. *American Journal of Community Psychology, 8*, 41–51.

Sandler, I. N., & Barrera, M. (1984). Toward a multi-method approach to assessing the effects of social support. *American Journal of Community Psychology, 12*, 37–52.

Satorra, A., & Bentler, P. M. (1990). Model conditions for asymptotic robustness in the analysis of linear relations. *Computational Statistics & Data Analysis.*

Scheck, D. C., & Emerick, R. (1976). The young male adolescent's perception of early childrearing behavior: The differential effects of socioeconomic status and family size. *Sociometry, 39*, 39–52.

Scheier, M. F., & Carver, C. S. (1985). Optimism, coping, and health: Assessment and implications of generalized outcome expectancies. *Health Psychology, 4*, 291–247.

Scheier, M. F., & Carver, C. S. (1989). Dispositional optimism and physical well-being: The influence of generalized outcome expectancies on health. *Journal of Personality, 57*, 1024–1040.

Scheier, M. F., Weintraub, J. K., & Carver, C. S. (1986). Coping with stress: Divergent strategies of optimists and pessimists. *Journal of Personality and Social Psychology, 51*, 1257–1264.

Stein, J. A., Newcomb, M. D., & Bentler, P. M. (1986). Stability and change in personality: A longitudinal study from early adolescence to young adulthood. *Journal of Research in Personality, 20*, 276–291.

Steinberg, L. D., Greenberger, E., Garduque, L., Ruggiero, M., & Vaux, A. (1982). Effects of working on adolescent development. *Developmental Psychology, 18*, 385–395.

Stewart, A. J. (1982). The course of individual adaption to life changes. *Journal of Personality and Social Psychology, 42*, 1100–1113.

Stewart, A. J., Sokol, M., Healy, J. M., Chester, N. L. (1986). Longitudinal studies of psychological consequences of life changes in children and adults. *Journal of Personality and Social Psychology, 50*, 143–151.

Turner, R. H. (1962). Some family determinants of ambition. *Sociology and Social Research, 46,* 397–411.

Velandia, W., Grandon, G. M., & Page, E. B. (1978). Family size, birth order, and intelligence in a large South American sample. *American Educational Research Journal, 15,* 399–416.

Zajonc, R. B. (1976). Family configuration and intelligence. *Science, 192,* 227–236.

Zajonc, R. B. (1979). The birth order puzzle. *Journal of Personality and Social Psychology, 37,* 1325–1341.

# 8 Developmental Systems and Family Functioning

Arnold Sameroff
*University of Michigan*

Models of child development have varied in the emphasis they place on contributions the characteristics of the person and characteristics of the environment make to later behavior. Although this debate can be treated as merely an academic discussion, it has important ramifications for the utilization of vast amounts of social resources. From intervention efforts that cost millions of dollars to the educational system that costs billions, practitioners rationalize their efforts on the basis of their developmental models. One of the major problems in such models is an inadequate conceptualization and differentiation of the environment. Bronfenbrenner and Crouter (1983) traced the history of empirical investigations of the environment and have shown how theoretical limitations have placed limits on the sophistication of research paradigms. The goal of this chapter is to expand on our understanding of the environment in order to lay a basis for more complex paradigms in both research and practice.

The significance of child and family characteristics for development can be viewed from two perspectives. The first is whether they make a contribution at all and the second is whether these contributions are active or passive ones. Reigel (1978) placed models of development into four categories reflecting various combinations of passive and active persons and passive and active environments. In the passive person–passive environment category he placed mechanistic theories that arose from the empiricist philosophy of Locke and Hume in which combinations of events that occur in the environment are imprinted into the minds of observing persons. This view has been the basis for learning theories in which factors such as the continuity, frequency, or recency of stimuli determine how they will be coded into the receiving mind.

In a second category, the passive person is combined with an active environ-

199

ment. In this category are Skinnerian approaches to behavior modification in which the conditioner actively structures the input to alter the person's behavior in particular directions, but where the person is assumed to make no contribution to the outcome independent of experience.

The third category contains the concept of the active person but retains the passive environment. In this grouping fall the cognitive theories of Piaget and the linguistic views of Chomsky. Piaget viewed the person as an active constructor of knowledge based on experience with the environment. The environment is a necessary part of development, but has no active role in structuring thought or action. Similarly, Chomsky viewed language development as the person's application of innate linguistic categories to linguistic experience. For neither theorist was the organization of experience a determinant of cognitive or language competence.

In the fourth category are models that combine an active person and an active environment. Riegel saw these models as deriving from Marx's interpretations of the dialectical nature of development in which the actions of the individual change reality, then, in turn, the changes in reality effect the behavior of the individual. Sameroff and Chandler (1975) captured this process in their transactional model of development. In this view, developmental outcomes are not a product of the initial characteristics of the child or the family or even their mechanistic combination. Outcomes are the result of the interplay between child and context across time, in which the state of one impacts on the next state of the other in a continuous dynamic process.

Arguments over appropriate theories have important implications for both research and clinical strategies. Unless one understands how development proceeds, there is little basis for attempts to alter it, either through prevention or intervention programs. The conclusion that I work toward here is that consideration of both nature and nurture are necessary for any developmental process and that the contributions of both are not only active, but interactive and transactive as well.

As is seen here, all development seems to follow a dynamic systems model. In this view, outcomes are never a function of the individual taken alone or the experiential context taken alone. Behavioral competencies are a product of the combination of an individual and his or her experience. To predict outcome, a singular focus on the characteristics of the individual, in this case the child, will frequently be misleading. What needs to be added is an analysis and assessment of the experiences available to the child.

## EVOLUTION OF DEVELOPMENTAL MODELS

The models that developmental researchers have used have evolved in complexity since the 1940s (Sameroff, 1987). Ancient theorists interpreted development as an unfolding of intrinsic characteristics as the child went through stages of

FIG. 8.1. Deterministic consti-
tutional model of development
(C1 to C4 represents state of the
child at successive points in
time).

$$C_1 \longrightarrow C_2 \longrightarrow C_3 \longrightarrow C_4$$

growth, from C1 to C2 to C3 in Fig. 8.1. The dictionary definition of *development* describes a photographic process in which some original image becomes clearer until the finished print appears. Everything in the grown-up child was inherent in the initial conditions, predominantly biological. Although geneticists argue that many developmental outcomes are inherent in the genes, the lack of significant correlations between measures of early behavior and later outcome have prevented the easy acceptance of this view.

This model was countered by environmental models in which each stage of development was determined by the contemporary context, analogous to Reigel's (1978) passive person–active environment category. If the context remained the same, the child remained the same. If the context changed, the child changed (see Fig. 8.2).

Risk research has produced evidence documenting the powerful effects of environmental factors on children's cognitive and socioemotional competence, especially parental mental health and social class (Broman, Nichols, & Kennedy, 1975; Golden & Birns, 1976; Werner & Smith, 1982). Efforts to understand developmental dysfunctions must be based on an analysis of how families that vary on dimensions such as social classes differ on the characteristics that foster or impede psychological development in their children.

In the Rochester Longitudinal Study (RLS) my colleagues and I also found social class and parental mental health to be associated with developmental risk (Sameroff, Seifer, & Zax, 1982). The RLS is a study of the development of several hundred children from birth through early adolescence assessing environmental factors as well as the cognitive and social competence of the children. We decided to subdivide the global variable of social class to see if we could identify factors more directly connected to the child that acted as environmental risks. These factors range from proximal variables like the mother's interaction with the child, to such intermediate variables as the mother's mental health, to distal variables such as the financial resources of the family.

When the sample of children in the RLS were 4 years old we assessed 10

FIG. 8.2. Deterministic environmental model of development (E1 to E4 represent experiential influences at successive
points in time).

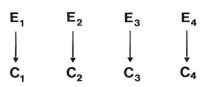

environmental variables that are correlates of socioeconomic status (SES) but not equivalents (Sameroff, Seifer, Barocas, Zax, & Greenspan, 1987). We then tested whether poor cognitive development in our preschool children was a function of low SES or the compounding of environmental risk factors found in low SES groups. The 10 environmental risk variables were as follows:

1. a history of maternal mental illness;
2. high maternal anxiety;
3. a parental perspectives score derived from a combination of measures that reflected rigidity in the attitudes, beliefs, and values that mothers had in regard to their child's development;
4. few positive maternal interactions with the child observed during infancy;
5. head of household in unskilled occupations;
6. minimal maternal education;
7. disadvantaged minority status;
8. single motherhood;
9. stressful life events; and
10. large family size.

When these risk factors were related to socioemotional and cognitive competence scores, major differences were found between those children with few risks and those with many. In terms of intelligence, children with no environmental risks scored more than 30 points higher than children with eight or nine risk factors (see Fig. 8.3).

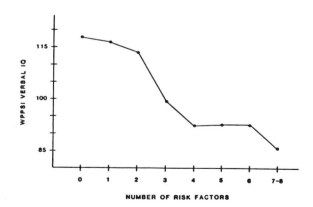

FIG. 8.3. Effects of multiple-risk scores on preschool intelligence (Sameroff et al., 1987).

These analyses of the RLS data were attempts to elaborate environmental risk factors by reducing global measures (e.g., SES) to component social and behavioral variables. We were able to identify a set of risk factors that was predominantly found in lower SES groups, but affected child outcomes in all social classes. Moreover, no single variables was determinant of outcome. Only in families with multiple risk factors was the child's competence placed in jeopardy. In the analyses of intellectual outcomes none of the children in the low multiple-risk group had an IQ below 85, whereas 24% of the children in the high multiple-risk group did. In a similar analysis of the effects of multiple risk on the socio-emotional competence of these 4-year-olds, 28 times as many children were identified as having clinical problems in the high-risk as in the low-risk group (Sameroff, Seifer, Zax, Barocas, & Greenspan, 1990).

Despite the demonstrated power of environmental effects, risk analyses still lack descriptions of the processes by which negative experiences have their effects. Such analyses as reported for the RLS offer an epidemiological black box that documents effects but not processes. An interactionist position would combine and extend separate analyses of environmental and child contributions as in Fig. 8.4. Here, continuity is carried by the child but moderated by possible discontinuities in experience. Anastasi (1958) is credited with the important interactionist conceptual breakthrough in pointing out that development could not occur without an environment. There is no logical possibility of considering development of an individual independent of the environment. Continuity could not be explained as a characteristic of the child because each new achievement was an amalgam of characteristics of the child and his or her experience. Neither alone would be predictive of later levels of functioning. If continuities were found, it was because there was a continuity in the relation between the child and the environment, not because of continuities in either taken alone.

Modern views of the determinants of intelligence or genetically related forms of psychopathology have adopted an additive, less dynamic version of the interactional model. In these views there is a biological predisposition that can produce a range of reactions depending on the addition of environmental factors (Zubin & Spring, 1977). In the Rosenthal (1970) diathesis stress model of schizophrenia, the genetic vulnerability only becomes manifest when there is an adequate amount of stress in the environment. There will be no schizophrenia if there is either vulnerability alone or stress alone.

More recent conceptualizations of the developmental model have incorporated effects of the child on the environment posited by Rheingold (1966) and Bell

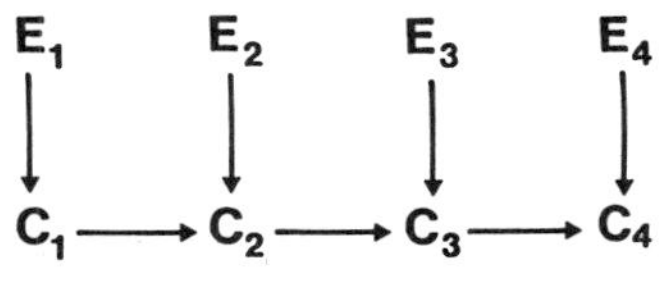

FIG. 8.4. Interactionist model of development.

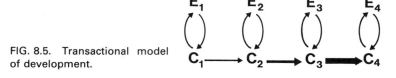

FIG. 8.5. Transactional model of development.

(1968). These dynamic interactionist (Thomas, Chess, & Birch, 1968) or transactional models (Sameroff & Chandler, 1975) add to the independent contributions of child and environment, characteristics of the environment that are conditioned by the nature of the child. Different characteristics of the child will trigger different responses from the environment (see Fig. 8.5).

There are a number of empirically validated examples of transactional processes in development (see Sameroff, 1987). One of the most compelling data sets emerges from the work of Patterson and his colleagues in a series of studies on the origins of antisocial behavior in childhood (Patterson, 1986). In the Patterson model, children who engage in noncompliant behavior (developmentally appropriate during early childhood) elicit inept disciplining from some parents that acts to reinforce the child's noncompliant behaviors characterized by whining, teasing, yelling, and disapproval. These behaviors escalate parental negative coercive responses that promote further child noncompliance eventuating in high-amplitude aggressive behaviors, including physical attack. When these aggressive noncompliant children enter the school setting they elicit poor peer acceptance that maintains their poor self-esteem and poor academic performance. This sequence from normal noncompliance to abnormal antisocial behavior and school failure has been demonstrated by Patterson to unfold in a developmental sequence of negative transactions.

The dynamic reciprocal interchanges between parent and child captured by the transactional model in Fig. 8.5 require further additions to complete the modern developmental model. Continuity is implied in the organization of the child's behavior by the series of arrows from C1 to C2 to C3 in Fig. 8.5. What must be added is continuity in the organization of experience, a series of arrows from E1 to E3 as found in Fig. 8.6.

In the RLS, we (Sameroff, Seifer, Baldwin, & Baldwin, 1989) examined such continuities in the development of children from birth through early adolescence,

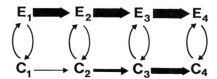

FIG. 8.6. Environmental regulation model of development.

assessing the cognitive and social competence of the children. The typical statistic reported in longitudinal research is the correlation between early and later performances of the children. We too found such correlations. Intelligence at 4 years of age correlated .72 with intelligence at 13 years of age, and the social competence scores at the two ages correlated .43. The usual interpretation of such numbers is that there is a continuity of competence or incompetence in the child. Such a conclusion cannot be challenged if the only assessments in the study are of the children.

In the RLS, environmental as well as child factors were examined. We were able to correlate environmental characteristics across time as well as child ones. We found that the correlation between environmental risk scores at the two ages was .76, as great or greater than any continuity within the child. Those children who had poor family and social environments at 4 years old still had them when they were 13 and probably would continue to have them for the foreseeable future. What appeared to be continuity of behavior in the child can be interpreted instead as a continuity in the characteristics of the environment. Whatever the child's ability for achieving high levels of competence, it was severely undermined by the continuing paucity of environmental support.

The complete model in Fig. 8.6 has consistency not only in the child but in the environment as well. There is a continuity in many of the basic characteristics of the environment that effect child development. Apparent continuities in the behavior of children may be an outcome of real continuities in the richness or paucity of experience provided by the caregiving environment at important developmental transitions.

## REGULATORY SYSTEMS IN DEVELOPMENT

What kind of dynamic theory would be necessary to integrate our current understanding of development? It must explain how the individual and the context work together to produce patterns of adaptive or maladaptive functioning and relate how to produce patterns of adaptive or maladaptive functioning and relate how such past or present functioning is carried forward in time (Sroufe & Rutter, 1984).

The genotype is considered to be the basic level of biological organization that regulates the physical outcome of each individual. There is a need for an analogous structure on the environmental side that regulates the social outcome of each individual. Such an organization has been proposed to describe the regulation of socialization patterns and has been labeled the *environtype* (Sameroff, 1985; Sameroff & Fiese, 1990). The environtype is composed of cultural, family, and parental subsystems that not only transact with the child but also transact with each other.

Developmental regulations at each of these levels are carried within codes: the cultural code, the family code, and the individual code of the parent. These codes regulate cognitive and socioemotional development so that the child ultimately will be able to fill a role defined by society. They are hierarchically related in their evolution and in their current influence on the child. The experience provided to the developing child is partially determined by the beliefs, values, and personality of the parents, partially by the family's interaction patterns and transgenerational history, and partially by the socialization beliefs, controls, and supports of the culture. To summarize the overall model of developmental regulation, the child's behavior at any point in time is a product of the transactions between the phenotype (i.e., the child), the environtype (i.e., the source of external experience), and the genotype (i.e., the source of biological organization; see Fig. 8.7).

## Cultural Code

The ingredients of the cultural code are a complex of characteristics that organize a society's childrearing system and that incorporate elements of socialization and education. These processes are embedded in sets of social controls and social supports. They are based on beliefs that differ in the amount of community consensus ranging from mores and norms to fads and fashions. It would be beyond the scope of this chapter to elucidate the full range of cultural regulatory processes that are potentially relevant to intervention efforts. As a consequence, only a few points are highlighted to clarify the dimensions of the cultural code.

Many common biological characteristics of the human species have acted to produce similar developmental agendas in most cultures. For example, in most cultures formal education begins between the ages of 6 and 8 when most children have reached the cognitive ability to learn from such structured experiences (Rogoff, 1981). However, there are historical and cross-cultural differences where changes in child behavior are emphasized or ignored. For example, informal education can begin at many different ages depending on the culture's attributions to the child. Some middle-class parents have been convinced that prenatal experiences will enhance the cognitive development of their children

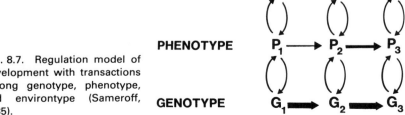

FIG. 8.7. Regulation model of development with transactions among genotype, phenotype, and environtype (Sameroff, 1985).

and consequently begin stimulation programs during pregnancy, whereas others believe it best to wait until the first grade before beginning formal learning experiences. Such examples demonstrate the variability of human developmental contexts, and the openness of the regulatory system to modification.

## Family Code

Just as the cultural code regulates the fit between individuals and the social system, family codes organize individuals within the family system. Family codes serve as guidelines for parental behavior in assigning roles, expressing emotions, and establishing rules of conduct. As in the cultural code, the family code is not synonymous with any one set of behaviors. Rather, family organization is coded along dimensions of beliefs, group practices, and interaction patterns.

Since the 1970s, a great deal of effort has been directed toward identifying patterns of parent–child interaction that may contribute to child outcome. Although issues of cause and effect have been addressed through sophisticated mathematical methodologies such as sequential analyses (e.g., Bakeman & Gottman, 1986; Sackett, 1979) and structural equation modeling (e.g., Bentler, 1987; Patterson, 1986), direct influences rarely account for a large proportion of the variance related to child outcome. A consistent finding has been that global aspects of the environment such as socioeconomic status regularly account for some of the variance (e.g., Sameroff et al., 1987) and microanalytic factors such as interaction patterns also account for some of the variance (e.g., Field, 1987). Intermediary between the cultural influences and individual interaction patterns are a series of factors that make up the family code.

The family regulates the child's development through a variety of processes that vary in their degree of representation and practice (Reiss, 1989). We (Sameroff & Fiese, 1990) considered four of these aspects of family organization to be on a dimension from most practiced to most represented. Families have *paradigms* that regulate how information is received by the family and is in operation when the family is together as a group. Families create *myths* that exaggerate roles within the family but are not topics open for discussion. Families tell *stories* that transmit values and orientations to other family members and anyone else who will listen. Families practice *rituals* that prescribe roles and ascribe meaning to family interactions. Family paradigms and myths cannot be reported as such by individual members but only come into play when two or more family members are together. Family rituals are most easily accessible for report and their practice can be described by most individual members of the family. Family stories are intermediate to rituals and paradigms being transmitted through narratives but also are dependent on the context or presence of other family members. These four components of the family code interact with components of the cultural code so that parents may indoctrinate the child into the social world while preserving the unique qualities of the family.

Assuming that child outcome is the result of a dynamic transactional process, the family code accounts for multiple influences on child development within the family context. Explicit rules, observed interactions, inferred emotions and shared beliefs all play a part in the family code. Different empirical strategies are called for in unearthing the components of the family code. Each component also implies different forms of intervention (Sameroff & Fiese, 1990).

*Family Paradigms.*    Family paradigms are beliefs that the family holds about the social world that can only be inferred from observations of family process (Reiss, 1981). Paradigms organize the behavior of family members in their attempts to deal with social institutions and individuals outside of the family unit. They reside within the family unit and are not considered characteristics of any one individual family member. They operate by filtering information through group processes. These characteristic styles of processing information have been shown to be related to how families respond to treatment in group settings and make decisions within the family (Reiss, 1981).

Family paradigms are the least articulated component of the family code. The importance of family paradigms is that they are manifested in family interactions, including how children are incorporated into group processes. The normal or disturbed behavior of children must to some degree be interpreted as an outgrowth of the family paradigm (Reiss, Oliveri, & Curd, 1981).

*Family Myths.*    Family myths are beliefs that have a strong influence on family process. They may highlight family roles but myths are not readily recountable by family members. Myths are not open for discussion, nor are they readily recognized as distortions (Ferreira, 1963). They may have a traumatic origin and frequently have a strong affective component (Kramer, 1985).

Family myths frequently provide a sense of continuity across generations. Individual family members carry with them their own beliefs and interpretations of their family of origin experiences and family heritage. Wamboldt and his colleagues (Wamboldt & Reiss, 1989; Wamboldt & Wolin, 1989) proposed that family myths influence mate selection and marital satisfaction and may even be changed through the marriage. They found that when new couples are faced with the task of defining for themselves what their newly created family will be like, they include beliefs about their parent's marital relationship. However, it is possible for an individual to be "rescued" from a family of origin myth by pairing with another individual with a healthier background and deliberately changing their myth (Bennett, Wolin, Reiss, & Teitelbaum, 1987).

*Family Stories.*    A third component of the family code that can be articulated by family members is family stories. They may contribute to the family code by emphasizing values and highlighting roles. Family stories can be told and heard by multiple members of the family. These stories provide a context in which children learn family roles as well as family values across generations. In particular, the content of family stories may be important in studying how values are transmitted in the family (Fiese & Sameroff, 1989; Reiss, 1989). These stories include the range of goals necessary to incorporate the child into the family and cultural system. Storytelling and narratives by their very nature organize experience in a way that will fit with the storyteller's understanding of the world (Sarbin, 1986) and identity (McAdams, 1989). In this regard, family stories provide a form of regulation that is influenced by the individual personality and experiences of the storyteller. Stories of a parent's childhood may transmit to the child what the parent considers important lessons of growing up as well as affective modifiers of salient childhood experiences.

Fiese (1990b) examined the relation between the thematic content of family stories and parent–child interaction patterns in a sample of mother and toddler pairs observed during a free-play period. Following the free-play period the mother was asked to tell her child a story "about when you were a little girl, when you were growing up." The mothers' stories were coded for thematic content along dimensions of play, affiliation, nurturance, rejection, and achievement. Mothers who told more affiliative, nurturant, and playful stories about their childhood engaged in more turn-taking and reciprocal interactions than mothers who told stories that included themes of rejection or achievement. However, mothers who told stories of their childhood that included themes of rejection or achievement tended to be less engaged overall and when they did interact with their toddler they tended to be more intrusive and directive.

Family stories may be a pathway for transmitting family of origin experiences to younger generations. The parent's representations of their family system may regulate, in part, how parents interact with their children.

If family stories provide a format for imparting lessons and values then it would be reasonable to predict that different themes would predominate according to social and developmental context. Fiese (1990b) found that mothers of 8- to 12-year-old boys told stories of their childhood that included themes of overcoming obstacles and facing adversity. These themes were not evident in the stories told to toddlers. From this dynamic perspective, family stories are adjusted to meet the demands of the family. Although family stories may provide a link across generations the connection is paired with the demands of the contemporary family.

*Family Rituals.*   Family rituals are the most self-aware aspects of the family code (Bossard & Boll, 1950). Family rituals may range from highly stylized religious observances such as first communion or bar mitzvahs to less articulated daily interaction patterns such as the type of greeting made when someone returns home. Rituals mark the beginning and end of life within a family but also regulate behavior on a daily basis. Families can easily identify ritual practices they hold as well as describe the routines they perform on a daily, weekly, or annual basis (Fiese & Kline, 1990; Wolin, Bennett, & Jacobs, 1988). Rituals are practiced by the whole family and are frequently documented. They may be times for taking photographs, exchanging gifts, or preserving mementos. The content of family rituals includes symbolic information as well as important preparatory phases, schedules, and plans. Rituals serve a regulatory function by assigning roles and providing meaning to family interactions.

The role of family rituals in regulating dysfunctional behavior has been most clearly demonstrated in families of alcoholics. In a study of married children of alcoholic parents, certain aspects of family rituals were identified as protective factors that guarded against the children becoming alcoholics (Wolin et al., 1988). Children who came from families that were able to preserve family rituals, such as distinctive dinner and holiday routines, were less likely to become alcoholics themselves. Wolin and his colleagues speculated that rituals provide stability for dysfunctional families.

A self-report measure of family rituals has been developed by Fiese and Kline (1990) to extend the interview research of Wolin et al. (1988). In the initial study using the Family Ritual Questionnaire (FRQ) with college students, the level of ritualization in the family was related to the child's feelings of security and belongingness as measured through a self-report of adolescent attachment to the family (Fiese & Kline, 1990). More specifically, the symbolic and affective qualities associated with family rituals were positively related to adolescent attachment.

In a second study using the FRQ (Fiese, 1990a), two distinct dimensions of family rituals were found: a ritual *meaning* factor and a ritual *routine* factor. The meaning factor included dimensions of regular occurrence, required attendance, symbolic significance, affective involvement, and deliberateness. The routine factor included dimensions of specific roles and detailed routines. The two factors were differentially related to measures of child outcome. The meaning factor was negatively related to a measure of anxiety, and positively related to self-esteem, but the routine factor was not significantly related to either.

To follow up on the studies of the intergenerational transmission of alcoholism, the family rituals of college students who reported problematic drinking in their family of origin were examined by Fiese (1990a). In accord with the findings of Wolin and Bennett (Bennett et al., 1987; Wolin et al., 1988) who had sampled self-identified children of alcoholics, children of alcoholics who reported low levels of family ritual meaning had significantly higher anxiety scores than children of alcoholics who reported high meaning levels or children of nonalcoholic families regardless of family ritual meaning level.

Family rituals may contribute to the family code by providing meaning to patterned interactions. Although it is probable that a certain amount of routine and regularity would have to exist in order for rituals to have a powerful influence, it is apparently the meaning associated with family rituals that is significantly related to child outcome. Sociologists have pointed out that when cultures create rituals the symbolic quality of patterned interactions transforms a routine into a ritual (Moore & Myerhoff, 1977). For the family it may be the meaning associated with routine interactions that transforms momentary interactions into central features of family process and organization.

## Individual Code of the Parent

There is clear evidence that parental behavior is influenced by the family and social context. When operating as part of a family, the behavior of each member is altered (Parke & Tinsley, 1987), frequently without awareness of the behavioral change (Reiss, 1981). However, there is also no doubt that individuals bring their own contribution to family interactions. The contribution of parents is determined much more complexly than that of young children, given the multiple levels that contribute to their behavior. The individualized interpretations that each parenting figure imposes on social and family practices are to a large extent conditioned by each parent's past participation in his or her own family's coded interactions, but they are captured uniquely by each member of the family. These individual influences further condition each parent's responses to his or her own child. Main and Goldwyn (1984) identified adult attachment categories that reflect parents' encoding of their interpretation of their attachment to their own parents. What is compelling about these adult attachment categories is that they operate across generations and are predictive of the attachment categories of the infants of these parents. In fact, these maternal representations have been better predictors of infant behavior than observational measures of the mother's actual interactions with the child.

In the Rochester Longitudinal Study one of the 10 risk factors we identified was called parental perspectives. This factor was a composite of three scales, the Sameroff and Feil (1985) Concepts of Development Questionnaire (CODQ), the Kohn (1969) parental values scale, and the Schaefer and Bell (1958) Parent Attitude Research Instrument (PARI). When the children in the study were 4 years old, their mothers completed all three scales. When the children were 13 years old their mothers completed the CODQ and the Kohn scales. One would think that there would be a great deal of plasticity in parent attitudes, beliefs, and values across the 9-year intervening period. In fact, there was not. When the 4- and 13-year measures were intercorrelated all the coefficients were in the 60s, all highly significant.

The stability of risk factors like low occupational and educational level, the things people do with their lives, is not terribly surprising. However, the stability of beliefs and values, the things people think about, is surprising. Both kinds of stability emphasize the importance of assessments of context as major regulators of how parents deal with children. It is important to recognize the parent as a major regulating agency, but it is equally important to recognize that parental behavior is itself embedded in social and family regulatory contexts (Goodnow, 1988).

## SUMMARY

In the history of models of child development there has been a movement from linear chains of causality to the complexity of transactional regulatory processes at multiple levels of living systems. Despite the desire to maintain simple models in psychology, advances in the complexity of models in biology and physics have provided ample justification for necessary changes. Models that focus on singular causal factors are inadequate for either the study or manipulation of developmental outcomes. By illuminating the multiple influences on development, one provides multiple opportunities for intervening in development. Because outcomes are not contained in initial conditions, each life trajectory has the opportunity to overcome early inadequacies if development fostering experiences are provided. On the other hand, the risks found in experience can offset early developmental achievements. The political context will have a large role in determining whether risk or protective features will characterize the child's environment. But it is behavioral science that will provide the explanations for how these processes operate and the mechanisms for improving them.

## REFERENCES

Anastasi, A. (1958). Heredity, environment, and the question, "How?" *Psychological Review, 75,* 81–95.

Bakeman, R., & Gottman, J. M. (1986). *Observing interaction: An introduction to sequential analysis.* Cambridge: Cambridge University Press.

Bell, R. Q. (1968). A reinterpretation of the direction of effects in studies of socialization. *Psychological Review, 75,* 81–95.

Bennett, L. A., Wolin, S., Reiss, D., & Teitelbaum, M. A. (1987). Couples at risk for alcoholism transmission: Protective influences. *Family Process, 26,* 111–129.

Bentler, P. M. (1987). Drug use and personality in adolescence and young adulthood: Structural models with nonnormal variables. *Child Development, 58,* 65–79.

Bossard, J.J.S., & Boll, E. (1950). *Ritual in family living.* Philadelphia: University of Pennsylvania Press.

Broman, S. H., Nichols, P. L., & Kennedy, W. A. (1975). *Preschool IQ: prenatal and early developmental correlates.* Hillsdale, NJ: Lawrence Erlbaum Associates.

Bronfenbrenner, U., & Crouter, A. C. (1983). The evolution of environmental models in development research. In P. H. Mussen (Series Ed.) & W. Kessen (Vol. Ed.), *Handbook of Child Psychology: Vol. 1. History, theories, and methods* (pp. 357–414). New York: Wiley.

Ferreira, A. J. (1963). Family myth and homeostasis. *Archives General Psychiatry, 9,* 457–463.

Field, T. M. (1987). Affective and interactive disturbances in infants. In J. Osofsky (Ed.), *Handbook of infant development* (2nd ed., pp. 972–1005). New York: Wiley.

Fiese, B. H. (1990a). *Dimensions of family rituals: The interplay between meaning and routine.* Unpublished manuscript.

Fiese, B. H. (1990b, April). *Family stories: Mothers stories of their childhood and relation to mother–toddler interaction in a free play setting.* Paper presented at the International Conference on Infant Studies, Montreal.

Fiese, B. H., & Kline, C. A. (1990). *Development of the Family Ritual Questionnaire.* Unpublished manuscript.

Fiese, B. H., & Sameroff, A. J. (1989). Family context in pediatric psychology: A transactional perspective. *Journal of Pediatric Psychology, 14,* 293–314.

Golden, M., & Birns, B. (1976). Social class and infant intelligence. In M. Lewis (Ed.), *Origins of intelligence: Infancy and early childhood* (pp. 125–143). New York: Plenum.

Goodnow, J. J. (1988). Parents' ideas actions, and feelings: Models and methods from developmental and social psychology. *Child Development, 59,* 286–330.

Kohn, M. L. (1969). *Class and conformity: A study in values.* Homewood, IL: Dorsey.

Main, M., & Goldwyn, R. (1984). Predicting rejection of their infant from mother's representation of her own experience: Implications for the abused and abusing intergenerational cycle. *Child Abuse and Neglect, 8,* 203–217.

McAdams, D. P. (1989). The development of a narrative identity. In D. M. Buss & N. Cantor (Eds.), *Personality psychology: Recent trends and emerging directions* (pp. 160–174). New York: Springer-Verlag.

Moore, S. F., & Myerhoff, B. G. (1977). *Secular ritual.* Amsterdam, The Netherlands: Van Gorcum.

Parke, R. D., & Tinsley, B. J. (1987). Family interaction in infancy. In J. Osofsky (Ed.), *Handbook of infant development* (2nd ed., 579–641). New York: Wiley.

Patterson, G. R. (1986). Performance models for antisocial boys. *American Psychologist, 41,* 432–444.

Reigel, K. F. (1978). *Psychology, mon amour: A countertext.* Boston: Houghton Mifflin.

Reiss, D. (1981). *The family's construction of reality.* Cambridge, MA: Harvard University Press.

Reiss, D. (1989). The represented and practicing family: Contrasting visions of family continuity. In A. J. Sameroff & R. N. Emde (Eds.), *Relationship disturbances in early childhood* (pp. 191–220). New York: Basic Books.

Reiss, D., Oliveri, M. E., & Curd, K. (1981). Family paradigm and adolescent social behavior. In H. D. Grotevant & C. R. Cooper (Eds.), *Adolescent development and the family. New Directions for Child Development* (Vol. 22, pp. 77–91). San Francisco: Jossey-Bass.

Rheingold, H. L. (1966). The development of social behavior in the human infant. In H. W. Stevenson (Ed.), Concept of development. *Monographs of the Society for Research in Child Development, 31* 5 (Whole No. 107).

Rogoff, B. (1981). Schooling and the development of cognitive skills. In H. C. Triandis & A. Heron (Eds.), *Handbook of cross-cultural psychology: Developmental psychology* (Vol. 4, pp. 233–294). Boston: Allyn & Bacon.

Rosenthal, D. (1970). *Genetic theory and abnormal behavior.* New York: McGraw-Hill.

Sackett, G. P. (1979). The lag sequential analysis of contingency and cyclicity in behavioral interaction research. In J. Osofsky (Ed.), *Handbook of infant development* (pp. 623–649). New York: Wiley.

Sameroff, A. J. (1985). *Can development be continuous?* Paper presented at annual meeting of American Psychological Association, Los Angeles.

Sameroff, A. J. (1987). The social context of development. In N. Eisenberg (Ed.), *Contemporary topics in developmental psychology* (pp. 273–291). New York: Wiley.

Sameroff, A. J., & Chandler, M. J. (1975). Reproductive risk and the continuum of caretaking casualty. In F. D. Horowitz, M. Hetherington, S. Scarr-Salapatek, & G. Siegel (Eds.), *Review of child development research* (Vol. 4, pp. 187–244). Chicago: University of Chicago Press.

Sameroff, A. J., & Feil, L. (1985). Parental concepts of development. In I. Sigel (Ed.), *Parent belief systems: The psychological consequences for children* (pp. 83–104). Hillsdale, NJ: Lawrence Erlbaum Associates.

Sameroff, A. J., & Fiese, B. H. (1990). Transactional regulations and early intervention. In S. J.

Meisels & J. P. Shonkoff (Eds.), *Handbook of early childhood intervention* (pp. 119–149). New York: Cambridge University Press.

Sameroff, A. J., Seifer, R., Baldwin, A. L., & Baldwin, C. (1989, April). *Continuity of risk from childhood to adolescence.* Paper presented at the biennial meetings of the Society for Research in Child Development, Kansas City.

Sameroff, A. J., Seifer, R., Barocas, R., Zax, M., & Greenspan, S. (1987). IQ scores of 4-year-old children: Social-environmental risk factors. *Pediatrics, 79,* 343–350.

Sameroff, A. J., Seifer, R., & Zax, M. (1982). Early development of children at risk for emotional disorder. *Monographs of the Society for Research in Child Development, 47*(7, Serial No. 199).

Sameroff, A. J., Seifer, R., Zax, M., Barocas, R., & Greenspan, S. (1990). Social-environmental risk and early competence. In C. Chiland (Ed.), *Yearbook of the International Association of Child and Adolescent Psychiatry and the Allied Professions (Vol. 9). The child and the family: New approaches to infant, child, adolescent and family mental health.* New York: Wiley.

Sarbin, T. R. (1986). The narrative as a root metaphor for psychology. In T. R. Sarbin (Ed.). *Narrative psychology: The storied nature of human conduct* (pp. 3–21). New York: Praeger.

Schaefer, E. S., & Bell, R. Q. (1958). Development of a parental attitude research instrument. *Child Development, 29,* 339–361.

Sroufe, L. A., & Rutter, M. (1984). The domain of developmental psychopathology. *Child Development, 55,* 17–29.

Thomas, A., Chess, S., & Birch, H. (1968). *Temperament and behavior disorders in children.* New York: New York University.

Wamboldt, F. S., & Reiss, D. (1989). Defining a family heritage and a new relationship identity: Two central tasks in the making of a marriage. *Family Process, 28,* 317–335.

Wamboldt, F. S., & Wolin, S. J. (1989). Reality and myth in family life: Changes across generations. In S. A. Anderson & D. A. Bagarozzi (Eds.), *Family myths: Psychotherapy implications* (pp. 141–166). New York: Haworth Press.

Werner, E. E., & Smith, R. S. (1982). *Vulnerable but invincible: A longitudinal study of resilient children and youth.* New York: McGraw Hill.

Wolin, S. J., Bennett, L. A., & Jacobs, J. S. (1988). Assessing family rituals. In E. Imber-Black, J. Roberts, & R. Whiting (Eds.), *Rituals and family therapy* (pp. 230–256). New York: Norton.

Zubin, J., & Spring, B. (1977). Vulnerability—A new view of schizophrenia. *Journal of Abnormal Psychology, 86,* 103–126.

# 9

# Epilogue: Unresolved Issues and Future Trends in Family Relationships With Other Contexts

Ross D. Parke
*University of California, Riverside*

This volume has raised a variety of issues that merit consideration by future researchers. The goal of this epilogue is to highlight the contribution of the preceding chapters and to underscore some of the unresolved problems and questions that this relatively new field faces.

## THE CHARACTERIZATION OF CONTEXT

One of the continuing concerns in this area is the development of a language for describing settings or contexts. To date, comparisons across contexts have been hampered by a lack of commonly used set of dimensions that would allow us to characterize contexts along similar lines. The value of the development of such dimensions is nicely illustrated by Cowan et al. (this volume) who note the importance of similarity between school and home for the prediction of academic and social adaptation. A variety of approaches to the problem of describing contexts have emerged (Cohen & Siegel, 1991), including a physical characteristics focus, a social systems approach, a relationship approach, and a regulatory approach. Perhaps the best-known illustration of the physical characteristics approach is Barker's (1968) ecological psychology approach, which stresses the importance of "behavior settings" that, in turn, constrain the behavior of individuals within those settings. However, this approach has proven to be of only limited value and has received less attention than other schemes. A second approach is Bronfenbrenner's social systems approach. Bronfenbrenner's (1979, 1986) characterization of four spheres or levels of social context continues to be a convenient taxonomy for organizing research findings. One of these levels is the microsystem, which refers to factors that directly impact on the child (e.g., family, peer group). In fact, as a field we have made considerable progress in describing microsystems such as the family (Dunn, 1988; Parke, 1988; Parke & Tinsley, 1987). As both the Cowan et al. and the Katz and Gottman chapters underscore, our understanding of the family has expanded to include the marital relationship as an important aspect of the family context. Moreover, progress is being made in describing different types of marriage and the impact of these types on children's peer relationships (Grych & Fincham, 1990; Katz & Gottman, this volume). In short, we are making considerable progress in expanding our understanding of the relationships within the family that are critical for understanding children's development. A second level—the mesosystem— refers to the combined impact of multiple systems (impact of peers, schools, extended families) or the influences among microsystems, whereby parent— child interaction influences the child's adaptation in the peer group or classroom. The exosystem refers to those settings that influence a child's development but in which the child does not directly participate or play a direct role. As Crouter (this volume) shows, parents' workplaces are prime examples of settings that have a profound impact on children even though children's own involvement and participation is minimal. Other examples of the exosystem might include the local school board, the zoning commission, or a school class attended by an older sibling. Finally, both mesosystems and exosystems are embedded within a set of ideological and institutional patterns of a particular culture or subculture as well as historical eras. This has been labeled the *chronosystem*. In his theoretical analyses, Sameroff (this volume) underscores and expands on Bronfenbrenner's chronosystem level in his discussion of ideology and culture as shaping factors that influence our behavior in various contexts.

Traditionally, research has been skewed toward understanding the microsystem to a large degree, with a primary focus on how factors within the family context influence children's outcomes. However, the hallmark of this volume is our movement toward understanding other levels of analyses. For example, much of the work can be characterized as operating at the mesosystem level, in which the interface between microsystems is explored. Examples include the chapters by Cowan et al. and Kellam et al. on the relationship between the family and adaptation to school, the McCarthy et al. chapter on the school links between family and young adult social and educational competence, the Parke et al. chapter on the links between family and peer systems, and Chase-Lansdale's work on the relationship between family and day care. Examples of the exosystem level of analysis are offered by Crouter in her exploration of the ways in which family and workplace interact to affect child and adult development.

A third approach involves describing settings in relationship terms (Hinde, 1979). This does not imply that the other approaches are without value, but suggests that psychological outcomes may often best be understood as products of differing kinds of relationships. Hinde (1979, 1992) offered a useful set of dimensions that could be applied to different settings such as schools, day-care settings, or the workplace. These dimensions include content, diversity, quality, relative frequency and patterning of interactions, the direction of the relationship (reciprocal vs. complementary), the degree of intimacy, the mutual understanding of the relationship, the degree of commitment, and the structural properties of the relationship (size and density). Although this is not an exhaustive taxonomy it is a useful starting point in beginning to describe different contexts using a common set of dimensions.

Sameroff's (1987, this volume) description of family-based regulatory mechanisms, such as paradigms, myths, stories, and rituals represents a fourth scheme that may have utility for describing regulatory mechanisms in other settings as well, using a common set of indices across contexts.

Combining social systems (Bronfenbrenner), relationship (Hinde) and regulatory (Sameroff) approaches will permit the description of the levels of organization that characterize complex settings and at the same time, not lose sight of the kinds of relationships that exist within each of these levels of organization and how these relationships are regulated. Bronfenbrenner's scheme is useful for alerting us to the multiple levels that are involved, although the Hinde and Sameroff approaches help us begin to describe the kinds of dimensions that can characterize common relationships and regulatory mechanisms across settings. Being able to conceptualize workplace, school, and family, for example, using a similar set of dimensions will be a major step in understanding how these settings will relate to one another.

## Linking Levels of Analysis Within and Across Contexts

A closely related issue in our efforts to characterize contexts concerns the distinction among levels of analysis within social contexts. Some progress has been made along these lines. In the case of the family, for example, distinctions between individual, dyadic, triadic, and family levels of analysis have been suggested (Elder, 1978; Parke, 1988; Parke, Power, & Gottman, 1979; Sigel & Parke, 1987). Moreover, as various authors in this volume (Cowan & Cowan; Katz & Gottman) suggest, it is important to distinguish among different types of dyadic and triadic relationships such as parent–child dyads, sibling dyads, or marital dyads. Similarly alliances among siblings or parents and a child each represent distinctive units of analysis. In other contexts such as the peer group, dyadic friendships have been distinguished from group membership or one's position in a peer group hierarchy (Hartup, 1986). Or consider the school system. The school can be viewed at the individual level, which includes pupils, teachers, and principals. In turn, each of these individuals develops various sets of dyadic relationships, with the child–teacher dyad receiving the most attention in the prior literature (Minuchin & Shapiro, 1983). The classroom level with its own norms, rules, and expectations represents another point of entry into the school system (Kellam, 1990). The school as the unit of analysis needs to be differentiated from individual and classroom levels because schools have distinctive atmospheres and characteristics as well (Bandura, 1991; Rutter, 1983). In turn, the school district level that sets overall policy for a number of schools needs to be distinguished. The kinds of relationships and regulatory mechanisms that characterize each of these levels within contexts can be described in similar ways that we discussed earlier. In addition, the links between these various levels of organization need to be described, if we are to understand how various levels within settings function to influence children's development. In summary, we need to give greater attention to the multiple levels of analysis that characterize contexts.

In turn, it is evident that we have little understanding of how different levels of organization within one context relate to similar or differing levels in other contexts. Our task of making connections across settings could be guided by these distinctions among levels of analysis. For example, within the family context individual, dyadic, and family levels of measurement might provide the opportunity to develop differing sets of skills, expectations, and attitudes. Family-level experience in which roles and rules governing group membership are learned would probably impact on children's ability to function in group settings such as play or work groups. On the other hand, dyadic relationships within the family would be expected to relate to the emergence of friendships or other dyadic relationships in school, work, or peer contexts (Park & Waters, 1989; Youngblade & Belsky, 1992). To date, we have ignored to a large degree these distinctions and instead often measured different levels of analysis in contexts that are being linked. Stronger relations may, in fact, be found if we recognize these distinctions when we choose our measurements in contexts that we wish to compare.

## Beyond the Family Setting: Describing Other Contexts

Another concern is the relative imbalance in the degree of attention paid to one or another setting that is being linked. To date, we have paid a disproportionate amount of attention to the family setting, while devoting less research attention to a description of extra-familial settings. Several illustrations flow from the chapters in this volume. As Chase-Lansdale notes, some of the difficulties in reconciling conflicting results concerning the impact of maternal employment on children's social and/or cognitive development are due to the fact that "the quality of child care was not measured" (p. 33). Similarly, Crouter stresses that "we will only fully understand work and family as settings when we pay equal attention to what is going on at work" (p. 22). A similar argument could be made about school and peer settings as well. Often, rich and detailed measures on the family side are linked with brief measures of the child's functioning in the other contexts. For example, Cowan et al. focus on teacher ratings and academic achievement, whereas Parke et al. rely on sociometric and teacher ratings. More effort to provide observational measures of the interaction patterns between children and teachers and peers in different contexts, such as various classroom activities as well as playground and lunchrooms would enhance these research programs. Katz and Gottman's reliance on direct observation of children's interactions with a best friend is a step in this direction, but a wider sampling of contexts beyond the home would be helpful.

## Neglected Contexts

It is clear that this volume only begins to address the myriad of contexts that merit consideration if we are to develop a comprehensive view of the links between families and other contexts. Little attention has been paid to the links between the family and religious institutions. Although a psychology and sociology of religion is emerging, scant attention has been paid to the interface between families and religious institutions (Thomas & Cornwall, 1990). Similarly more attention needs to be given to family links with various parts of the legal and social service systems, such as courts, adoption agencies, and welfare and employment agencies. Finally, it is not only formal contexts that need to be considered but informal ones as well, such as neighborhoods and playgrounds (Cupp, Spitzer, Isley-Paradise, Bentley, & Parke, 1992; Medrich, Roizen, Rubin, & Buckley, 1981).

## BIDIRECTIONALITY OF INFLUENCE

Although it is often assumed (at least implicitly) that the direction of influence in these studies is a unidirectional process, it is important to underscore that this is a bidirectional process. In many chapters, it is assumed that the direction of influence is from the family to other contexts: For example, the family influences children's behavior in school (Cowan et al., Kellam), in day care (Chase-Lansdale), or within peer group settings (Katz-Gottman; Parke et al.; McCarthy et al.). In other chapters, the assumption is that the direction of influence flows from work contexts—as indexed by maternal employment—to family relationships. Chase-Lansdale and Crouter both provide several findings that suggest that employment may negatively (or positively) impact family relationships and, in turn, children's development.

Interestingly, it seems to be that when adults are the family members that are involved in extra-familial settings, the direction of influence flows from outside contexts back to the family. When children are involved in outside activities (e.g., schools, peers, etc.) it is assumed that the family influences their adaptation in these contexts. To date we know much less about the impact of extra-familial contexts on family functioning than vice-versa. However, work on job loss, work stress, and school experience (Elder, 1974, 1991; Reppetti, 1989, 1993) is beginning to correct this imbalance by showing clearly that experiences of family members in outside contexts, in turn, can alter the nature of family functioning. It is important to underscore that children's as well as adults' experiences in extra-familial settings are influential. Historically, the emphasis has been on the experience of adults in work settings, for example, but it is important to consider children's experiences in school settings, for example on their subsequent family relationships.

## MULTIPLE PATHWAYS BETWEEN FAMILY AND OTHER CONTEXTS

First, family and other contexts are linked in multiple ways. In several chapters throughout the volume, illustrations of the myriad of ways in which family and other systems are linked have been examined. Indirect and direct pathways (Parke et al., 1989) between family and other contexts have been illustrated in this volume. Indirect pathways describe the impact of relationships among family members as well as the cognitive and behavioral processes that evolve from these interactions. Examples of indirect influence include the Cowan et al., Gottman-Katz, and Parke et al. chapters. Direct pathways involve parental efforts to promote and manage children's experiences in other contexts. These include a variety of parental roles such as designers, mediators, supervisors, and consultants (Ladd & Coleman, in press). Both Chase-Lansdale's work on parents' management of children's day-care experience and Parke et al.'s discussion of parent as provider of opportunities for peer contact illustrate this second type—the direct influence pathway. Progress has been gained in our understanding of these direct modes of parental influence (Bhavnagri & Parke, 1991; Ladd, Profilet, & Hart, 1992; Lollis & Ross, 1992; Parke & Bhavnagri, 1989).

Although further work is clearly needed in exploring both of these pathways, little effort has been made to explore how the strategies represented by them operate in combination to produce their impact on children's functioning in extra-familial settings. This array of socialization strategies that is available to parents can be viewed as analogous to a "cafeteria model" in which various combinations of items can be chosen or ignored in variously sized portions (Parke et al., 1992). Do all combinations produce equally socially competent children, or are some "ingredients" in this mix more important than others? Do different combinations produce different, but equally well-adjusted children—in recognition of the fact that developmental adaptations may be achieved through multiple pathways? Can heavy investment in one set of strategies compensate for limited utilization of another mode of influence? For example, Howes (1990) found that a high-quality relationship with a day-care provider can, in part, compensate for an insecure attachment relationship with a primary caregiver in the home. In this case, a parental management decision (e.g., to enroll a child in day care) may offset a poor parent–child relationship.

## NATURE OF LINKING PROCESSES

Two stages of research are evident in this domain of research. First, we have been in a descriptive phase in which the links between settings have been established. For example, variations in family patterns are, in turn, related to outcomes or behaviors of family members in other settings such as schools, peer groups, or neighborhoods (e.g., MacDonald & Parke, 1984; Putallaz, 1987). A second phase involves the identification of the processes that account for and/or explain the reasons for the links between family and other social settings. There is little agreement concerning the nature of these linking processes, but cognitive and emotional processes have been given a prominent role by some theorists (Grych & Fincham, 1990; Katz & Gottman; this volume; Parke, Cassidy, Burks, Carson, & Boyum, 1992; Sroufe & Fleeson, 1986).

Within the cognitive realm, attachment theorists (Eliker, Englund, & Sroufe, 1992; Sroufe & Fleeson, 1986) suggest the role of working models as mediating mechanisms. This approach has been useful for organizing findings that link early family experience to later adaptation to peers (Eliker et al., 1992; Sroufe, 1993) as well as subsequent parent–infant relationships (Bretherton & Waters, 1985). However, its heuristic value as a framework for examination of family links to other contexts such as work contexts remains to be explored. Moreover, questions of how these working models develop, the nature of the dimensions that characterize these "working models" and their structure and organization all need further elaboration and specification. Similarly, the issue of whether children develop single or multiple models needs to be explored more closely (Fox, Kimmerly, & Schafer, 1991; Main & Weston, 1981).

Alternative types of cognitive models beyond "working models" merit consideration, as well. A great deal of attention has been devoted to the role of children's social information-processing models (Dodge, 1986; Ladd & Crick, 1989) in understanding the processes underlying variations in children's peer relationships, for example, but less attention has been given to the origins of these social information-processing differences in the family or to the value of this approach for accounting for other types of extra-familial relationships. Do similar sets of processes guide parental decision making about social situations? Are parental social information-processing processes related to the similar processes in their children? Do parents have similar ways of solving family issues and issues arising in other contexts, or do they have different approaches to issues in different settings? Answers to these types of questions would begin to reveal patterns of similarities and differences across adults and children and provide a clearer picture of the nature of representational models of social behavior across family systems and other social systems.

Emotional regulatory processes have also been suggested as candidates to explain the links between family and other social contexts (see Chapters by Katz & Gottman and Parke et al.). However, more work needs to be done in terms of both specification of the aspects of emotional regulation that merit consideration and the role of the family in the socialization of these emotional processes.

Finally, a fusion between models that focus on cognitive processes and models that champion emotional processes would be of value because it is clear that both cognitive and emotional processes play important roles in this area. Moreover, it is evident that there is room for emotional variables in cognitive models as well as vice versa. For example, theories of working models within the attachment tradition clearly emphasize the role of emotion within relationships (Sroufe & Fleeson, 1986). Similarly, information processing (Dodge, 1991) as well as attribution theorists (Grych & Fincham, 1990) have stressed the importance of including emotions in their theories. On the other side, emotion-oriented researchers are increasingly recognizing the role that cognition plays in their theories (Parke et al., this volume). The main obstacle to a better fusion of these two classes of variables is the development of theoretical language and measurement systems that will allow a dialogue across different theoretical paradigms. The interplay among these possible linking processes needs more attention because cross-context transfer is likely to be a multiply determined phenomenon.

Finally, the extent to which similar processes are useful for explaining links between the family and different settings needs to be examined. Are a similar or common set of processes involved in all links between the family and other contexts or are there setting or context specific processes? These questions are just beginning to be formulated and no clear answers are yet available.

## ARE SETTINGS ALWAYS LINKED?

In our enthusiasm to document links between settings, we have not given sufficient consideration to the possibility that settings may make independent contributions to children's development. Settings, in short, may not always be linked, which may have some beneficial effects for children. Particularly in the case of children who come from family settings with poor parent–child relationships, the capacity to develop independent sets of relationships with individuals in outside settings may be an important developmental buffer. For example, Howes (1990) showed that children can develop distinctive patterns of attachment with their parents and with their child-care workers. Children with poor child–parent attachment relationships who, in turn, developed a high-quality attachment relationship with an adult in a child-care context were better in their socioemotional development. The conditions under which there is not transfer or generalizability across settings is an issue that deserves much more attention, especially if there are marked differences in the quality of care and opportunities across settings.

## DEVELOPMENTAL ISSUES

Developmental issues have received only a small amount of attention. However, it is highly likely that the links will shift in meaningful ways across development.

Parents' strategies will also shift across development from direct, didactic approaches to more subtle more indirect strategies as the child matures. In turn, the role of the child as an active shaper of his or her relationships with extra-familial contexts will change across development. Adult development needs to be considered as well, because this will alter the adults roles in extra-familial settings such as the workplace (Elder, 1974, 1991; Parke, 1988).

The influence of families on children may not be equally evident at all developmental periods. As McCarthy et al. note in their chapter, the direct influence of families on outcomes in early adulthood was less evident than the impact of individual factors, such as personal beliefs, values, and lifestyle. They noted that:

> Family characteristics of the late adolescent are, of course, important influences on personal beliefs, values, and lifestyle that have been shown to contribute more directly to predicting adult competence and thus are important mediators. It is also possible that family influences may have had an earlier impact (during childhood and early adolescence) on generating the personal values, beliefs, and lifestyle that are conducive to the subsequent development of the late adolescents' individual characteristics and thus to young adults sense of competency and efficacy . . . these family influences may not contribute directly to the development of adult competence once their impact has been originally registered earlier in life. (pp. 192–193)

This work suggests that greater attention needs to be paid to the timing of outcome assessments and to distinctions between direct and indirect effects at different points in the child's developmental cycle.

Development needs not to be limited to age-related issues in a narrow sense of biologically based shifts. Development needs to be viewed from a sociocultural viewpoint as well. This viewpoint recognizes the culturally controlled social agenda that determines the timing of the child's entry into various social settings such as the transition to elementary school or junior high school or the work force (Parke, 1988). The value of this cultural agenda perspective on development is that it focuses our attention on important transitions between the family and other settings. In turn, it suggests that transition periods may be a fruitful way to examine the institution–family linkage question. Transitions may be periods that are particularly likely to illuminate more clearly the central processes that link family and other contexts (Cowan, 1991).

Similarly, prior distinctions between normative and non-normative transitions may be a useful distinction to introduce into this literature. Are the processes governing family links with normative transitions to school, day-care, or work settings similar to non-normative transitions such as job loss, divorce, adoption, or criminal activity that introduce the family to institutions in unanticipated and nonscripted fashion?

## VARIATIONS IN FAMILY RELATIONSHIPS
## WITH OTHER SOCIAL CONTEXTS

One of the lessons derived from this volume is that greater attention needs to be given to issues of generalizability. This issue assumes several forms.

*Historical Continuity.* Is it appropriate to assume that family relationships with other social contexts can be accounted for by the same set of principles in different historical periods? Probably not! However, we still know relatively little about the nature of this historical variation. Historical analyses can serve several functions. First, history can provide unique opportunities to assess the generalizability of our explanatory principles in different historical periods. Historical variations such as war, famine, or economic depression represent important and powerful natural experiments that permit opportunities for theory and model testing, often under conditions that are much more drastic than developmental researchers could either ethically or practically engineer or produce in either the laboratory or the field. Elder's (1974) exploration of economic depression on family functioning and life course development of children is a classic example of this approach. Current work (Conger & Elder, in press) in which similar issues of the impact of economic hardship are being addressed in the 1980s and 1990s provides a unique opportunity to assess the historical boundedness of the family–employment relationships. Tracing how historical shifts in family organization in turn alters peer group relationships would be an interesting and profitable enterprise. For example, during wartime the increased degree of father absence accompanied by a higher percentage of mothers in the workplace and children in day care provides unique opportunities to assess family–peer relationships. Cross-time comparisons between earlier periods and the present era, in which day-care enrollment are high would provide interesting insights concerning how the historical period conditioned family–peer relationships and how the impact of day care on families has changed.

*Cultural Continuity.* Just as history provides us with naturally occurring variations, so do cross-cultural contexts provide opportunities for exploring the boundary conditions of our theories. Social scientists increasingly recognize that culture shapes the nature, timing, and rate of social development. This recognition is part of our shift away from endorsement of a positivistic assumption that psychological laws of development are applicable universally. At a minimum, the necessity of examining the assumption by replicating findings in other cultural contexts is increasingly common, whereas in a stronger form it is assumed that culture organizes behavioral patterns in fundamentally unique ways (see Rogoff, 1990; Whiting & Edwards, 1988).

Variations in family organization and structure that is evident in different societies represents one point of departure. Do extended family arrangements produce different relationships with other social contexts than nuclear family types? Different role arrangements for household members provides opportunities to examine variations in mother versus father contributions to children's and adult's functioning in other settings. In the case of peer contexts, are peer relationships different in cultures where older siblings are required to assume caregiving responsibility for younger siblings? In turn, are subsequent peer relationships different as a consequence of siblings versus parents as the primary socialization agent? How do variations in the organization of peer groups change across cultures? Are they largely informal or is contact between age mates limited to formal settings? Are groups limited to single age groups or do they involve multiple ages in single groups? Similar sets of questions could be raised about the organization of child care, schools, or work across different cultures.

How is the family's role modified by other institutions. The role that parents play may shift in organizing peer contacts varies considerably as a function of schooling. In cultures with no formal schooling, parental involvement in peer group activities may assume a more major role than in cultures where school attendance is normative.

Similarly, attitudes toward schooling and the relationship between families and schools vary across cultures such as the United States and Japan (Stevenson & Stigler, 1992). Moreover, interesting differences in academic achievement across ethnic groups (e.g., Asian, African, and Hispanic) in American culture can, in part, be accounted for by differences in parenting styles and peer processes. To take a final example, attitudes toward maternal employment, as Chase-Lansdale notes, vary across ethnic lines, with African-American women being more accepting than White females of extra-familial employment. In turn, these attitudinal differences may alter the impact of these experiences on families—women as well as their children. Cross-cultural and within-culture comparisons offer important opportunities to test the generalizability of our prior findings concerning the links between families and other contexts.

## INTERVENTION: AN UNDERUTILIZED RESEARCH STRATEGY

Intervention efforts can be undertaken for several reasons. Although the goal is generally to improve the social life of the target child or family another central reason for interventions is to provide a test of a theoretical position.

In terms of target, it has been fashionable to focus on the individual (child or parent) as the target of the intervention. Improving children's classroom behavior or their relationships with other children has been the goal of numerous earlier intervention programs (Furman & Robbins, 1985; Ladd & Mize, 1983). In the past, researchers have focused largely on measuring shifts in behavior in the setting (e.g., school/classroom) in which the intervention is located.

This is also a useful strategy as a way of examining how changes in children's behavior in the peer/school or day-care context can modify family relationships. This is a beginning step in unraveling the direction of influence issue and in particular to see how shifts in child functioning in extra-familial settings can alter relationships, within the family setting. It simply requires that another set of measures of family relationships be secured, in addition to the outcomes centered at the intervention site. However, a wider variety of contexts need to be targeted for intervention purposes. Although schools and peer contexts have been utilized frequently, as Crouter (this volume) notes, the impact of interventions at the work site on family functioning have been relatively infrequent. These represent interesting opportunities for future research.

Individual parents or perhaps the parent–child dyad have often been the targets of intervention. Techniques of discipline, beliefs, and knowledge are systematically modified and, in turn, the impact on (a) parent–child relationships are examined and (b) children's relationships in other contexts are scrutinized to determine if shifts, in fact, have occurred. Patterson's (1982) work is an example of this type of strategy. Chase-Lansdale (this volume) also provides several examples, including the impact of aiding a mother who leaves the welfare system on both her own development and her child's subsequent progress.

Work is only beginning to appear on the impact of interventions aimed at both parents and children simultaneously (Chase-Lansdale, Paikoff, & Brooks-Gunn, 1990), but holds the promise of having "additive or multiplicative positive effects on children's development" (Chase-Lansdale, this volume, p. 37).

Other types of interventions involve targeting neither individuals nor dyads, but the links across contexts. These include (a) programs (Epstein, 1989) that provide opportunities for parents to become involved in the activities of the institution (e.g., school) through mechanisms such as notes to parents and (b) parent–teacher conferences that provide opportunities for parents to become more aware of not only their child's behavior in these settings, but may increase parental sense of efficiency in terms of their ability to modify or alter their children's behavior in these extra-familial settings.

Alternatively, interventions can also be targeted at the setting itself, such as a neighborhood. For example, increasing safety or improving access to play spaces for children may, in turn, alter parental actions on behalf of their children. In this case, the shifts occur in terms of "opportunity structures" (Cochran, Larner, Riley, Gunnarsson, & Henderson, 1990) that are available to parents, who, in turn, permit their children access to these resources. This type of intervention could be viewed as a modification of parental gate keeping, by reorganizing the availability of resources. A variety of other interventions at the level of the community such as increased day care for young children could be viewed within this framework.

# CONCLUSION

It is clear that this volume raises more questions than it answers. In a sense, this volume can serve as an invitation to others to join in the search for answers to the central question: How do families and other institutions relate to one another? It is our hope that the questions are sufficiently intriguing that the invitation will be taken up by others.

# REFERENCES

Bandura, A. (1991). *Efficacy and schools.* Unpublished manuscript, Stanford University, Stanford, CA.

Barker, R. G. (1968). *Ecological psychology.* Stanford, CA: Stanford University Press.

Bhavnagri, N., & Parke, R. D. (1991). Parents as direct facilitators of children's peer relationships: Effects of age of child & sex of parent. *Journal of Social & Personal Relationships, 8,* 423–440.

Bretherton, I., & Waters, E. (Eds.) (1985). Growing points in attachment theory and research. *Monographs of the Society for Research in Child Development, 50,* (1–2) Serial No. 209.

Bronfenbrenner, U. (1979). *The ecology of human development.* Cambridge, MA: Harvard University Press.

Bronfenbrenner, U. (1986). Ecology of the family as a context for human development: Research perspectives. *Developmental Psychology, 22,* 723–742.

Chase-Lansdale, P. L., Paikoff, R., & Brooks-Gunn, J. (1990). Research and programs for adolescent mothers: Missing links and future promises. Unpublished manuscript, University of Chicago, Chicago, IL.

Cochran, M., Larner, M., Riley, D., Gunnarsson, L., & Henderson, C., Jr. (1990). *Extending families: The social networks of parents and their children.* Cambridge, England, and New York: Cambridge University Press.

Cohen, R., & Siegel, A. W. (1991). A context for context: Toward an analysis of context and development. In R. Cohen & A. W. Siegel (Eds.), *Context and development.* Hillsdale, NJ: Lawrence Erlbaum Associates.

Conger, R., & Elder, G. (Eds.). (in press). *Economic hardship and families.* New York: Plenum.

Cowan, P. A. (1991). Individual and family life transitions: A proposal for a new definition. In P. A. Cowan & E. M. Hetherington (Eds.), *Family transitions* (pp. 3–30). Hillsdale, NJ: Lawrence Erlbaum Associates.

Cupp, R., Spitzer, S., Isley-Paradise, S., Bentley, B., & Parke, R. D. (1992, June). *Children's social acceptance: The role of parents' perceptions of the neighborhood.* Poster presented at the annual meeting of the American Psychological Society, San Diego, CA.

Dodge, K. A. (1986). A social information processing model of social competence in children. In M. Perlmutter (Ed.), *Minnesota symposium on child psychology* (Vol. 18, pp. 77–126). Hillsdale, NJ: Lawrence Erlbaum Associates.

Dodge, K. A. (1991). Emotion and social information processing. In J. Garber & K. A. Dodge (Eds.), *The development of emotion regulation and dysregulation* (pp. 159–181). New York: Cambridge University Press.

Dunn, J. (1988). Relations among relationships. In S. Duck (Ed.), *Handbook of personal relationships* (pp. 193–209). New York: Wiley.

Elder, G. (1974). *Children of the Great Depression.* Chicago: University of Chicago Press.

Elder, G. H. (1991). Family transitions, cycles, and social change. In P. A. Cowan & E. M. Hetherington (Eds.), *Family transitions* (pp. 31–56). Hillsdale, NJ: Lawrence Erlbaum Associates.

Elder, G. H., Jr. (1978). Family history & the life course. In T. K. Hareven (Ed.), *Transitions: The family and the life course in historical perspective* (pp. 17–64). New York: Academic Press.

Eliker, J., Englund, M., & Sroufe, L. A. (1992). Predicting peer competence and peer relationships in childhood from early parent-child relationships. In R. D. Parke & G. W. Ladd (Eds.), *Family-peer relationships: Modes of linkage* (pp. 77–106). Hillsdale, NJ: Lawrence Erlbaum Associates.

Epstein, J. L. (1989). The selection of friends: Changes across the grades and in different school environments. In T. Berndt & G. Ladd (Eds.), *Peer relationships in child development* (pp. 158–187). New York: Wiley.

Fox, N. A., Kimmerly, N. L., & Schafer, W. D. (1991). Attachment to mother/attachment to father: A metaanalysis. *Child Development, 62,* 210–225.

Furman, W. J., & Robbins, P. (1985). What's the point? Issues in the selections of treatment objectives. In B. Schneider, K. Rubin, & J. Ledingham (Eds.), *Children's peer relationships: Issues in assessment an intervention* (pp. 41–54). New York: Springer-Verlag.

Grych, J. H., & Fincham, F. D. (1990). Marital conflict and children's adjustment: A cognitive-contextual framework. *Psychological Bulletin, 108,* 267–290.

Hartup, W. W. (1986). On relationships & development. In W. W. Hartup & Z. Rubin (Eds.), *Relationships and development* (pp. 27–50). Hillsdale, NJ: Lawrence Erlbaum Associates.

Hinde, R. A. (1979). *Towards understanding relationships.* London: Academic Press.

Hinde, R. A. (1992). Developmental psychology in the context of other behavioral sciences. *Developmental Psychology, 28,* 1018–1029.

Howes, C. (1990). Can the age of entry into child care and the quality of child care predict adjustment in kindergarten? *Developmental Psychology, 26,* 292–303.

Kellam, S. G. (1990). Developmental epidemiological framework for family research on depression and aggression. In G. R. Patterson (Ed.), *Depression and aggression in family interaction* (pp. 11–48). Hillsdale, NJ: Lawrence Erlbaum Associates.

Ladd, G. W., & Coleman, J. (in press). Parent's management of peer relationships. In B. Spodek (Ed.), *Handbook of early education.* New York: Plenum.

Ladd, G. W., & Crick, N. R. (1989). Probing the psychological environment: Children's cognitions, perceptions and feelings in the peer culture. In M. Maehr and C. Ames (Eds.), *Advances in motivation and achievement: Motivation enhancing environments* (Vol. 6, pp. 1–44). Greenwich, CT: JAI.

Ladd, G. W., & Mize, J. (1983). A cognitive-social learning model of social skill training. *Psychological Review, 90,* 127–157.

Ladd, G. W., Profilet, S. M., & Hart, C. H. (1992). Parents' management of children's peer relations: Facilitating & supervising children's activities in the peer culture. In R. D. Parke & G. W. Ladd (Eds.), *Family–peer relationships: Modes of linkage* (pp. 215–253). Hillsdale, NJ: Lawrence Erlbaum Associates.

Lollis, S., & Ross, H. (1992). Parents as direct influences on peer relationships. In R. D. Parke & G. W. Ladd (Eds.), *Family–peer relationships: Modes of linkage* (pp. 255–281). Hillsdale, NJ: Lawrence Erlbaum Associates.

MacDonald, K. B., & Parke, R. D. (1984). Bridging the gap: Parent–child play interaction & peer interactive competence. *Child Development, 53,* 1265–1277.

Main, M., & Weston, D. R. (1981). The quality of toddlers' relationship to mother & to father: Related to conflict behavior and the readiness to establish new relationships. *Child Development, 52,* 932–940.

Medrich, E. A., Roizen, J. A., Rubin, V., & Buckley, S. (1982). *The serious business of growing up: A study of children's lives outside school.* Berkeley: University of California Press.

Minuchin, P. P., & Shapiro, E. K. (1983). The school as a context for social development. In P. H. Mussen (Series Ed.) & E. M. Hetherington (Vol. Ed.), *Handbook of child psychology:* Vol. 4. *Socialization, personality, and social development* (pp. 197–274). New York: Wiley.

Park, K. A., & Waters, E. (1989). Security of attachment & preschool friendships. *Child Development, 60,* 1076–1081.

Parke, R. D. (1988). Families in life-span perspective: A multilevel developmental approach. In E. Hetherington, R. Lerner, & M. Perlmutter (Eds.), *Child development in life-span perspective* (pp. 159–190). Hillsdale, NJ: Lawrence Erlbaum Associates.

Parke, R. D., & Bhavnagri, N. P. (1989). Parents as managers of children's peer relationships. In D. Belle (Ed.), *Children's social networks and social supports* (pp. 241–259). New York: Wiley.

Parke, R. D., Cassidy, J., Burks, V. M., Carson, J., & Boyum, L. (1992). Familial contribution to peer competence among young children: The role of interactive & affective processes. In R. D. Parke & G. W. Ladd (Eds.), *Family–peer relationships: Modes of linkage* (pp. 107–134). Hillsdale, NJ: Lawrence Erlbaum Associates.

Parke, R. D., MacDonald, K., Burks, V., Carson, J., Bhavnagri, N., Barth, J., & Beitel, A. (1989). Family and peer systems: In search of the linkages. In K. Kreppner & R. M. Lerner (Eds.), *Family systems and life-span development,* (pp. 65–92). Hillsdale, NJ: Lawrence Erlbaum Associates.

Parke, R. D., Power, T. G., & Gottman, J. M. (1979). Conceptualization & quantifying influence patterns in the family triad. In M. E. Lamb, S. J. Suomi, & G. R. Stephenson (Eds.), *Social interaction analysis: Methodological issues* (pp. 231–253). Madison: University of Wisconsin Press.

Parke, R. D., & Tinsley, B. J. (1987). Family interaction in infancy. In J. D. Osofsky (Ed.), *Handbook of infant development* (2nd ed., pp. 579–641). New York: Wiley.

Patterson, G. R. (1982). *A social learning approach: Coercive family processes.* Eugene, OR: Castilla.

Putallaz, M. (1987). Maternal behavior & children's sociometric status. *Child Development, 58,* 32–44.

Repetti, R. L. (1989). Effects of daily workload on subsequent behavior during marital interaction: The roles of social withdrawal and spouse support. *Journal of Personality and Social Psychology, 57,* 651–659.

Repetti, R. L. (1993, April). *The effects of daily social and academic experiences on children's subsequent interactions with parents.* Poster presented at the Biennial Meeting of the Society for Research in Child Development, New Orleans, LA.

Rogoff, B. (1990). *Apprenticeship in thinking: Cognitive development in social context.* New York: Oxford University Press.

Rutter, M. (1983). School effects on pupil progress: Research findings & policy implications. *Child Development, 54,* 1–29.

Sameroff, A. J. (1987). The social context of development. In N. Eisenberg (Ed.), *Contemporary topics in developmental psychology* (pp. 273–291). New York: Wiley.

Sigel, I. E., & Parke, R. D. (1987). Structural analysis of parent-child research models. *Journal of Applied Developmental Psychology, 8,* 123–137.

Sroufe, L. A., Carlson, E., & Shulman, S. (1993). *The development of individuals: From infancy through adolescence.* In D. Funder, R. D. Parke, C. Tomlinson-Keasey and K. Widaman (Eds.), *Studying lives through time: Approaches to development and personality.* Washington, DC: American Psychological Association.

Sroufe, L. A., & Fleeson, J. (1986). Attachment and the construction of relationships. In W. W. Hartup & Z. Rubin (Eds.), *Relationships and development* (pp. 51–72). Hillsdale, NJ: Lawrence Erlbaum Associates.

Stevenson, H. W., & Stigler, J. W. (1992). *The learning gap.* New York: Simon & Schuster.

Thomas, D. W., & Cornwall, M. (1990). Religion and family in the 1980's: Discovery and development. *Journal of Marriage and the Family, 52,* 983–992.

Whiting, B. B., & Edwards, C. P. (1988). *Children of different worlds: The formation of social behavior.* Cambridge: Harvard University Press.

Youngblade, L. M., & Belsky, J. (1992). Parent-child antecedents of 5-year-olds close friendships: A longitudinal analysis. *Developmental Psychology, 28,* 700–713.

# Author Index

# Subject Index